AAT LEVEL 4

Drafting and Interpreting Financial Statements

AAT Level 4

Drafting and Interpreting Financial Statements

(Q22 1.1)

Published by Accountext

The content of this pack is frequently updated but on occasion, changes to legislation or accounting standards may not be reflected until sometime after implementation.

Accountext Publishing Ltd
First Floor Unit B,
Meltex House
65-67 Kepler
Tamworth
B79 7XE

www.accountext.co.uk

Introduction

The manual is split into chapters from 1 to 8 and contains many exercises. You should start at the beginning and work through each chapter in order. Should you become stuck at any point, ensure you review the content again – a second or third reading often helps.

The manual contains a number of icons to provide assistance along the way:

The Activity icon indicates that you have an activity to complete at that stage of the manual. Activities aid learning – have a go and then check where the answer came from.

When you see this icon, an answer to the activity you have carried out, will be displayed. Take time to appreciate how the answer was arrived at.

Where you see this icon an example is provided. This may be an illustration of a document that is used in business or an illustration of how a calculation or activity is to be completed.

Take note. This is information that is important or information that you may need for examination purposes.

This is one of the most important icons – it represents a requirement for you to complete an online assessment.

This page is left intentionally blank.

Contents

Chapter 1: Background to Financial Accounting

By the end of this chapter you should:

- Understand the reporting frameworks that underpin financial reporting
- Understand the purpose of accounting standards
- Understand how the financial statements of limited companies differ from those of sole traders and partnerships
- Understand the different accounting concepts and definitions
- Understand the concepts and principles that underlie the preparation and presentation of financial statements for external users.

The Global Importance of Accounting

For centuries businesses traded with each other and accountants have recorded these transactions in the accounts of the company. Whilst accounting is broadly similar around the world, each country has slightly different interpretations. Whilst most trade was between companies in the same country this didn't matter too much; however, the world is a very different place now and with the rapid growth of global trade, helped by technological advances such as the internet and political changes, much trade is undertaken between companies in different countries.

Leaving aside problems caused by language, currency and culture, a major issue of global trade is that financial statements prepared in one country can be prepared on a slightly different basis to those prepared in a another country.

The International Accounting Standards Board (IASB)

Since 1973, the IASB has been responsible for developing a single set of accounting standards with a view to them being used consistently around the world.

These standards were initially called International Accounting Standards (IASs), and since 2001 they have been issued as International Financial Reporting Standards (IFRSs). The purpose of these standards is to harmonise the way in which accountants deal with transactions around the world – so that financial statements can be more easily and usefully compared. This is particularly important given the increasingly global nature of both business ownership and trading.

Where Are We Now?

Since 2005 it has been mandatory for all large EU companies to report under the IASB accounting standards. In the UK, this means that all listed companies (i.e. listed on the London stock market) have had to prepare financial statements on this basis. Other UK companies and businesses can still prepare financial statements in line with UK standards (UK Generally Accepted Accounting Practice or UK GAAP), although this will change in years to come.

Other countries around the world have not fully adopted the IASB standards are indicated in white on the map below.

Source: www.ifrs.org

Why Are Consistent Standards Important?

Lots of business decisions are based on the information contained within financial statements. Users of financial statements need to have confidence that the information is consistent and reliable – otherwise they are more likely to make poor decisions, which could result in lost profits, business closures, job losses and so on.

With the increase in global trade this is even more important.

The objective of the IASB is ***"to develop, in the public interest, a single set of high quality, understandable and enforceable global accounting standards that require high quality, transparent and comparable information in financial statements and other financial reporting to help participants in the world's capital markets and other users make economic decisions".***

So the idea is that by having a **single set** of **global accounting standards**, it won't matter if you are investing in, or trading with, a company in America, Europe, China or anywhere else in the world, you will understand the financial statements and be confident in what they are telling you.

Of course, it is not easy developing one set of standards which would be acceptable to businesses, governments and accountants around the world, and there is still a degree of discord about what should and should not be included. One thing seems certain, though – the drive to find an acceptable common global approach to accounting will not be going away any time soon.

In the UK, it is not allowable under UK GAAP to value inventory under the Last In First Out method in a company's financial statements – and yet in the USA this is a perfectly acceptable and commonly used method. This illustrates the difficulties faced in arriving at one single global set of accounting standards.

As we move towards this '*single set of …enforceable global accounting standards*' it is important that accountants – and accounting students – are familiar with the current position, particularly because they are already mandatory for some limited companies in the UK (ie listed UK companies).

The Conceptual Framework

Accountants have struggled for many years to produce a single set of rules which are applicable in all circumstances – this is essentially the objective of the International Accounting Standards Board. However, it is nigh-on impossible to produce just one set of rules which will cover all eventualities, especially in an area as complex as international finance.

In 1989 the IASB issued its ***Conceptual Framework for Financial Reporting***, and this was revised in 2010. The Conceptual Framework is not an accounting standard in its own right; it doesn't tell accountants how to account for a certain type of transaction. Instead, it aims to provide guidance on the underlying concepts which must be considered when preparing financial information – it is an attempt to define the nature and purpose of accounting.

The main purpose of the Framework is to:

- assist in the development of future IFRS and the review of existing standards by setting out the underlying concepts.
- promote harmonisation of accounting regulation and standards by reducing the number of permitted alternative accounting treatments.
- assist the preparers of financial statements in the application of IFRS, which would include dealing with accounting transactions for which there is not (yet) an accounting standard.

Without a conceptual framework, it is highly likely that accountants would disagree about the purpose and presentation of financial statements even more strongly than they do already!

The Conceptual Framework provides us with:

- the objective of Financial Reporting
- the main users of financial statements
- the underlying assumptions on which all financial statements should be prepared
- the qualitative characteristics of useful financial information.

These are covered in more detail in the following pages.

GAAP or IAS / IFRS?

As we saw earlier, the vast majority of UK businesses can still prepare their financial statements using UK GAAP (Generally Accepted Accounting Practice). It is expected that in years to come an increasing number of businesses in the UK will be obliged to prepare accounts under the International Accounting Standards / International Financial Reporting Standards.

All AAT exam questions in this unit are based on the International Accounting Standards, rather than UK GAAP. You will be expected to have both theoretical knowledge of certain IAS/IFRS, as well as the ability to apply them practically in the production of financial statements. Don't worry, though – you don't need to know all of them – the list of IAS/IFRS which fall within this Unit is shown in the back of this book.

The Objective of Financial Statements

Of course, if we are trying to produce a set of standards which will apply to the preparation of financial statements, the starting point is to be absolutely clear:

- Why we need financial statements in the first place.
- Who will use the financial statements we have produced, and for what reasons.

Answering these two questions will allow the standards to be framed in such a way that they make the financial statements fit for purpose.

We saw earlier that the IASB produced the 'Conceptual Framework for Financial Reporting' which identified the objective of financial reporting as ***"...to provide financial information about the reporting entity that is useful to existing and potential investors, lenders and other creditors in making decisions about providing resources to the entity".***

This definition gives us a really good starting point in thinking about why accountancy is so important. The role of the accountant is essentially to **prepare and present information which is used to inform business decisions** – and the accounting standards provide a framework for doing this.

So what business decisions are we talking about? Well, this will very much depend on who is using the accounting information, since each user's needs are different.

The Different Users of Financial Statements

We can identify the different groups of users of financial statements. Whilst there will be similarities between the reasons for which each group uses the statements, each group will have its own focus or needs.

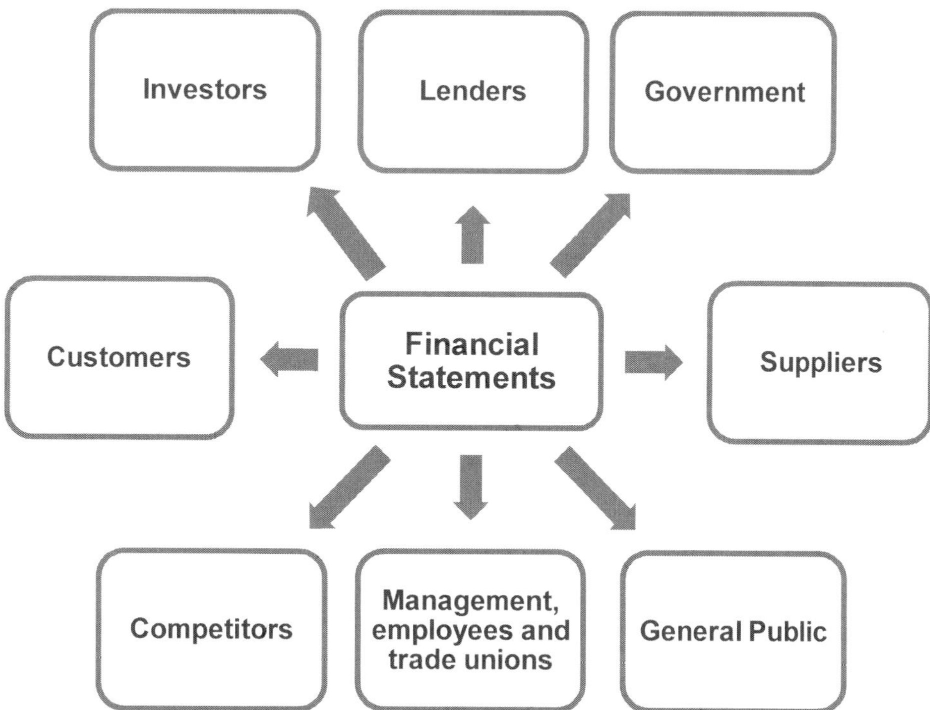

The Importance of Investors

If you invest in a Limited Company, you become a part owner of that company. Many limited companies are small and may only have a small number of shareholders (maybe even only one) – but the bigger limited companies (and particularly PLCs) may have several thousand shareholders. Although most shareholders have the right to vote at Annual General Meetings, they do not take part in the day-to-day management of the company. They rely on the financial statements to present a *true and fair* view of the financial position and performance of the company, so that they can judge whether to maintain their shareholding in the business.

Ultimately, the current (and potential) investors of the business are the **most important** of the users identified above – because they are the owners (and potential owners) of the business.

Therefore, the objective of financial reporting puts them at the forefront of the reason why we have financial statements, alongside lenders (such as banks) and other creditors (e.g. suppliers).

These three groups have most to lose if a company goes out of business, and therefore their needs are central in designing a single set of financial statements.

Because most shareholders are not involved in the day to day management of the business (in larger organisations), management serve an important dual function. Not only must they act to ensure the business achieves its objectives, they must also act to ensure that the shareholders' financial investment in the business is protected. This responsibility is known as the **stewardship** function of management.

STEWARDSHIP: "Management responsibility, not only for the custody and safekeeping of enterprise resources, but also for their efficient and profitable use and for protecting them to the extent possible from unfavourable economic impacts of factors in the economy, such as inflation or deflation and technological and social changes."

The financial statements act as a primary method of allowing shareholders to judge how well the directors of a business are performing their stewardship function. In some cases, the results of the business presented through the financial statements may be so poor that the shareholders decide to remove one or more of the directors.

The Underlying Assumptions

There are two underlying assumptions (recognised in the Conceptual Framework) which underpin the way in which all financial statements are produced. These form the foundations for preparing financial statements for organisations of all sizes. If either of these underlying assumptions were not used, the financial statements would look very different indeed, and it would not be possible to meaningfully compare one set of statements with another.

GOING CONCERN

The financial statements are assumed to have been prepared on the basis that the entity will continue in business for the foreseeable future, and the enterprise has neither the intention nor the need to liquidate or curtail materially the scale of its operations. This is particularly important for the way in which assets and liabilities are valued.

ACCRUALS BASIS

The financial statements are prepared under the accruals basis. The effects of transactions and other events are recognised when they occur and not when the cash is received or paid. It is the opposite to the *cash basis of accounting*, where transactions are recorded according to when they are paid or received.

The Accounting Concepts

In addition to the underlying assumptions of going concern and accruals, there are a number of other accounting concepts which are an essential part of producing financial statements. These are:

THE BUSINESS ENTITY CONCEPT

This means that the financial statements are prepared purely from the perspective of the business – they do not include any valuations of personal assets or liabilities of the owners.

This is easily demonstrated by probably the very first double entry transaction you will ever have made:

John invests £10,000 of his own money into a new business: The double entry would be to Debit Bank, Credit Capital. This illustrates how accounting keeps the assets and liabilities of the owners separate to those of the business.

MATERIALITY

The Conceptual Framework and IAS 1 provides the definition of materiality as "*Information is material if omitting it or misstating or obscuring it could reasonably be expected to influence the decisions that the primary users of general purpose financial statements make on the basis of financial statements, which provide financial information about a specific reporting entity*".

Remember the objective of financial statements is "to provide financial information about the reporting entity that is useful to existing and potential investors, lenders and other creditors in making decisions about providing resources to the entity" – in other words, the whole purpose of preparing financial statements is to enable others to make decisions. ***Material*** information is therefore any information which will affect this decision-making process and whether to recognise an asset is ultimately is a matter of judgement.

Materiality will be set at a different level depending on the size of the organisation; for a small business spending £300 on a new printer would be material and so you would expect it to be shown separately in the financial statements; however, for a large multi-national this would not be a material transaction. It would still need to be accounted for, of course, but would not be shown separately.

Materiality allows us to tackle two fundamental questions when preparing financial statements:

- Should a transaction be included in the financial statements, or just a note to the accounts?
- Should a transaction be shown separately, or aggregated with other similar transactions?
- What Makes Accounting Information Useful?
  Information is useful if it helps people to make better decisions.

PRUDENCE

Prudence essentially means adopting a cautious approach when preparing financial statements. Gains or profits should only be recognised in the accounts when they have actually been made, whilst losses should be recorded as soon as it becomes probable they will arise. This is to ensure that income and assets are not overstated in the accounts, while expenses and liabilities are not understated.

There are many applications of this concept with which you will already be familiar – IAS 2, for example, requires inventories and work-in-progress to be valued at the **lower** of cost and net realisable value. This is a prudent valuation as it does not include unrecognised profits (i.e. before the inventory has been sold) – but if the items are damaged their loss in value is recognised immediately. Similar, any provisions or estimates of doubtful or irrecoverable debts, or the provision for depreciation against the value of non-current assets, are measures aimed at not overstating the value of the company's assets.

CONSISTENCY

Financial statements should be prepared using the same accounting techniques and valuation bases as previous statements – this is to help make the statements more comparable over time. Whilst organisations have some freedom in choosing their valuation bases (e.g. choosing whether to use FIFO or AVCO for inventories, or whether to depreciate non-current assets on a straight line or diminishing balance basis), they should then continue to use these bases in future years. Organisations should not simply change these bases year-on-year just to show better figures. If the directors decide that a change is required (e.g. to meet a change in legislation or regulation) then the nature of that change, and its impact, must be shown clearly in the financial statements.

Activity 1.1

In preparing the financial statements for Anderson Ltd for the year ended 31 March 20X7, the managing director Julian Anderson has raised a number of concerns. These are:

1. The company bank account paid for an extension and swimming pool to be paid for at Julian's country house.
2. At 31 March 20X8 there is an unopened box of A4 paper in the stationery cupboard which have not been included in the figure for 'closing inventory', and Julian feels this is wrong.
3. Julian has said that he wants to include the proceeds of a large sale to a new customer in this year's accounts. Although the contract has not actually been signed yet, Julian is confident it should all go through in the next few weeks.
4. Anderson Ltd is experiencing significant cash flow problems and it is considered quite likely that the company will have to go into liquidation in the next few months.

Required

For each of the concerns, identify which one (or more) of the accounting concepts should be applied in determining the correct approach to dealing with them.

Concern	Accounting Concept
1.	
2.	
3.	
4.	

What Makes Information Useful

There are two fundamental characteristics of useful information.

These are:

- **relevance** and;
- **faithful representation.**

There are also four supporting (enhancing) characteristics of:

- **comparability**
- **verifiability**
- **timeliness**
- **understandability**.

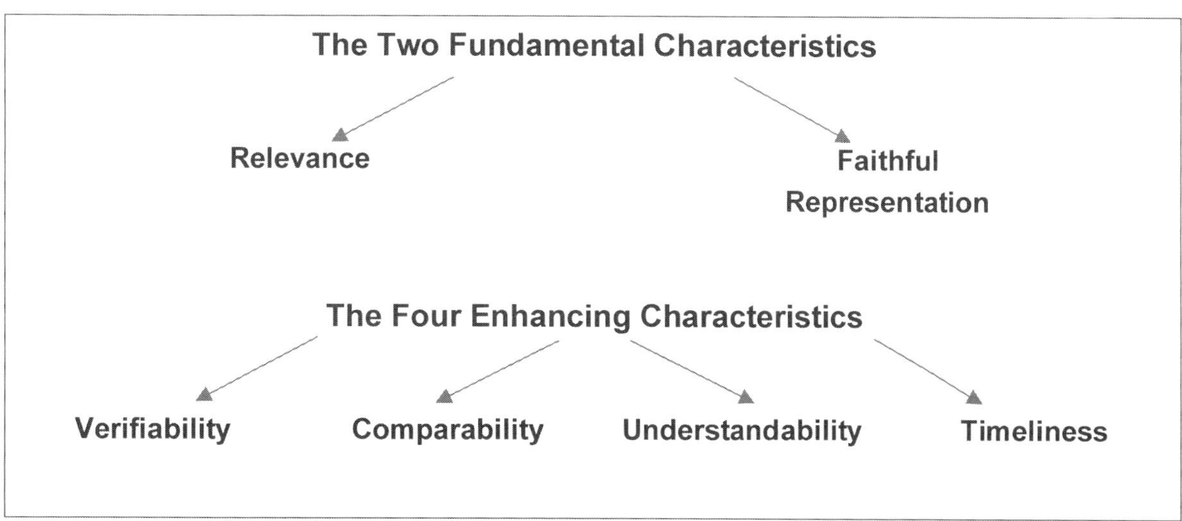

RELEVANCE:

Information is **relevant** if it:

- Is capable of making a difference in the decision-making process.

  And either

- Has **predictive** value – it allows the user to make predictions about future events, *or*

- Has **confirmatory** value – it allows the user to confirm past evaluations.

FAITHFUL REPRESENTATION:

Information is **faithfully representative** if it:

- Corresponds to the effect of transactions or events
- As far as possible, is:
  - Complete
  - Neutral
  - Free from error

This means that the figures presented in the financial statements match what actually happened or existed.

The four supporting characteristics of useful information are:

Comparability

If information is to be comparable, and to allow subjective judgements to be drawn from it, it must be comparable with other and similar information. Financial statements in particular should have comparability – users need to know that if they wish to compare the financial statements of two different companies that they have been prepared on the same basis. Variations such as use of different accounting bases (e.g. different methods and rates of depreciation) can have a significant impact on the information contained within the statements. Similarly, if we are comparing two or more sets of information over time, changes in legislation or regulation may make the process of comparing two seemingly similar sets of information quite misleading. One of the key roles of accounting standards is to ensure that financial statements are as comparable as possible – no matter where in the world they are produced.

Verifiability

Information needs to be trustworthy – anybody using the information should be able to do so with confidence that it is as accurate as possible, and has been prepared truthfully and fairly. Verifiability means that the information (and the original sources of it) can be checked – this provides greater assurance to the user. For example, financial statements which have been audited have a higher degree of verifiability than those which have not – the user has greater assurance because the figures presented in the statements have been verified by an independent third party (the auditors).

Timeliness

To be useful, information must be made available on a timely basis. For example, if you were planning on going on a picnic tomorrow, it would be no use checking the weather forecast in a week's time – it would be too late. Timeliness of financial statements is an issue, because organisations need time to prepare the relevant data and then to prepare and issue the statements. However, the longer they are allowed to do this, the less useful the information may be useful for users. There is often a trade-off between accuracy and timeliness – the sooner the information is required the more likely there may be estimates (or even errors) within it.

Understandability

Information should be presented as logically, clearly and concisely as possible. Large tables of numerical data, or long-winded sentences full of jargon, are difficult for the majority of users to understand. It may be beneficial to users to include pictures or other diagrams, and to include 'headlines' which are then supported by more complex or detailed information in appendices at the back of a report.

It is acknowledged that not all users of financial statements are 'experts' – and so they should be presented in such a way as to make them understandable to the layperson – someone with little or no financial knowledge. This can create difficulties, as by definition much of the data contained within financial statements is specialist in nature. However, most companies do try to present their financial statements supported by other, more accessible, information.

Make sure you know the fundamental and enhancing characteristics.

Key Definitions

Relevance
- capable of influencing decisions

Faithful Representation
- information must be complete, neutral and free from error.

Comparability - it is possible to compare an entity over time and also with similar entities at the same point in time.

Verifiablility - this provides assurance to users that the information is credible and relaible.

Timeliness - information must be provided to users in a timescale that is suitable for their decision making purposes

Understandability - information must be understood by a wide range of potenial users.

Example 1.1

Tesco plc incorporate a number of features to help make their financial statements more useful for users. Their annual reports can be accessed here:

https://www.tescoplc.com/investors/reports-results-and-presentations/results-and-presentations/

Among the features are short videos, an interactive pdf which makes accessing relevant parts of the statements easier, and access to statements from previous years (improving comparability).

Regulation and Legislation

The accountancy profession must operate within a framework of both **regulation** and **legislation**. **Regulation** is imposed by the accountancy profession itself (e.g. International Accounting Standards (IAS) and International Financial Reporting Standards (IFRS)), or by other bodies. Although not legally binding, accountants must adopt and implement the regulations in their work; otherwise they will face sanctions including (potentially) expulsion from the profession.

Legislation is the law under which companies must operate. UK companies must operate under UK law. There are many pieces of legislation affecting UK companies, such as the Health and Safety at Work Act (1974) and assorted pieces of employment legislation. However, the Act which most affects accountants within limited companies is the Companies Act (2006).

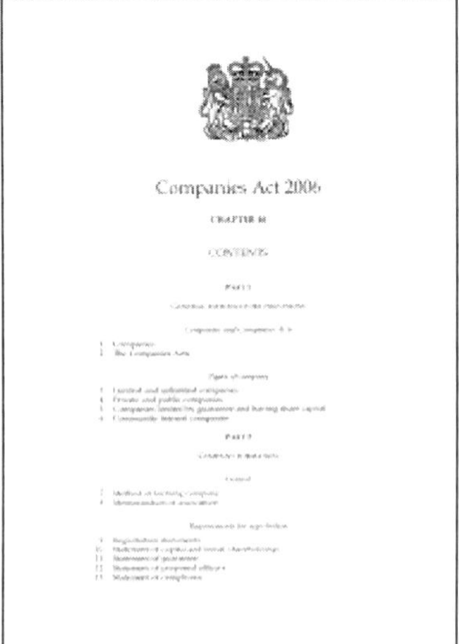

Companies Act 2006

The Companies Act (2006) contains many provisions which focus on formation, administration and governance of limited companies. It also imposes significant responsibilities and duties on the directors of any limited company – failure to meet these is a criminal offence which could result in fines or imprisonment.

The directors are responsible for keeping proper company accounting records, preparing the annual financial statements and having these audited if required (see below). Once the financial statements have been prepared, the directors must ensure they are presented to shareholders at an Annual General Meeting (AGM), and once approved by the shareholders must ensure they are filed with the Registrar of Companies (Companies House).

Annual financial statements must normally be filed with the Registrar of Companies no more than nine months after the end of the accounting period to which they relate.

The Financial Statements of Limited Companies

The requirement for limited companies to prepare financial statements is enshrined in the Companies Act (2006). The layout and content of these financial statements is directed by both the Companies Act and also the relevant accounting regulations and standards (IAS and IFRS). The requirements are therefore significantly more regulated than for sole traders or partnerships.

Under the Companies Act (2006), all limited companies (Ltd and plc) must present the following:

- A Statement of Financial Position (SFP).
- A Statement of Profit or Loss and Other Comprehensive Income (SPLOCI).
- Group (Consolidated) Accounts where a company has subsidiaries.
- A Directors' Report.

IAS 1 also requires that companies present the following statements:

- A Statement of Changes in Equity.
- A Statement of Cash Flows.

Some limited companies are required by law to have their accounts audited – although most small businesses no longer need this. For private limited companies, unless their articles of association state that the financial statements **must** be audited (or the shareholders specifically request an audit), they will be exempt from this requirement so long as they meet two of the following criteria:

- an annual turnover of no more than £10.2 million
- assets worth no more than £5.1 million
- 50 or fewer employees on average

Make sure you know what information each of the financial statements provides for users.

The Financial Statements	
Statement of Financial Position	•Assets and liabilities •Financial health and stength
Statement of Profit or Loss	•Performance over the past period •Other gains and losses
Statement of Changes in Equity	•How the ownership (equity) of the business has changed over the past period
Statement of Cash Flow	•The financial adaptability of the business •Cash flows in and out of the business

The Elements of the Financial Statements

You should be familiar with the accounting equation:

ASSETS – LIABILITIES = EQUITY (or **CAPITAL** for sole traders and partnerships).

This equation underpins the financial statements – and in particular the structure of the Statement of Financial Position. Until now, you have probably been happy to think of an asset as 'something the business owns' and a liability as 'something the business owes' – and as everyday working definitions these are fine. However, the IASB has defined the five **elements of financial statements** more completely, and you need to understand and recall each of these five definitions.

The conceptual framework identifies and defines five elements of financial statements. These are:

- **Assets** – An asset is *"a present economic resource controlled by the entity as a result of past events. An economic resource is a right that has the potential to produce economic benefits"*.
- **Liabilities** – A liability is *"a present obligation of the entity to transfer an economic resource as a result of past events"*.
- **Equity** – Equity is *"the residual interest in the assets of the entity, after deducting all its liabilities"*.
- **Income** – Income is *"Increases in assets or decreases in liabilities that result in increase in equity, other than those relating to contributions from holders of equity claims"*.
- **Expense** – Expenses are *"Decreases in assets or increases in liabilities that result in decreases in equity, other than those relating to distributions to holders of equity claims"*.

Although these definitions may seem lengthy and complex, it is essential that you learn them as you could be tested on one or more of them in your exam. These definitions are more 'in depth' than you will have come across before – and this is because they must be consistently applicable across all possible accounting transactions.

Example 1.2

The definition of an asset (from IAS 1) is *"a present economic resource controlled by the entity as a result of past events"*.

You will note that this definition refers to **control** of an asset rather than ownership. This is because in some situations (e.g. a long-term 'finance' lease) an organisation is deemed to control the asset even if it does not legally own it (you will study this further under IFRS 16 later in this text). In such situations, the item should still be recognised as an asset in the organisation's Statement of Financial Position, even though it does not hold legal ownership of it.

Assessment 1

You are now required to log-in to your ROGO account to complete your online assessment before progressing on to the next chapter.

This page is left intentionally blank.

Chapter 2: Financial Statements of Limited Companies

By the end of this chapter you should:

- Understand the effect of international accounting standards on the presentation, valuation and disclosure of items within the financial statements.
- Be able to make appropriate entries in the statements in respect of information extracted from a trial balance and additional information.
- Be able to draft statements of profit or loss and other comprehensive income.
- Be able to draft statements of financial position.

Introduction

Entity concept

The entity concept means that a business and its owner(s) are treated as separate entities for accounting purposes.

Accountants and bookkeepers are duty bound to keep the business and its activities separate from those of its owners. This means the financial statements only focus on the transactions of the business and not the owners to show a measure of the performance of the business in terms of making a profit or loss.

The entity concept is important because if the business transactions are jumbled with those of the owners, or even other businesses, then this does not provide an accurate position of the business, or the owners, and the usability of the financial accounts are deemed useless.

Using the entity concept and keeping the transactions separate helps to:

- Separate the taxation for the business and the owner.
- Separate and measure the performance of a business in terms of profitability.
- Separate the cash flows of the business and the owner.

Models of Business Ownership

There are different legal structures that businesses adopt. The type of structure will determine the liability that is imposed on the owners, the amount of paperwork that is legally required and the amount of tax to be paid by that business. You should be familiar with these from your Level 2 and Level 3 studies.

There are profit seeking structures and non-profit seeking structures. There are three common profit seeking business structures:

- **Sole trader** (managed and owned by one person)
- **Partnerships** (managed and owned by two or more people)
- **Limited Liability Partnership (LLP)** (separate entity, managed and owned by two or more people)
- **Companies** (separate entity, managed by directors, owned by shareholders)

Companies

Sole traders and partnerships are **unincorporated businesses**. Sole traders and partnerships have unlimited liability, meaning there is no legal difference between the business and the owners. This means that the owner's personal assets maybe at risk for the liabilities or obligations of the business.

Limited companies and Limited Liability Partnerships (LLP) are **incorporated businesses**.

We can form a company or LLP by 'incorporation'.

Incorporation is the legal process that is used to form a company or LLP. This enables the business to be recognised as a separate legal entity from its owners, unlike sole traders and partnerships.

This means that any liability to its owners is limited to the amount they have invested and cannot be held personally responsible for the debts of the company. This is called limited liability which means the owner's personal assets and finances are protected.

There are two types of limited companies:

PRIVATE COMPANY LIMITED BY SHARES (LTD)

And

PUBLIC LIMITED COMPANY (PLC)

PRIVATE LIMITED COMPANIES

A limited company has shareholders, who own a 'share' of the business.

Each shareholder has **limited liability**, which means that they are only liable to lose the amount they have invested in the business should it fail. Conversely, sole traders and partnerships have **unlimited liability**, whereby if the business fails they may be forced to sell private assets (e.g. houses or cars) to meet the business's debts.

Shareholders who own **Ordinary Shares** in the company are entitled to vote at the Annual General Meeting on key matters regarding the management of the company; however, the day to day running of the company is entrusted to **directors** who are appointed by the shareholders. Directors can, of course, also be shareholders in the business.

Whereas sole traders and partners take **drawings** from the business, shareholders in a limited company receive **dividends**, which represent their share of the profits of the business which have not been retained (e.g. for future investment in new assets).

Limited companies pay **Corporation Tax** on their profits, whereas sole traders and partnerships are taxed on profits under Income Tax legislation.

Limited companies must comply with the requirements of the **Companies Act 2006.** This wide-ranging piece of legislation includes requirements on how limited companies must be established, the roles and responsibilities of directors, the requirement for financial statements to adhere to certain requirements, requirements on when **external audit** is required and many other aspects of corporate law.

Limited companies must submit an annual return and file a copy of their financial statements, to **Companies House** each year.

Approximately 37% of all UK businesses are limited companies.

Although many limited companies are significantly larger than sole traders and partnerships, at the start of 2021 it was estimated that approximately 951,000 (out of 2 million active limited companies) were one-person businesses – essentially sole traders who had chosen to set up as a limited company. This is often due to perceived tax advantages or the potential advantage of limited liability.

There were 6.0 million private sector businesses in the UK in 2020, which was an increase of 112,700 compared to 2019. These range from very large, well known businesses such as Tesco, BP and Unilever, to the many hundreds of thousands of sole traders such as plumbers and hairdressers, plasterers and accountants.

In 2020, there were 2.5 million more businesses than in 2000, which shows an increase of 72% over the whole 20-year period.

Source: https://www.gov.uk/government/statistics/business-population-estimates-2020/

PUBLIC LIMITED COMPANIES

Some of the most well-known companies are Public Limited Companies, including:

Public Limited Companies carry the letters PLC after their name (e.g. Marks and Spencer PLC).

The main difference between a Private Limited Company and a Public Limited Company is that a Public Limited Company can offer its shares for sale to the general public. This generally makes it easier for a plc to raise capital (finance).

Listed PLCs are simply those which list their shares for sale on the **Stock Exchange**. Since 2006, listed PLCs have been required to prepare their annual financial statements under the International Accounting Standards (IAS) and International Financial Reporting Standards (IFRSs). Non-listed PLCs still have the choice as to whether to prepare their financial statements under IAS/IFRS, or according to UK Generally Accepted Accounting Practice (UK GAAP) – see Chapter 1 for further information.

The second likely difference between a Public and a Private Limited company is that PLCs tend to be larger, with more shareholders to whom the directors of the company are accountable.

The Differences Between Sole Traders and Limited Companies

At Level 3 you studied how to produce the financial statements ('the accounts') for both sole traders and partnerships. Although the fundamental principles of accounting remain the same, there are some key differences in the way in which the financial statements are produced for limited companies.

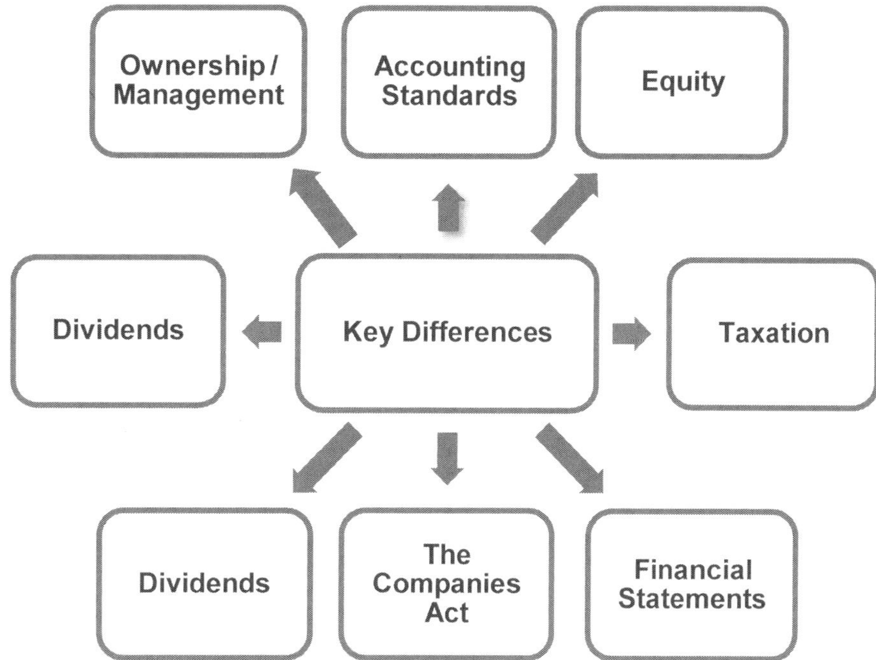

OWNERSHIP / MANAGEMENT:

In most cases a sole trader not only owns the business but they are also the main manager of the business, responsible for planning and making decisions. As we have seen, a limited company may have many different owners. In such a case, the owners are not involved in the day-to-day management of the company; instead they entrust the management function to a board of managers (or directors). These directors are often shareholders (owners of the business) themselves, but they manage the company on behalf of all shareholders.

ACCOUNTING STANDARDS:

All businesses prepare their accounts within the general framework of UK Generally Accepted Accounting Practice (UK GAAP). However, publicly listed companies (i.e. those whose shares are listed for public sale on the stock market) must, as we have seen, prepare accounts in line with the International Accounting Standards (IAS and IFRS).

EQUITY:

A key concept in accounting for limited companies is ***equity*** – this is defined as "*...the owners' residual interest in the assets of the entity, after deducting all its liabilities*" – in other words, the value of the business which is owned by the shareholders rather than that which has been financed by loans which would have to be paid back to lenders. The owners' equity is made up of the amounts they have originally invested, retained earnings and other gains and losses. For a sole trader or partnership, this is broadly equivalent to ***capital***.

DIVIDENDS:

A sole trader will take money out of their business through ***drawings*** – these are a reduction in capital invested in the business. Owners of a limited company do not take drawings; instead, they receive ***dividends*** – a return based on the level of profits made by the business and determined by the directors of the company.

TAXATION:

Sole traders are liable to pay income tax on the profits of their business; limited companies pay ***Corporation Tax***. The rules for these two types of tax are quite different. Directors will also pay income tax on the dividends that they receive (you will study tax in more detail if you choose the optional taxation units at this level).

LIMITED LIABILITY:

Sole traders and partnerships are held personally responsible for any debts incurred by the business; essentially, if the business fails the financial burden falls on the owner, who may have to sell personal assets such as cars or a house to repay debts. Shareholders in a limited company enjoy ***limited liability***, which means that their personal liability in the event of the company failing is limited to the amount which they invested.

THE COMPANIES ACTS 2006:

The Companies Acts are the legislative framework under which limited companies must operate. They cover a broad range of aspects of corporate regulation, including the duties of directors, the requirement to issue financial statements, the documentation required to set up a company, including the ***Memorandum and Articles of Association***, regulations around ***auditing*** and many other aspects (the Act itself is almost 700 pages long!). The provisions of the Companies Act only apply to limited companies, not to sole traders or partnerships.

FINANCIAL STATEMENTS:

There is a far greater emphasis on limited companies producing financial statements in a prescribed format; the precise format used will depend on whether the company prepares its financial statements under UK GAAP or the international financial reporting standards. In this unit you will study the requirements for producing financial statements under the international financial reporting standards.

The Financial Statements

Sole traders and partnerships generally produce financial statements ('the accounts') for two (or possibly three) main user groups:

- The owners – so they can see how much profit (or loss) has been made during the financial period, and to enable them to calculate any tax implications.
- Banks – who have lent, or may be approached to lend, money to the business.
- Potential buyers of the business (if it is for sale).

Limited companies – because they are generally much bigger enterprises – have a wider group of **stakeholders**.

A stakeholder is **any individual, organisation or group who have an INTEREST in the business** – this is anyone who could affect or be affected by the decisions and actions of the business. Stakeholders can be **internal** or **external** to the business.

Be careful not to confuse stakeholders with shareholders – all shareholders are stakeholders but not all stakeholders are shareholders!

Internal stakeholders are likely to include:

- Shareholders
- Managers
- Staff

External stakeholders could include:

- Potential investors
- Lenders
- Customers
- Suppliers
- Local communities
- The Government
- Trade Unions
- The general public / local community

Because limited companies tend to be larger, and have a higher public profile, (and therefore more external stakeholders), more people are likely to be interested in their financial statements than for a sole trader or partnership.

In Chapter One we looked at the different **users** of financial statements – you can see here that any stakeholder in the business is potentially interested in using the financial statements for that entity – the users and the stakeholders are essentially the same group.

Although many limited companies in the UK still prepare their financial statements according to UK GAAP, the AAT have stated that you will only be assessed against the relevant IAS/IFRS. A list of these can be found at the end of the book.

Under IAS 1 ***Presentation of Financial Statements***, limited companies **<u>must</u>** produce the following on at least an annual basis:

- Statement of Profit or Loss and Other Comprehensive Income
- Statement of Financial Position
- Statement of Cash Flows
- Statement of Changes in Equity
- Notes to the Financial Statements, including a statement of the company's accounting policies

These statements must clearly display the name of the company, the period the financial statements are prepared for, the currency the statements are presented in (e.g. £, € or US $) and the level of rounding used in the statements (e.g. £000, £million).

Furthermore, the Companies Act **also** requires limited companies to produce:

- A directors' report
- An auditors' report (where an audit has been carried out)

The Statement of Financial Position

The Statement of Financial Position provides measures of the company's financial stability and liquidity at the end of the financial period. It is based on the accounting equation, in the form:

ASSETS = LIABILITIES + EQUITY

The layout of the Statement of Financial Position is a little different to that which you have met before for sole traders and partnerships – all limited companies must use this layout to ensure consistency between financial statements. The pro-forma layout is shown below.

Statement of Financial Position for XXXXXX Ltd as at 31st December 20XX		
	£000	**£000**
ASSETS		
Non-Current Assets		
Intangible Assets		
Investments		
Property, Plant and Equipment		
Current Assets		
Inventories		
Trade and Other Receivables		
Cash and Cash Equivalents		
TOTAL ASSETS		
EQUITY AND LIABILITIES		
Equity		
Share Capital		
Share Premium		
Retained Earnings		
Revaluation Reserve		
Total Equity		
Non-current Liabilities		
Bank loans		
Current Liabilities		
Trade and Other Payables		
Tax Payable		
Total Liabilities		
TOTAL EQUITY AND LIABILITIES		

We can see that assets are shown at the top of the statement, with non-current assets shown first, and then current assets. There is no need to show different classes of non-current assets (e.g. land and buildings, motor vehicles etc) – they are all grouped together as '**Property, Plant and Equipment'** and shown at their carrying value. **Intangible assets** are covered in more detail in Chapter 4, and include items such as copyrights, patents and licences.

The 'bottom half' of the statement shows the company's **equity**, including a number of **reserves**. It then shows the **non-current liabilities** e.g. bank loans or loan stock (debentures) and **current liabilities**.

Total Assets will be equal to **Total Equity and Liabilities.**

The Statement of Profit or Loss and Other Comprehensive Income

The Statement of Profit or Loss and Other Comprehensive Income measures the financial performance of the company over the accounting period, in terms of whether it made a profit or loss. In addition to its **trading profit or loss** (i.e. the profit or loss arising from the company's normal day-to-day activities), the statement also includes **other comprehensive income**, such as any gain or loss arising due to the revaluation of a non-current asset. Such a gain or loss does not form part of the company's 'normal' profits, and so is shown separately.

Again, the layout of the Statement of Profit or Loss and Other Comprehensive Income for limited companies (under IAS 1) is more rigidly prescribed than for sole traders or partnerships – meaning that each company must prepare its statement in the same way. This is to improve **consistency** of presentation between companies. However, the layout is significantly more simplistic than for most sole traders and partnerships, because the company's expenses are simply classified as either:

- Cost of Sales
- Distribution Costs
- Administrative Expenses
- Finance Costs

The pro-forma layout for a Statement of Profit or Loss and other Comprehensive Income is shown on the following page.

Statement of Profit & Loss and Other Comprehensive Income
For the year ended 31st December 20XX

	£000
Revenue	
Cost of Sales	
GROSS PROFIT	
Distribution Costs	
Administrative Expenses	
PROFIT FROM OPERATIONS	
Finance Costs	
PROFIT BEFORE TAX	
Tax	
PROFIT FOR YEAR FROM CONTINUING OPERATIONS	
Other Comprehensive Income	
TOTAL COMPREHENSIVE INCOME FOR THE YEAR	

You will note that there are far fewer items in the Statement than you covered for sole traders and partnerships. For example, **Cost of Sales** is shown as a single item, whilst expenses are classified as described in the pro-forma. You will not see individual expenses such as rent, salaries and wages or purchases shown separately on the statement. However, further information on items such as depreciation and employee benefit expenses must be included in the **Notes to the Accounts**.

Preparing the Statements

The starting point for preparing the Statement of Financial Position (SFP) and the Statement of Profit or Loss and other Comprehensive Income (SPLOCI) is usually the trial balance. Once this has been produced, there will then usually be a series of adjustments which will need to be carried out. These adjustments reflect that the company may identify some transactions which have not previously been accounted for, unresolved errors or accounting adjustments at the year end. The types of adjustments you will see in tasks should mostly already be familiar to you from your previous studies.

Typical adjustments include:

- Calculation of the depreciation expense for the year.
- Dealing with irrecoverable or doubtful debts / doubtful receivables.
- Dealing with closing inventories.
- Accrued and prepaid expenses and income.
- Corrections to errors in the way transactions have been accounted for.
- Inclusion of the tax charge for the year.
- Revaluation of non-current assets.
- Changes in other reserves.

NOTE: It is assumed that at this stage of your studies you are reasonably familiar with the idea of year-end adjustments. You will come across many examples and activities in this text which will allow you to practice them further, but if you feel you need to 'freshen up' your knowledge you are strongly advised to revise these areas from your earlier studies (e.g. AAT Level 3 Advanced Diploma).

Example 2.1

Flytea Ltd are preparing the financial statements for the year ended 31st December 20X7. The following adjustments need to be made. Identify the correct debit and credit entries which should be made to the accounts.

a) IT equipment with a carrying value of £25,000 at 1st January 20X7 need to be depreciated. The equipment was all purchased on 1st January 20X4 and is being depreciated on the straight line basis over five years. It has not been calculated for year ended 31st December 20X7. Depreciation of IT equipment is treated as an administrative expense by Flytea Ltd.

b) Motor vehicles which cost £100,000 on 1st January 20X5 have not been depreciated for the year ended 31st December 20X7. Motor vehicles are depreciated on a 40% diminishing balance basis, with the charge for depreciation being treated by Flytea Ltd as a distribution cost.

c) On 3rd February 20X8, Flytea Ltd received a telephone bill for £660, relating to the period 1st November 20X7 to 31st January 20X8.

d) An invoice for £450 for motor vehicle repairs (a distribution cost) was incorrectly coded to photocopier repairs (an administrative expense).

e) Land and buildings owned by Flytea Ltd were revalued for the first time in December 20X7, resulting in a revaluation reserve of £25,000.

Answer

(Note that in these answers, SPLOCI refers to the Statement of Profit or Loss and Other Comprehensive Income, whilst SFP refers to the Statement of Financial Position.)

a) IT equipment with a carrying value of £25,000 at 1st January 20X7 needs to be depreciated. The equipment was all purchased on 1st January 20X4 and is being depreciated on the straight line basis over five years. It has not been calculated for year ended 31st December 20X7. Depreciation of IT equipment is treated as an administrative expense by Flytea Ltd.

Debit	**Administrative Expense (SPLOCI)**	**£12,500**
Credit	**Accumulated Depreciation (SFP)**	**£12,500**

The assets were bought on 1st January 20X4 and have an estimated useful life of five years. On the 1st January 20X7, the carrying value of £25,000 represents two more years of estimated useful life, so the asset is being depreciated at £12,500 per year (we can calculate that the asset must have cost £62,500 when it was first bought).

b) Motor vehicles which cost £100,000 on 1st January 20X5 have not been depreciated for the year ended 31st December 20X7. Motor vehicles are depreciated on a 40% diminishing balance basis, with the charge for depreciation being treated by Flytea Ltd as a distribution cost.

Debit	**Distribution Cost (SPLOCI)**	**£14,400**
Credit	**Accumulated Depreciation (SFP)**	**£14,400**

The vehicles are depreciated 40% diminishing balance, so in the third year (20X7) this will be:

Year ended 31/12/X5 £100,000 x 40% = £40,000

Year ended 31/12/X6 £60,000 x 40% = £24,000

Year ended 31/12/X7 £36,000 x 40% = £14,400

c) On 3rd February 20X8, Flytea Ltd received a telephone bill for £660, relating to the period 1st November 20X7 to 31st January 20X8.

Debit	**Administrative Expenses (SPLOCI)**	**£440**
Credit	**Accruals (SFP)**	**£440**

2/3 of the bill relates to the year ended 31st December 20X7, so an accrual for £440 needs to be made.

d) An invoice for £450 for motor vehicle repairs (a distribution cost) was incorrectly coded to photocopier repairs (an administrative expense).

Debit	**Distribution Costs (SPLOCI)**	**£450**
Credit	**Administrative Expenses (SPLOCI)**	**£450**

e) Land and buildings owned by Flytea Ltd were revalued for the first time in December 20X7, resulting in a revaluation reserve of £25,000.

Debit	**Land and Buildings (SFP)**	**£25,000**
Credit	**Revaluation Reserve (SFP)**	**£25,000**

*Although the adjustments are to items in the Statement of Financial Position, the revaluation gain **will** be shown in Other Comprehensive Income.*

Activity 2.1

Kelspa Ltd is preparing its year end accounts at 31st March 20X8. It has a number of adjustments which need to be. For each, identify the correct double entry to be made.

a) Inventories at the close of business on 31st March 20X8 were valued at £182,000. Included within this figure is some inventory which had been valued at £6,000 but which is now only worth £3,500 due to damage.

b) Depreciation has not yet been charged for the year ending 31st March 20X8.

The company had buildings which cost £4,000,000, and plant and equipment with a carried down value at 1st April 20X7 of £140,000.

Depreciation is to be provided for as follows:

i Buildings	2% Straight Line Basis
ii Plant and Equipment	20% Reducing Balance Basis

The Depreciation charge for the year is to be allocated 50% to cost of sales, 25% to distribution costs and 25% to administrative expenses.

c) Land (which is not to be depreciated) is included in the Trial Balance at a cost of £1,500,000. It is to be revalued to £1,670,000 and this revaluation is to be included in the financial statements as at 31st March 20X8.

d) Administrative expenses of £19,200 owing are to be provided for.

e) An insurance contract for distribution lorries for the year 1st April 20X7-31st March 20X8 costing £5,800 is included in the Administrative Expense in the trial balance.

f) The Corporation Tax charge for the year of £23,000 is to be provided for.

g) The provision for doubtful receivables is to be maintained at 2%. At 31st March 20X8, the balance of trade receivables was £138,000, and the provision for doubtful receivables was £2,520. Adjustments to the doubtful receivables account should be included in Administrative Expenses.

h) Interest on a 6% loan of £200,000 for the period 1st October 20X7 to 31st March 20X8 has yet to be paid and must be provided for.

Example 2.2

You are working on the financial statements of Bridgemoor Ltd for the year ended 31st December 20X7. The trial balance as at that date is shown below:

	£000	£000
Ordinary Share Capital		2,480
Share Premium Reserve		320
Revaluation Reserve 1st January 20X7		450
Retained earnings at 1st January 20X7		3,010
Trade and Other Payables		610
Land and buildings – at cost	4,450	
Plant and equipment – at cost	2,650	
Land and buildings – accumulated depreciation		400
Plant and equipment – accumulated depreciation		985
Trade and Other Receivables	885	
Accruals		35
Prepayments	24	
8% Loan Repayable 20Y5		400
Interest Paid	16	
Sales		2,175
Purchases	990	
Sales Returns	15	
Purchase Returns		10
Distribution Costs	540	
Administrative Expenses	320	
Cash & Cash Equivalents	225	
Inventories at 1st January 20X7	655	
Provision for Doubtful Debts		15
Final Dividend for 20X6	55	
Interim dividend for 20X7	65	
	10,890	**10,890**

The following additional information is available:

- Inventories at the close of business on 31st December 20X7 were valued at £820,000.
- The tax charge for the year has been estimated at £81,000.
- Land which had cost £2,900,000 has been revalued by a professional valuer at £3,100,000. No adjustment has yet been made to the trial balance, but the revaluation is to be included in the financial statements for the year ended 31st December 20X7.
- Only six months interest on the loan has been included in the trial balance.

Task 1

Identify which of the items in the trial balance will be included in the Statement of Financial Position, and which would be included in the Statement of Profit or Loss and Other Comprehensive Income by ticking the appropriate column.

Answer

	In SFP	In SPLOCI
Ordinary Share Capital	✓	
Share Premium Reserve	✓	
Revaluation Reserve at 1st January 20X7	✓	
Retained earnings at 1st January 20X7	✓	
Trade and Other Payables	✓	
Land and buildings – at cost	✓	
Plant and equipment – at cost	✓	
Land and buildings – accumulated depreciation	✓	
Plant and equipment – accumulated depreciation	✓	
Trade and Other Receivables	✓	
Accruals	✓	
Prepayments	✓	
8% Loan Repayable 20Y5	✓	
Interest Paid		✓
Sales		✓
Purchases		✓
Sales Returns		✓
Purchase Returns		✓
Distribution Costs		✓
Administrative Expenses		✓
Cash & Cash Equivalents	✓	
Inventories at 1st January 20X7		✓
Provision for Doubtful Debts	✓	
Final Dividend for 20X6	✓	
Interim Dividend for 20X7	✓	
Tax charge for the year		✓
Inventories at 31st December 20X7	✓	✓

Task 2

Prepare the following workings for entries in the financial statements.

Cost of Sales	**£000**
Inventories at 1st January 20X7	655
Purchases	990
Purchase returns	(10)
Inventories at 31st December 20X7	(820)
Cost of Sales	815

Property, Plant & Equipment	**£000**
Total PPE at cost	7,100
Accumulated Depreciation	(1,385)
Revaluation	200
Carrying Value of PPE at 31 December 20X7	5,915

Trade and Other Receivables	**£000**
Trade Receivables	885
Provision for Doubtful Debts	(15)
Prepayments	24
Trade and Other Receivables at 31 December 20X7	894

Trade and Other Payables	**£000**
Trade Payables	610
Accruals	35
Interest on Loan	16
Trade and Other Receivables at 31 December 20X7	661

Note: Interest on the loan for year = £400,000 x 8% = £32,000. Only £16,000 of this has been accounted for so we need to set up an accrual for £16,000.

Revaluation Reserve	**£000**
Balance at 1st January 20X7	450
Revaluation of Property in 20X7	200
Balance at 31st December 20X7	650

Retained Earnings	£000
Balance at 1st January 20X7	3,010
Profit for Year Ended 31st December 20X7 (from SPLOCI)	372
Dividends	(120)
Balance at 31st December 20X7	3,262

Task 3

Prepare the Statement of Profit or Loss and Other Comprehensive Income and the Statement of Financial Position for the year ended 31st December 20X7.

Bridgemoor Ltd **Statement of Profit & Loss and Other Comprehensive Income** **For the year ended 31st December 20X7**	
	£000
Revenue	2,160
Cost of Sales	815
GROSS PROFIT	**1,345**
Distribution Costs	540
Administrative Expenses	320
PROFIT FROM OPERATIONS	**485**
Finance Costs	32
PROFIT BEFORE TAX	**453**
Tax	81
PROFIT FOR YEAR FROM CONTINUING OPERATIONS	**372**
Other Comprehensive Income	200
TOTAL COMPREHENSIVE INCOME FOR THE YEAR	**572**

Statement of Financial Position for Bridgemoor Ltd as at 31st December 20X7		
	£000	**£000**
ASSETS		
Non-Current Assets		
Intangible Assets		
Investments		
Property, Plant and Equipment	5,915	
Current Assets		
Inventories	820	
Trade and Other Receivables	894	
Cash and Cash Equivalents	225	
	1,939	
TOTAL ASSETS		**7,854**
EQUITY AND LIABILITIES		
Equity		
Share Capital	2,480	
Share Premium	320	
Retained Earnings	3,262	
Revaluation Reserve	650	
Total Equity	6,712	6,712
Non-current Liabilities		
Bank loans	400	
Current Liabilities		
Trade and Other Payables	661	
Tax Payable	81	
	742	
Total Liabilities		1,142
TOTAL EQUITY AND LIABILITIES		**7,854**

Activity 2.2

Murray Mince Ltd is a frozen food manufacturer which prepares its financial statements to 31st December each year. You have the Trial Balance as at 31st December 20X4 for Murray Mince Ltd below:

	£000	£000
Ordinary Share Capital		2,500
Share Premium Reserve		200
Revaluation Reserve		600
Retained earnings at 1st January 20X4		1,480
Trade and Other Payables		104
Land and buildings – at cost	3,250	
Plant and equipment – at cost	1,060	
Land and buildings – accumulated depreciation		1,080
Plant and equipment – accumulated depreciation		210
Trade and Other Receivables	300	
Accruals		24
Prepayments	16	
6% Loan Repayable 20Y4		400
Interest Paid	12	
Sales		841
Purchases	265	
Sales Returns	18	
Purchase Returns		7
Distribution Costs	188	
Administrative Expenses	107	
Cash & Cash Equivalents	1,577	
Inventories at 1st January 20X4	198	
Provision for Doubtful Debts		10
Final Dividend for 20X3	225	
Interim dividend for 20X4	240	
	7,456	**7,456**

Additional Information:

1. Inventories at the close of business on 31st December 20X4 were valued at £214,000. Included within this figure is some inventory which had been valued at £12,000 but which is now only worth £2,000 due to damage.
2. Depreciation has not yet been charged for the year ending 31st December 20X4. Depreciation is to be provided for as follows:

i.	Buildings	5% Straight Line Basis
ii.	Plant and Equipment	8% Reducing Balance Basis

    The Depreciation charge for the year is to be allocated 50% to cost of sales, 25% to distribution costs and 25% to administrative expenses.
3. Land (which is not to be depreciated) is included in the Trial Balance at a cost of £850,000. It is to be revalued to £990,000 and this revaluation is to be included in the financial statements as at 31st December 20X4.
4. Distribution costs of £16,000 owing are to be provided for.
5. A maintenance contract for administrative equipment for the year 1st January 20X5 - 31st December 20X5 costing £3,000 is included in the Administrative Expense in the trial balance.
6. The Corporation Tax charge for the year of £27,000 is to be provided for.
7. The provision for doubtful debts is to be maintained at 4%.
8. Interest on the loan for the second half of 20X4 has yet to be paid and must be provided for.
9. All operations are continuing.

You are required to prepare the Statement of Profit or Loss for the year ended 31st December 20X4 and the Statement of Financial Position as at the same date.

STATEMENT OF PROFIT OR LOSS – WORKINGS

Depreciation Charge	£000
Buildings *Workings*	
Plant and Equipment *Workings*	
Total	
To Cost of Sales	
To Distribution Costs	
To Administration Expenses	

Revenue	£000
Sales	
Less Sales Returns	
Total	

Cost of Sales	£000
Opening Inventories	
Purchases	
Less Purchase Returns	
Depreciation Charge	
Less Closing Inventories	
Total	

Distribution Costs	£000
Distribution Costs (from TB)	
Depreciation	
Accruals	
Prepayments	
Other Adjustments	
Total	

Administration Costs	£000
Administration Expenses (from TB)	
Depreciation	
Accruals	
Prepayments	
Provision for Doubtful Receivables – Adjustment	
Other Adjustments	
Total	

Finance Costs	£000
Interest Paid (from TB)	
Accruals	
Total	

Taxation	£000
Tax charge for year (from notes)	
Adjustments for under/over payment in previous year	
Total	

Statement of Profit & Loss and Other Comprehensive Income
For the year ended 31st December 20X4

	£000
Revenue	
Cost of Sales	
GROSS PROFIT	
Distribution Costs	
Administrative Expenses	
PROFIT FROM OPERATIONS	
Finance Costs	
PROFIT BEFORE TAX	
Tax	
PROFIT FOR YEAR FROM CONTINUING OPERATIONS	
Other Comprehensive Income	
TOTAL COMPREHENSIVE INCOME FOR THE YEAR	

STATEMENT OF FINANCIAL POSITION – WORKINGS

Property, Plant and Equipment	£000
Land and Buildings at cost	
Land and Buildings – Accumulated Depreciation	
Revaluation	
Plant and Equipment – at cost	
Plant and Equipment – Accumulated Depreciation	
Depreciation Charge for the Year	
Total	

Trade and Other Receivables	£000
Trade and Other Receivables	
Prepayments	
Provision for Doubtful Debts	
Total	

Retained Earnings	£000
Retained Earnings at 1st January 20X4	
Profit for Period	
Dividends Paid	
Retained Earnings at 31st December 20X4	

Trade and Other Payables	£000
Trade and Other Payables	
Accruals	
Accrued Interest	
Total	

Statement of Financial Position for Murray Mince Ltd as at 31st December 20X4

	£000	£000
ASSETS		
Non-Current Assets		
Property, Plant and Equipment		
Current Assets		
Inventories		
Trade and Other Receivables		
Cash and Cash Equivalents		
TOTAL ASSETS		
EQUITY AND LIABILITIES		
Equity		
Share Capital		
Share Premium		
Retained Earnings		
Revaluation Reserve		
Total Equity		
Non-current Liabilities		
Bank loans		
Current Liabilities		
Trade and Other Payables		
Tax Payable		
Total Liabilities		
TOTAL EQUITY AND LIABILITIES		

Activity 2.3

Chartwell Ltd is an engineering company which prepares its financial statements to 31st March each year. You have the Trial Balance as at 31st March 20X8 below:

	£000	£000
Ordinary Share Capital		3,000
Share Premium Reserve		280
Revaluation Reserve		410
Retained earnings at 1st April 20X7		2,580
Trade and Other Payables		265
Land and buildings – at cost	5,900	
Plant and equipment – at cost	990	
Land and buildings – accumulated depreciation		1,064
Plant and equipment – accumulated depreciation		190
Trade and Other Receivables	300	
Accruals		30
Prepayments	19	
8% Loan Repayable 20Y2		500
Interest Paid	20	
Sales		1,085
Purchases	481	
Sales Returns	10	
Purchase Returns		14
Distribution Costs	153	
Administrative Expenses	121	
Cash & Cash Equivalents	882	
Inventories at 1st April 20X7	208	
Provision for Doubtful Debts		6
Final Dividend for 20X7	180	
Interim dividend for 20X8	160	
	9,424	**9,424**

Additional Information:

1. Inventories at the close of business on 31st March 20X8 were valued at £275,000. Included within this figure is some inventory which had been valued at £8,000 but which is now only worth £3,000 due to damage.

2. Depreciation has not yet been charged for the year ending 31st March 20X8. Depreciation is to be provided for as follows:

   i. Buildings 4% Straight Line Basis

   ii. Plant and Equipment 10% Reducing Balance Basis

   The Depreciation charge for the year is to be allocated 50% to cost of sales, 25% to distribution costs and 25% to administrative expenses.

3. Land (which is not to be depreciated) is included in the Trial Balance at cost of £1,600,000. It is to be revalued to £1,900,000 and this revaluation is to be included in the financial statements as at 31st March 20X8.

4. Distribution costs of £19,000 owing are to be provided for.

5. A maintenance contract for administrative equipment for the year 1st January 20X8-31st December 20X8 costing £12,000 is included in full in the Administrative Expense in the trial balance.

6. The Corporation Tax charge for the year of £32,000 is to be provided for.

7. The provision for doubtful debts is to be maintained at 3%.

8. Interest on the loan for the second half of 20X7-X8 has yet to be paid and must be provided for.

9. All operations are continuing.

You are required to prepare the Statement of Profit or Loss for the year ended 31st March 20X8 and the Statement of Financial Position as at the same date.

STATEMENT OF PROFIT OR LOSS – WORKINGS

Depreciation Charge	£000
Buildings	
Plant and Equipment	
Total	
To Cost of Sales	
To Distribution Costs	
To Administration Expenses	

Revenue	£000
Sales	
Less Sales Returns	
Total	

Cost of Sales	£000
Opening Inventories	
Purchases	
Less Purchase Returns	
Depreciation Charge	
Less Closing Inventories	
Total	

Distribution Costs	£000
Distribution Costs (from TB)	
Depreciation	
Accruals	
Prepayments	
Other Adjustments	
Total	

Administration Expenses	£000
Administration Expenses (from TB)	
Depreciation	
Accruals	
Prepayments	
Provision for Doubtful Receivables – Adjustment	
Other Adjustments	
Total	

Finance Costs	£000
Interest Paid (from TB)	
Accruals	
Total	

Taxation	£000
Tax charge for year (from notes)	
Adjustments for under/over payment in previous year	
Total	

Statement of Profit & Loss and Other Comprehensive Income **For the year ended 31st March 20X8**	**£000**
Revenue	
Cost of Sales	
GROSS PROFIT	
Distribution Costs	
Administrative Expenses	
PROFIT FROM OPERATIONS	
Finance Costs	
PROFIT BEFORE TAX	
Tax	
PROFIT FOR YEAR FROM CONTINUING OPERATIONS	
Other Comprehensive Income	
TOTAL COMPREHENSIVE INCOME FOR THE YEAR	

STATEMENT OF FINANCIAL POSITION – WORKINGS

Property, Plant and Equipment	£000
Land and Buildings at cost	
Land and Buildings – Accumulated Depreciation	
Revaluation	
Plant and Equipment – at cost	
Plant and Equipment – Accumulated Depreciation	
Depreciation Charge for the Year	
Total	

Trade and Other Receivables	£000
Trade and Other Receivables	
Prepayments	
Provision for Doubtful Receivables	
Total	

Retained Earnings	£000
Retained Earnings at 1st April 20X7	
Profit for Period	
Dividends Paid	
Retained Earnings at 31st March 20X8	

Trade and Other Payables	£000
Trade and Other Payables	
Accruals	
Accrued Interest	
Total	

Statement of Financial Position for Chartwell Ltd
as at 31st March 20X8

	£000	£000
ASSETS		
Non-Current Assets		
Property, Plant and Equipment		
Current Assets		
Inventories		
Trade and Other Receivables		
Cash and Cash Equivalents		
TOTAL ASSETS		
EQUITY AND LIABILITIES		
Equity		
Share Capital		
Share Premium		
Retained Earnings		
Revaluation Reserve		
Total Equity		
Non-current Liabilities		
Bank loans		
Current Liabilities		
Trade and Other Payables		
Tax Payable		
Total Liabilities		
TOTAL EQUITY AND LIABILITIES		

Assessment 2

You are now required to log-in to your ROGO account to complete your online assessment before progressing on to the next chapter.

Chapter 3: Equity

By the end of this chapter you should:

- Understand the term Equity and how it is calculated in the statements.
- Be able to draft statements of changes in equity.

Introduction

Equity is shown in the Statement of Financial Position. We saw in Chapter 2 that equity is defined as:

"The owners' residual interest in the assets of the entity, after deducting all its liabilities."

This definition indicates that equity is the amount of value which 'belongs' to the owners of the business, once all the liabilities of the business have been taken into consideration. It reflects the accounting equation (rearranged) as below:

Equity = Assets - Liabilities

As a reminder, the equity section of the Statement of Financial Position contains the following items:

Share Capital	X
Share Premium Reserve	X
Revaluation Reserve	X
Retained Earnings	X
Total Equity	X

We shall look at each of these in turn.

Share Capital

This is the amount of money invested in the company by its shareholders. When a company is first created, it nominates an amount of **Authorised Share Capital**. This is the **maximum** value of shares it is allowed to sell over its lifetime. However, the company does not necessarily issue all of these shares when it is first incorporated – most companies will retain some 'spare' shares which it can issue in the future so that it can raise finance when it is required. Therefore, the **Issued Share Capital** is the actual number of shares issued to shareholders at any point in time – and this will often be less than (but never more than) the authorised share capital.

There are two major classes of shares in limited companies – **ordinary shares** and **preference shares**.

Ordinary Shares are the main type of shares issued by companies. When an investor purchases ordinary shares, they are in effect purchasing a 'share' of the company. Whilst smaller companies may have a 100% shareholder who owns all the issued shares in the company, most larger companies are owned by several – or thousands of – different owners. This part-ownership of a company entitles each shareholder to vote on decisions at the company's Annual General Meeting. Furthermore, if the company makes a profit after tax it will often **declare a dividend** – this means that each shareholder receives a 'portion' of the profit based on the proportionate number of shares they own. Companies will not usually pay all profits back to shareholders in the form of dividends, however – they will usually keep some profits back for future investment in the business. These are known as **retained profits**. If the company fails, however, ordinary shareholders are unlikely to receive the full value of their investment back – indeed, in many cases they may receive nothing at all.

Preference shares are issued by companies to investors in order to raise finance. They are generally less risky for investors, as should the company fail they are more likely to receive at least some of their investment back as they are entitled to receive payment **before** the ordinary shareholders. Preference shareholders are also entitled to receive dividends before ordinary shareholders – this means in years when the company performs badly, preference shareholders will still receive a dividend when ordinary shareholders may not. However, preference shares do not carry voting rights (meaning preference shareholders have no say at all in how the company is managed) and are entitled to a fixed dividend each year (e.g. 6%). In years when the company performs well, preference shareholders may receive a lower dividend than ordinary shareholders. For these reasons, preference shares are not usually included in the equity section of the Statement of Financial Position, and are instead included as non-current liabilities of the company.

Rights Issues

Companies can elect to issue to new shares to the general market. However, they may prefer to offer a **rights issue**, which is an offer made to existing shareholders to buy more shares at a discounted rate. This is done to reward existing shareholders, and may also make it easier for the company to sell the required number of shares in order to raise the required funds.

A rights issue is made by offering exiting shareholders the 'right' to buy more shares – the maximum number of shares each shareholder can buy is determined by the size of their current shareholding. For example, in a 1 for 3 offer, shareholders can purchase 1 new share for every 3 that they already own. In a 4 for 1 offer, they could buy 4 new shares for each one owned.

Example 3.1

Biggles Ltd makes a rights issue of new £1 ordinary shares to existing shareholders on a 2:3 basis at a price of £2.50 per share. All shares offered in the rights issue are taken up by existing shareholders.

Prior to the issue, Biggles Ltd had 90,000 ordinary £1 issued shares. The share premium reserve was £25,000 and the retained earnings of the company were £390,000.

Required

a) Calculate the total number of issued shares after the rights issue.

b) Show the double entry to record the rights issue.

c) Show the equity section of the Statement of Financial Position after the rights issue.

Answer

a) Previously issued	=	90,000 shares	
Rights Issue	=	60,000 shares	*(90,000 x 2/3)*
Total	=	150,000 shares	

b) **Dr** Bank	£150,000
Cr Ordinary Share Capital	£60,000
Cr Share Premium Account	£90,000

c) Equity Section (extract)

Ordinary Shares	£150,000
Share Premium A/c	£115,000
Retained Earnings	£390,000
Total Equity	£655,000

Bonus Shares

Whilst rights issues are the issue of new shares to existing shareholders, a **bonus issue** is simply the issuing of new shares to existing shareholders at zero cost – the shareholder simply receives a number of 'free' shares. A bonus issue does not therefore raise any additional funds for the company.

A bonus issue is usually made by a company to enable it to reclassify its non-share reserves. Under the Companies Act (2006), some equity reserves are not distributable – this means that funds held in these reserves may not be distributed to shareholders as dividends. Examples of non-distributable reserves are the share premium and the revaluation reserve. By converting non-distributable reserves to distributable share reserves, a company has more freedom in how it chooses to pay dividends to its shareholders.

Example 3.2

Boggles Ltd makes a bonus issue of new £1 ordinary shares to existing shareholders on a 1:6 basis, using the share premium account. All shares offered in the bonus issue are taken up by existing shareholders.

Prior to the issue, Boggles Ltd had 60,000 ordinary £1 issued shares. The share premium reserve was £35,000 and the retained earnings of the company were £210,000.

Required

a) Calculate the total number of issued shares after the bonus issue.

b) Show the double entry to record the bonus issue.

c) Show the equity section of the Statement of Financial Position after the bonus issue.

Answer

a) Previously issued	=	60,000 shares	
Bonus Issue	=	10,000 shares	*(60,000 x 1/6)*
Total	=	70,000 shares	

b) **Dr** Share Premium A/c £10,000

Cr Ordinary Share Capital £10,000

c) Equity Section (extract)

Ordinary Shares	£ 70,000
Share Premium A/c	£ 25,000
Retained Earnings	£210,000
Total Equity	£305,000

Share Premium Reserve

When a company issues ordinary shares, each share has a **nominal value** (also called a **face value** or **par value**). This is the minimum price for which the shares can be issued. For example, many ordinary shares have a nominal value of £0.50 or £1.00, meaning that when the company issues new shares they cannot be issued for a lower price than that. However, often when an established company makes a new share issue it will do so with the shares valued at a higher price. The difference between the actual issue price and the nominal value is the **share premium**. It arises because the value of each share (measured as a proportion of the value of the company at the time of issue) is higher than the nominal value established when the company was incorporated.

Example 3.3

Baggles Ltd has authorised share capital of 1,000,000 ordinary shares with a nominal value of £1.00 each. On 31st May 20X3 it has 400,000 of these shares in issue. The value of the company on this date is £8,000,000. On 1st June 20X3, the company issues a further 100,000 ordinary shares. These are sold to investors for £20 each.

The revised company valuation on 1st June 20X3 is £10,000,000 (£8,000,000 + £2,000,000 new investment). The share valuation on 31st May was (£8,000,000 / 400,000) = £20 per share. The valuation on 1st June remains £20 (£10,000,000 / 500,000). Investors are therefore paying £20 for each £1 ordinary share – and the premium is therefore £19 per share.

The accounting entries required for the new share issue would be:

Dr Bank	**£2,000,000**	*(100,000 x £20)*
Cr Share Capital	**£100,000**	*(100,000 x £1 nominal value)*
Cr Share Premium	**£1,900,000**	*(100,000 x £19 premium)*

Note that only the nominal value is credited to the Share Capital Account, with the premium being credited to the Share Premium Account. The value of the Share Capital Account in the Statement of Financial Position on 1st June (after the issue) would therefore be £500,000, representing the issued share capital of 500,000 £1 ordinary shares shown at their nominal value.

Activity 3.1

On 31st December 20X7, Buggles Ltd had the following equity section within its Statement of Financial Position.

Equity

Ordinary Shares (£1)	£400,000
Share Premium Account	£ 96,000
Retained Earnings	£120,000
	£616,000

On 1st April 20X8, the company makes a 1:5 rights issue at a price of £3.20 per share. All shares under the rights issue were taken up by existing shareholders.

On 1st October 20X8, the company then makes a 1:10 bonus issue, using the share premium account. All shares offered in the bonus issue are taken up by existing shareholders.

Required

a) Calculate the total number of issued shares after the rights issue.

b) Show the double entry to record the rights issue.

c) Show the equity section of the Statement of Financial Position after the rights issue.

d) Calculate the total number of issued shares after the bonus issue.

e) Show the double entry to record the bonus issue.

f) Show the equity section of the Statement of Financial Position after the bonus issue.

Revaluation Reserve

When a company purchases property, plant or equipment (PPE) it will record the asset at its original cost. This asset will then be depreciated each year according to the company's policy. Whilst most assets will decline in value over their life, some assets – particularly property – will increase in value. When this happens, the assets could become undervalued in the accounts. Whilst accountants must always follow the concept of prudence, and not recognise unrealised gains, they must also at the same time ensure that the financial statements present a true and fair view of the financial position of the company.

Therefore, companies are permitted to value their assets on either of the following bases:

- **The cost model** – where non-current assets are valued at their historic cost, less accumulated depreciation.
- **The revaluation model** – whereby non-current assets are valued at their 'fair value' less any subsequent accumulated depreciation.

You will learn more about this in Chapter 4 but for now should recognise that some assets (particularly property) may be revalued and the higher value shown in the Statement of Financial Position.

When this happens the Property account is debited with the amount of the revaluation, and the Accumulated Depreciation account is also debited (to remove any depreciation which has previously been charged on those assets), whilst a Revaluation Reserve is credited with the same amount.

Dr **Property at Cost**

Dr **Accumulated Depreciation**

Cr **Revaluation Reserve**

The carrying value in the non-current assets section of the Statement of Financial Position will be the revalued amount. The company should continue to charge depreciation on the asset after revaluation.

Example 3.4

Stephenson Ltd owns a number of properties in London. In the Statement of Financial Position as at 1st May 20X3 these were shown at their combined historic cost of £8.9 million, less accumulated depreciation of £1.3 million. There were no additions or disposals during the financial year ended 30th April 20X4, but during the year the properties were professionally revalued at a combined valuation of £11.4 million.

Required

Show the double entry required to reflect the revaluation of the properties.

Answer

The carrying value of the property at 30th April 20X3 is £7,600,000 (£8.9 million - £1.3 million). After revaluation, the carrying value should be £11,400,000.

The double entry would be:

Dr **Property at Cost** **£2,500,000**

(increasing from £8.9 million to £11.4 million)

Dr **Accumulated Depreciation** **£1,300,000**

(removing the previously accumulated depreciation)

Cr **Revaluation Reserve** **£3,800,000**

(reflecting an increase in the value of the business which, in turn, represents an increase in the value of the equity).

Retained Earnings

We saw earlier that any profits (after tax) made by a company belong to its shareholders. Payment of profits to shareholders are called **dividends.** Companies will not usually pay all their profits to shareholders, as they will wish to hold some of this money back to pay for investment in non-current assets, or to provide a buffer against potential future poor years.

Any profits not paid out in the form of dividends are **retained profits**. They still ultimately belong to the shareholders, and so increase the value of the equity in the business. Dividends are not treated as an expense, and so do not appear in the Statement of Profit or Loss and Other Comprehensive Income. Instead, they are a distribution of profits, and so reduce the level of equity in the business by being deducted from the profit for the year – only the retained profits are included in equity.

The double entry for the payment of dividends is therefore:

Dr Dividends (SFP)

Cr Bank

Companies will often pay an **Interim Dividend** part-way through the year. This is a 'part' dividend based on the profits the directors predict the company will make for the year. It means that shareholders do not have to wait until after the financial statements have been approved before they can receive a payment. A second dividend payment is then **proposed** at the Annual General Meeting based on the actual profit, and if this is approved by the shareholders becomes the **Final Dividend** for the year.

The Statement of Changes in Equity

Statement of Changes in Equity is a particularly useful report for shareholders in the business. It breaks down the changes which have occurred in the equity section of the Statement of Financial Position over the previous twelve months.

A pro-forma Statement of Changes in Equity is shown below:

	Share Capital £000	Share Premium £000	Revaluation Reserve £000	Retained Earnings £000	Total Equity £000
Balance at start of year	X	X	X	X	X
Changes in Equity					
Comprehensive Income			X	X	X
Dividends				(X)	(X)
Issue of Share Capital	X	X			X
Balance at end of year	X	X	X	X	X

The reserves which appear in the equity section of the Statement of Financial Position are listed across the top of the Statement along with their balances at the start of the year. Any events which lead to changes in these balances during the year are then recorded in the appropriate columns. So, for example, any revaluation of non-current assets during the year (which can be found in the Statement of Profit or Loss and Other Comprehensive Income) are recorded in the Revaluation Reserve column. Retained earnings are increased by any profits made (from the SPLOCI) and reduced by any dividends paid (from the SFP). If new share capital has been issued during the year, this is shown as both Share Capital (the nominal value of the issue) **and** as Share Premium (the difference between the actual and nominal values of the issue).

Example 3.5

In the year ended 31st March 20X4, Perez Ltd made an operating profit after tax of £580,000. During the year the following events occurred:

- There was a revaluation of freehold properties owned by the company, resulting in a gain of £110,000.
- The company issued 30,000 new £1 ordinary shares, raising £50,000 new capital.
- A dividend of £250,000 was made to shareholders.

Equity balances as at 1st April 20X3 were:

Share Capital	£125,000
Share Premium	£40,000
Revaluation Reserve	£ 0
Retained Profits	£186,000

Required

Prepare the Statement of Changes in Equity for the year ended 31st March 20X4.

	Share Capital £000	Share Premium £000	Revaluation Reserve £000	Retained Earnings £000	Total Equity £000
Balance at start of year	125	40	0	186	351
Changes in Equity:					
Comprehensive Income			110	580	690
Dividends				(250)	(250)
Issue of Share Capital	30	20			50
Balance at end of year	155	60	110	516	841

Activity 3.2

In the year ended 31st August 20X5, Bronski Ltd made an operating profit after tax of £63,000. During the year the following events occurred:

There was a revaluation of freehold properties owned by the company, resulting in a gain of £92,000. The company issued 20,000 new £0.50 ordinary shares, raising £18,000 new capital.

A dividend of £31,000 was made to shareholders.

Equity balances as at 1st September 20X4 were:

Share Capital	£100,000
Share Premium	£ 28,000
Revaluation Reserve	£ 12,000
Retained Profits	£155,000

Required

Prepare the Statement of Changes in Equity for the year ended 31st August 20X5.

	Share Capital £000	Share Premium £000	Revaluation Reserve £000	Retained Earnings £000	Total Equity £000
Balance at start of year					
Changes in Equity:					
Comprehensive Income					
Dividends					
Issue of Share Capital					
Balance at end of year					

Assessment 3

You are now required to log-in to your ROGO account to complete your online assessment and midpoint assessment before progressing on to the next chapter.

Chapter 4: Assets

By the end of this chapter you should:

- Understand the requirements and application of the accounting standards for:
    - Assets
    - Intangible assets
    - Leases
    - Impairments
    - Research and development
    - Goodwill
    - Inventories

Introduction

All companies need to invest in assets in order to operate their business on a day to day basis. Accountants differentiate between:

Current Assets – these are assets which have an estimated useful life of less than twelve months, and which are 'transitionary' in nature; that is, the valuation of them changes on a day to day basis.

Examples of current assets include inventories, trade and other receivables (including prepayments), cash and cash equivalents (such as short-term bank deposits).

Non-Current Assets – these are assets which the company plans to keep and use on a regular basis over an extended period of time – at least for the next twelve months. By using these assets in its day-to-day business, the company expects to be able to generate profits now and in the future.

Examples of non-current assets include land, buildings, vehicles, plant and machinery and office equipment. These are aggregated together and shown as the single item **Property, Plant and Equipment** in the Statement of Financial Position for limited companies.

Other examples of non-current assets include investments (assets such as properties or shareholdings in other companies which are not used on a day-to-day basis in the business, but which nevertheless are expected to generate future profits), and intangible assets (which will be considered in more detail later in this chapter).

Definition of an Asset

We saw in Chapter 1 that an asset is defined as:

"A present economic resource controlled by the entity as a result of past events."

This definition extends and formalises our basic understanding of what an asset is. There are a number of important aspects to this definition:

- The business does not necessarily have to **own** an item for it to be considered an asset; it may be enough that it simply **controls** the item. This is particularly important when trying to identify the difference between a **short term lease** and a **finance lease**. This is considered in more detail later in this chapter in IFRS 16 *Leases*.

- **Future economic benefits** must be expected to flow to the entity – this means that to consider an item as an asset the business must expect to be able to generate profits from it in the future. This has implications for how businesses value items which have outlived their useful economic life but which the company still own. If an item is not expected to be able to be used to generate profits, it cannot be considered to be an asset.

IAS 16 Property, Plant and Equipment

You should already be familiar with the different types of tangible non-current (fixed) assets owned by a business. Tangible simply means that the asset can be seen and touched – that it has **physical substance**. Examples of tangible assets include:

- Land
- Buildings
- Machinery
- Office equipment
- Fixtures and fittings
- Motor vehicles

Non-current means that the asset is expected to be used over more than one period (i.e. for longer than twelve months). Not all non-current assets are tangible (and you will learn about some **intangible** assets further on in this chapter), but IAS 16 only deals with the tangible assets of Property, Plant and Equipment (PPE).

Property, Plant and Equipment is therefore defined as:

"Tangible assets held for use in the production or supply of goods and services, which are expected to be used for more than one period."

Remember, also, the definition of an asset from the conceptual framework:

"A present economic resource controlled by the entity as a result of past events…"

The reason businesses own assets, is to use them in the future in order to generate income – if an asset (e.g. a dilapidated old machine) is no longer capable of earning income in the future it should no longer be regarded as an asset.

IAS 16 considers important accounting concepts in dealing with non-current assets, including:

- When to **recognise** an asset (i.e. when to show it in the financial statements).
- When and how to depreciate non-current assets.
- How to record the carrying value (net book value) in the financial statements.

IAS 16 links with other IASs in your studies in the following way:

IAS 16 only considers **tangible** assets; intangible assets (e.g. research and development) are considered in IAS 38.

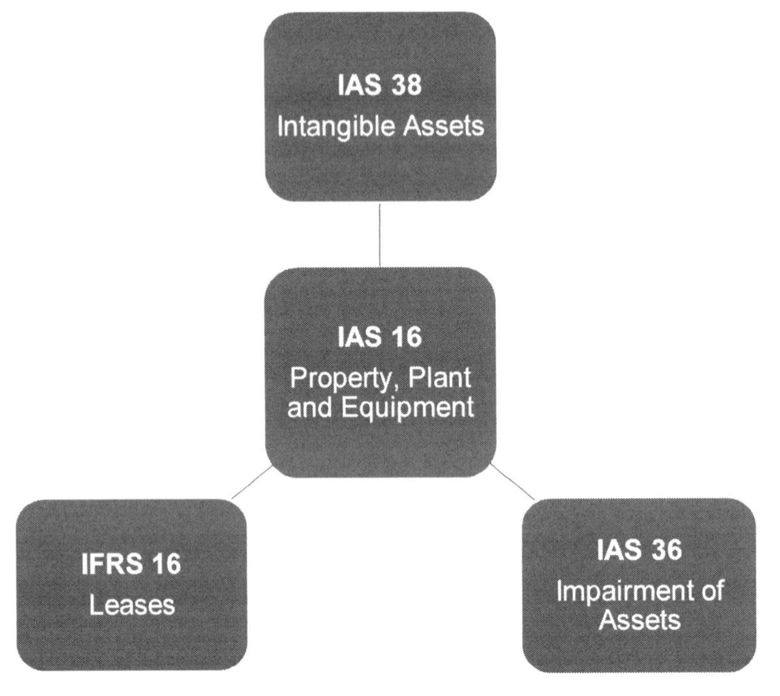

IFRS 16 considers the factors which determine whether an entity has the right to use or control an asset and the ways these should be accounted for.

IAS 36 considers how to account for reductions in value of assets – e.g. when an asset is damaged in some way.

A thorough understanding of IAS 16 will help you to understand the key issues in accounting for non-current assets, and also to understand the wider issues in these other IASs.

Recognition of Assets

One key issue is to identify when an asset should be **recognised** – that is, when it should be shown in the financial statements. There are two key criteria which must be met:

a. It is **probable** that future economic benefits will flow to the entity.

b. The cost of the asset must be **reliably measured.**

Only if both of these criteria are met should the asset be recorded in the accounts.

Non-current assets should be recorded at their **Historic Cost** (i.e. the amount paid) in the first instance; this will include not only the initial purchase price but also costs such as:

- Costs of site preparation.
- Delivery and handling costs.
- Installation costs.
- Professional fees (e.g. architects, engineers or surveyors).
- Testing the asset before bringing it into use.

However, the following items must be treated as revenue expenditure and charged to the Statement of Profit or Loss in the period in which they are incurred:

- Administration and other general overhead costs.
- Start-up costs of a new business (or a new part of an existing business).

In addition, the following items of expenditure (which are incurred after the asset has been brought into use) can be included in the carrying value (Net Book Value) of the asset:

- The regular replacement of parts of the asset (e.g. major components in a production line).
- The cost of regular inspections, where these are required in order to continue the operation of the asset (e.g. safety inspections on aircraft or ships).

However, costs of day-to-day servicing, including the cost of small parts should **not** be included in the cost of the asset, and instead must be treated as a **revenue cost**, and recognised as an expense in the Statement of Profit or Loss for the period in which the expenditure is incurred.

Example 4.1

Arthur Ltd purchased a new machine for its engineering plant in September 20X7.The new machine is to be used in the production of a brand new product, the Vistor.

The cost of the machine was £87,500 plus VAT. In addition, the company incurred additional expenses of:

Site preparation fees	£8,000
Delivery and installation	£5,600
Architects fees	£2,300
Testing costs	£2,950
Advertising costs promoting the new product	£6,200

In November 20X7, the company spent £1,850 re-calibrating the machine and a further £980 cleaning it, following a faulty batch of production.

How should Arthur Ltd recognise the asset in the financial statements at their year end of 31st March 20X8?

Answer

The machine appears to meet the recognition criteria of:

a. It is **probable** that future economic benefits will flow to the entity.

b. The cost of the asset must be **reliably measured.**

Therefore, the asset should be recorded in the Statement of Financial Position as a tangible non-current asset. Recognition should be at the Historic Cost of the asset.

This would include:

Cost of machine	£87,500	(VAT not capitalised if VAT registered)
Site preparation	£ 8,000	
Delivery/installation	£ 5,600	
Architects' fees	£ 2,300	
Testing costs	£ 2,950	
TOTAL	£106,350	

This figure will be included in Machinery at Cost as at 31st March 20X8.

The advertising costs, re-calibration costs and cleaning costs are not included in the cost of the asset, and instead must be treated as an expense in the Statement of Profit or Loss for the year ending 31st March 20X8.

Valuation of Assets

We have seen above that when an asset is first acquired it should be recorded in the accounts at the Historic Cost. Following this, the business must then decide which of the following two valuation models it wishes to choose when recording the asset in subsequent financial statements.

Cost Model – you are already familiar with this model – the asset is carried in the financial statements at its historic cost, less accumulated depreciation and accumulated impairment losses.

Revaluation Model – here, the asset is re-valued periodically (perhaps every 3-5 years, or even annually). The asset must be re-valued to its **fair value**, and then shown in the financial statements at its fair value minus subsequent depreciation and impairment losses (see IAS 36).

Definition of Fair Value:

"The price that would be received to sell an asset, or paid to transfer a liability, in an orderly transaction between market participants at the measurement date (i.e. the date of the valuation)."

This definition comes from IFRS 14 Fair Value which is outside your studies at Level 4, but you should still be able to recall and apply this definition.

This means that the **fair value** of an asset is based on an objective, market-based valuation of the asset – whether or not the entity actually intends to keep or sell the asset is irrelevant. For the purposes of this unit, it can be assumed that **fair value** is the same as **market value.**

If the entity chooses to adopt the revaluation model, then **all** assets in the same class must also be valued using this basis. This means, for example, that if the entity chooses to adopt the revaluation model for property, then **all** property owned by the entity must be valued in this way.

Any assets being valued under the revaluation model must be re-valued regularly – this is to ensure that the carrying amount of the asset in the financial statements does not differ materially from its fair value at that date.

Example 4.2

Jerzy Ltd owns three properties. One of these is in the centre of London, and was purchased one year ago for £2.5 million. It has been charged with accumulated depreciation of £100,000.

Jerzy Ltd had the property professionally re-valued at £4.2 million at the end of the accounting period.

Jerzy Ltd could choose to value the property in either of the following ways:

a. **Cost model.**

   Valued at £2,500,000 - £100,000 = £2,400,000

b. **Revaluation model.**

   Valued at £4.2 million. Note that we do not deduct the accumulated depreciation at this stage, as the accounting date matches the revaluation date.

If Jerzy Ltd decide to adopt the revaluation model, then they must also have their other two properties re-valued and included in the financial statements at these revaluations. However, other classes of assets (e.g. machinery or vehicles) could continue to be valued under the cost model.

ACCOUNTING FOR THE INCREASE IN VALUE

Where an asset is re-valued upwards:

Dr Asset at cost

Cr Revaluation Reserve

... with the increase in value. The increase in value is also shown in the Statement of Profit or Loss and Other Comprehensive Income (as other Comprehensive Income).

Where an asset is re-valued downwards:

Dr Expense in the Statement of Profit or Loss

Cr Asset at cost

... with the decrease in value.

These accounting entries reflect the accounting concept of ***prudence*** – the gain in value is not recognised in the Statement of Profit or Loss because it has not actually been realised yet, whilst any downward revaluation is recognised immediately as a loss, even though the asset has not actually been sold and so the loss has not actually happened.

Example 4.2 continued ...

Continuing the earlier example, if Jerzy Ltd adopts the revaluation model for property, it would debit its Property account with £1,800,000 (because the property has been re-valued from £2.4 million to £4.2 million). It would create a revaluation reserve (which is a non-distributable reserve within the equity section of the Statement of Financial Position) with the same amount.

However, if the revaluation **reverses** a previous valuation, then the process is slightly different:

For an upwards revaluation which reverses a previous downwards revaluation:

Dr Asset at cost

Cr Income in the Statement of Profit or Loss

The earlier downwards revaluation will have previously been treated as an expense, so this will 'match' the subsequent upwards revaluation against this. This can only be done to the extent of reversing the earlier downwards revaluation.

For a downwards revaluation which reverses a previous upwards revaluation:

Dr Revaluation Reserve (this reduces the balance in the revaluation reserve)

Cr Asset at cost

Example 4.3

Pepe Ltd values its land according to the revaluation model. It purchased the property in 20X0 for £700,000, and in 20X3 it was re-valued to £900,000. In 20X7, it was again re-valued, this time to £780,000, and then five years later, in 20Y2 it was re-valued again to £950,000.

The accounting entries would be:

20X0:	**Dr Land at cost**	**£700,000**	
	Cr Bank	**£700,000**	being the original purchase
20X3	**Dr Land at cost**	**£200,000**	
	Cr Revaluation Reserve	**£200,000**	being the revaluation to £900,000
20X7	**Dr Revaluation Reserve**	**£120,000**	
	Cr Land at cost	**£120,000**	as a reversal of the previous gain, this is not charged as an expense to the Statement of Profit or Loss.
20Y2	**Dr Land**	**£170,000**	
	Cr Revaluation Reserve	**£170,000**	being the revaluation to £950,000

Depreciation

You should be familiar with depreciation from your earlier studies.

Definition: *"Depreciation is the systematic allocation of the depreciable amount of an asset over its useful life."*

The ***depreciable amount*** is the cost less any estimated residual value (i.e. the realistic and prudent estimate of what the asset could be sold for at the end of its economic life).

The ***estimated useful life*** is the length of time, or number of units of production, for which an asset is expected to be able to be used.

The residual value, and the estimated useful life, should both be reviewed at least annually to ensure they remain realistic. If the estimates change, then this should be accounted for in the financial statements.

There are many different ways to calculate the depreciation charge for the year for an asset; the exact method chosen will be chosen by the reporting entity.

The most common methods of depreciating non-current assets are:

- **Straight Line Method**
  The original cost, minus any residual amount, is depreciated over the estimated useful life of the asset. An identical amount of depreciation is charged in each year.

- **Diminishing Balance (Reducing Balance) Method**
  The carrying value of the asset is reduced each year by a fixed percentage. This means that the asset will suffer higher depreciation charges in the early years of ownership in comparison to the straight line basis. However, over the useful life of the asset the total depreciation charged would be the same. This is most commonly applied to assets which quickly lose value, such as motor vehicles.

The following diagram shows how an asset is depreciated by the Straight Line method. The original cost of the asset is £30,000, with an estimated useful life of 10 years and no expected residual value. The asset is depreciated at (£30,000-£0)/10 = £3,000 per year. The plotted dots show the annual depreciation charge, which is constant each year, whilst the line shows that the carrying value (the value of the asset in the accounts) reduces each year by this constant amount.

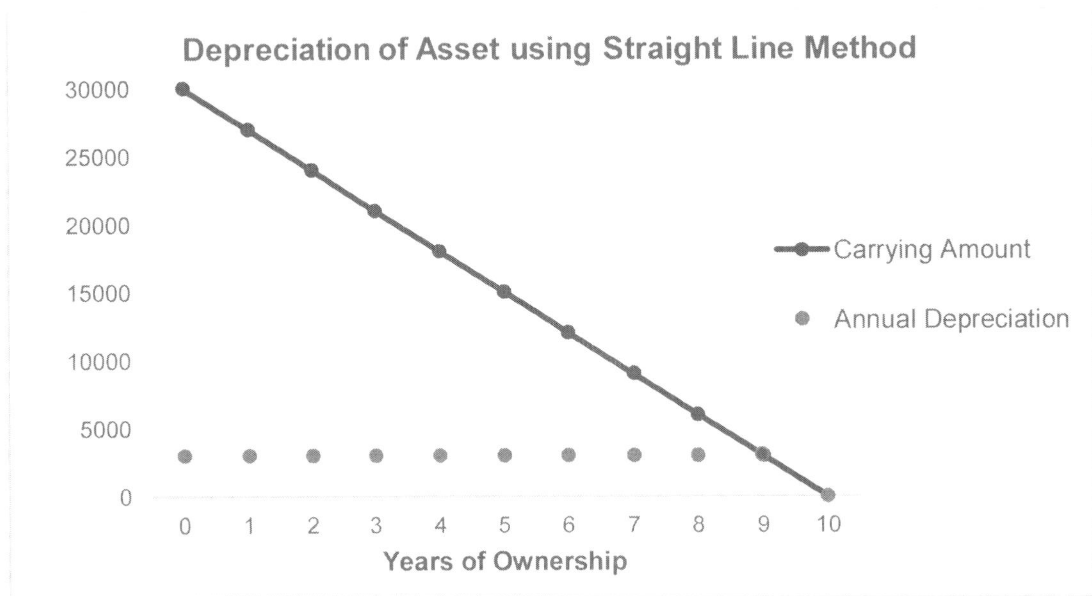

The next diagram shows the same asset being depreciated by the Reducing Balance method, at a rate of 40% per year. You should note how the line (the carrying value) falls much more quickly in the early years of ownership, but then 'flattens off' in the late years. The amount of depreciation charged against profits in the earlier years (shown by the dots) is much higher, but again reduces in later years.

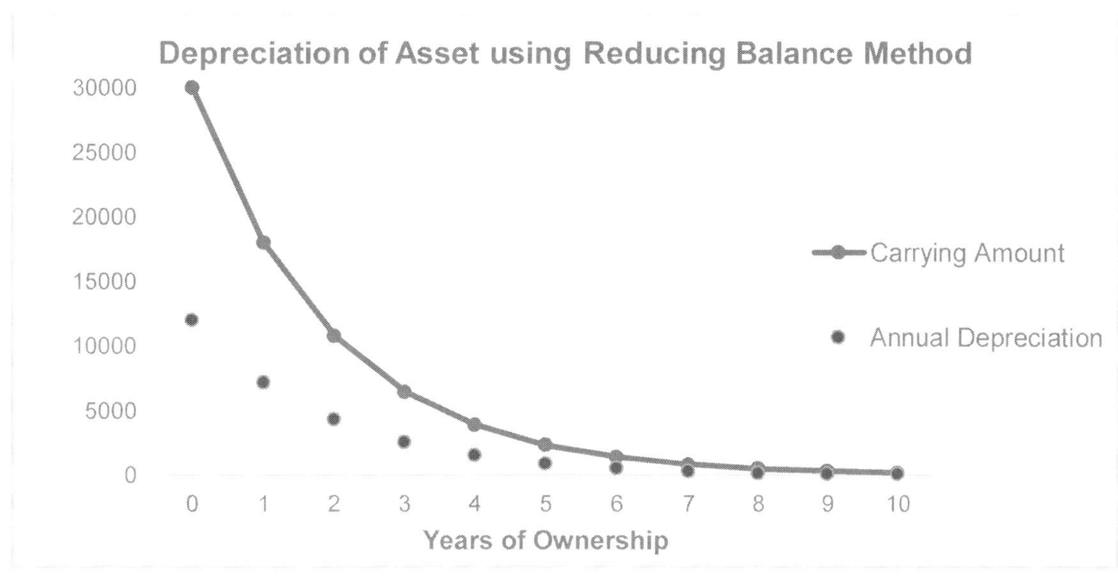

Both methods result in a final carrying value of (approximately) £0 after ten years of ownership.

Example 4.4

An aeroplane has been purchased by Southall Airlines for £100 million. It is expected to have a useful life of 20,000 'cycles' – a 'cycle' is classed as a take-off and landing (regardless of how many miles are flown in each flight). Once this limit has been reached, the aircraft could be sold for £20 million.

The depreciation rate could therefore be determined by:

(£100 million - £20 million) / 20,000 cycles = £4,000 per cycle.

During the first six years of ownership the number of 'cycles' flown is as follows, along with the depreciation charged each year, and the carrying value of the aircraft at the end of each year:

	No of 'cycles'	Depreciation Charge	Carrying Amount at end of year
Year 1	480	£1,920,000	£98,080,000
Year 2	520	£2,080,000	£96,000,000
Year 3	580	£2,320,000	£93,680,000
Year 4	460	£1,840,000	£91,840,000
Year 5	540	£2,160,000	£89,680,000
Year 6	550	£2,200,000	£87,480,000

Depreciation – Other Aspects

The entity should choose the most appropriate method of depreciation which best reflects this actual pattern by which the asset's economic benefits are consumed. This should be reviewed at least annually – and if there is a change in the pattern of usage of economic benefits then the depreciation method should be changed – however, this would only happen very rarely.

Determining the expected useful life of an asset is obviously subjective; however, the following factors must be taken into account:

- The expected usage (capacity) of the asset.
- The expected physical wear of the asset (e.g. operating conditions, planned maintenance). However, simply because a company incurs expenditure on maintenance does **not** mean that it does not have to charge depreciation.
- Possible technological or commercial obsolescence, caused by changes in technology or changes in demand for the product which is made by the asset.
- Any legal or other restrictions on the use of the asset (e.g. the terms of any lease agreement).

Freehold Land is never depreciated (except see below) – this is because land is deemed to have an indefinite useful life. The exception to this would be for land such as mines or quarries, where part of the value of the land is the element which will ultimately be mined, and therefore does not have an infinite useful life.

Leasehold Land, on the other hand, is depreciated based on the remaining life of the lease.

Accounting for Depreciation

The annual charge to depreciation is debited to the Statement of Profit or Loss as an expense. This may be allocated across different expenses such as Cost of Sales (e.g. for production assets), Administration Expenses (e.g. for office assets) and Distribution Expenses (e.g. for warehouses and delivery vehicles).

The annual charge is then credited to the Accumulated Depreciation account for each class of assets (e.g. Accumulated Depreciation – Motor Vehicles). This Accumulated Depreciation reduces the carrying amount of the assets which are shown in the Statement of Financial Position.

Motor Vehicles - At cost					
Dates	Details	£	Date	Detail	£
01/01/20X3	Bank	20,000			

Motor Vehicles - Accumulated Depreciation					
Dates	Details	£	Date	Details	£
			31/12/20X3	Depreciation	4,000
			31/12/20X4	Depreciation	4,000
			31/12/20X5	Depreciation	4,000
					12,000

Each year the Statement of Profit or Loss is charged with a Depreciation Expense of £4,000

The carrying amount of this Motor Vehicle at 31st December 2015 is £20,000 - £12,000 = £8,000

DERECOGNITION

We considered earlier the criteria for recognition of Property, Plant and Equipment; when the asset has been disposed of (e.g. sold or scrapped) we must **derecognise** it – that is, remove it from the financial statements.

Any gain or loss arising on disposal (i.e. the difference between the **disposal proceeds** and the **carrying amount at the time of disposal**) must be accounted for in the Statement of Profit or Loss and Other Comprehensive Income.

DISCLOSURE IN THE FINANCIAL STATEMENTS

IAS 16 also defines the items which a reporting entity must disclose in its financial statements:

- The basis for determining the carrying amount.
- The depreciation method(s) used.
- The estimated useful lives of assets, or the depreciation rates (%) used.
- The gross carrying amount (the original cost).
- Accumulated depreciation at the beginning and end of the accounting period.
- Accumulated impairment losses at the beginning and end of the accounting period.
- A reconciliation of the carrying amount at the beginning and end of the accounting period:
    - Additions
    - Disposals
    - Acquisitions through business combinations (e.g. mergers)
    - Any increases in value caused by revaluations
    - Any impairment losses
    - Any reversal of impairment losses
    - Depreciation
    - Any other changes.

Example 4.5

You work for Stepney Ltd, a manufacturing company.

The company purchased a new machine on 1st January 20X5 for use in the production process at a cost of £120,000. Data relating to the machine is presented below:

MACHINE 897/DR		
Estimated Life – 5 years		
Estimated Residual value at end of 5 years - £9,400		
Estimated Production –	20X5	20,000 kg
	20X6	40,000 kg
	20X7	65,000 kg
	20X8	45,000 kg
	20X9	30,000 kg
		200,000 kg

Required:

Calculate the depreciation expense recognised in the Statement of Profit or Loss, and the carrying amount of the asset in the Statement of Financial Position at the end of each year using:

a. Straight Line Method
b. Reducing Balance Method (using 40% per annum)
c. Units of Output Method

a. Straight Line Method

	Depreciation Expense for year	**Carrying Value at end of year**
20X5	*£22,120*	*£97,880*
20X6	*£22,120*	*£75,760*
20X7	*£22,120*	*£53,640*
20X8	*£22,120*	*£31,520*
20X9	*£22,120*	*£9,400*

b. Reducing Balance Method

	Depreciation Expense for year	Carrying Value at end of year
20X5	*£48,000*	*£72,000*
20X6	*£28,800*	*£43,200*
20X7	*£17,280*	*£25,920*
20X8	*£10,368*	*£15,552*
20X9	*£6,220*	*£9,332*

Note that the reducing balance will not always leave the final carrying amount at exactly the same figure as the depreciable amount, and an adjustment in the final year (in this case £68) may be necessary.

c. Units of Output Method

	Depreciation Expense for year	Carrying Value at end of year
20X5	*£11,060*	*£108,940*
20X6	*£22,120*	*£86,820*
20X7	*£35,945*	*£50,875*
20X8	*£24,885*	*£25,990*
20X9	*£16,590*	*£9,400*

Activity 4.1

1. Define 'depreciation'

"The _______________ __________________ of the _______________ amount of an asset over its ______________________________."

2. Define 'fair value'

"The ___________ that would be _____________ to ___________ an __________ or ___________ to _____________ a ________________ in an ___________________ transaction between _______________________ at the ________________________."

3. What are the two models which an entity may choose by which to value its Property, Plant and Equipment?
   a. Impairment Model
   b. Cost Model
   c. Revaluation Model
   d. Depreciating Model
   e. Diminishing Model
   f. Fair Value Model

4. Which of the following costs could be included in the cost of a new industrial sanding machine?
   a. Costs of site preparation
   b. Costs of testing the asset before being brought into use
   c. Cost of professional fees (e.g. architect or surveyor)
   d. Cost of ongoing maintenance contract for the machine
   e. Cost of initial delivery of the machine
   f. Cost of replacement sanding discs for the machine

5. If an asset is revalued upward, the double entry is to debit the bank and credit the revaluation reserve. True/False?

6. Which type of land may be depreciated?
   a. A freehold quarry
   b. Freehold land without planning permission
   c. Freehold land with planning permission for industrial development
   d. Freehold land with derelict property
   e. Leasehold land

7. Which of these methods of depreciation would be most likely to result in equal depreciation expenses each year?
   a. Reducing Balance Method
   b. Straight Line Method
   c. Units of Output Method

8. Which of these is the depreciable amount of an asset?
    a. The total amount of depreciation charged to date
    b. The amount at which the asset is shown in the financial statements
    c. The original cost of the asset less any estimated residual amount
    d. The percentage rate at which depreciation is calculated in the diminishing balance method

9. When, according to IAS 16, should an asset be recognised in the financial statements?
    a. When it is possible that it will result in future economic benefits flowing to the entity, and the value of the asset can be reliably measured.
    b. When it is probable that it will result in future economic benefits flowing to the entity, and an approximate estimate of the value of the asset can be made.
    c. When it is certain that it will result in future economic benefits flowing to the entity, and the value of the asset can be reliably measured.
    d. When it is probable that it will result in future economic benefits flowing to the entity, and the value of the asset can be reliably measured.
    e. When it is possible that it will result in future economic benefits flowing to the entity, and an approximate estimate of the value of the asset can be made.

IFRS 16 Leases

In January 2019, IFRS 16 Leases replaced *IAS 17 Leases*. IFRS 16 requires all leased items to be initially recognised as assets in the financial statements of the user. There is no longer a distinction between operating and finance leases, all leases are now effectively being treated as finance leases.

For the users of leased items, all leases will be recorded in the Statement of Financial Position as liabilities, at the present value of the future lease payments, along with an asset reflecting the right to use the asset over the lease term.

IFRS 16 Objective

IFRS 16 sets out the principles for the recognition, measurement, presentation and disclosure of leases.

The objective is to ensure that lessees and lessors provide relevant information in a manner that faithfully represents those transactions. This information gives a basis for users of financial statements to assess the effect that leases have on the financial position, financial performance and cash flows of an entity.

What is a Lease?

A lease - A contract, or part of a contract, that conveys the right to use an asset (the **underlying asset**) for a period of time in exchange for consideration. [IFRS 16 Appendix A]

In simple terms, a lease contract is an agreement between the **LESSOR** (who owns the asset) and the **LESSEE** (who leases the asset).

The **lessor** is usually a finance company that allows the right to use an asset for the stated period of time in exchange for consideration (payment).

The **lessee** is the entity that gained the right to use the asset for the stated period of time in exchange for consideration (payment).

Therefore, the lessee has the right of use of the asset in exchange for payment made to the lessor.

Companies do not always buy their assets outright. Instead, they will often **lease** assets from another company. Leasing is an effective flexible source of financing by which a company can gain the right to use and control non-current assets.

Non-current assets which are often leased include:

- Plant and machinery
- Vehicles

Identifying a lease

A contract is, or contains, a lease if it conveys the right to control the use of an identified asset for the period of time in exchange for consideration. [IFRS 16:9]

To assess whether a contract conveys the right to control the use of an identified asset for a period of time, an entity shall assess whether, throughout the *period of use*, the customer has both of the following:

a) the right to obtain substantially all of the economic benefits from use of the identified; and
b) the right to direct the use of the identified asset.

Control is conveyed where the customer has both the right to direct the identified asset's use and to obtain substantially all the economic benefits from that use. [IFRS 16:B9]

If we consider the definition of an asset – *a present economic resource controlled by the entity as a result of past events* - we can see that it is not essential that the asset is actually owned by the company – it only has to **control** the asset.

For example, if a company has a contract to lease a vehicle from a finance company for 3 years, the lessee has the control and the right to use and control the vehicle over that period of time as long as the agreed lease payments are made.

Accounting for Leases by the Lessee

Recognition

The leased asset will be **recognised at fair value and depreciated** over the length of the lease.

A lease liability will also be **recognised at the present value** of the minimum lease payments. This liability will then **decrease over the lease period** until it has been **completely repaid** by the end of the agreement.

Therefore, at the start of the lease the lessee will recognise a 'right of use' of the **asset** and the **lease liability**.

DR Property, Plant and Equipment / Right of use asset

CR Lease Liability

Initial Measurement

At the date of commencement, the lessee will measure the **'right of use asset'** at cost, and this will appear in the Statement of Financial Position in the non-current assets (PPE or 'Right of use' assets). This cost includes the total lease liability together with any lease payment made at or before the start date, plus any direct costs incurred by the lessee.

At the date of commencement, the lessee will measure the **lease liability** at the **present value** of the lease payments that are paid over the term of the lease.

Over an extended period of time, the time value of money will decrease, meaning that £1 earned or spent in 1901 would be worth significantly more than £1 in 2022. Therefore, we 'discount' projected cash flows to show them in today's values (the present value).

We will use discount factors to calculate to the present value of the lease, although in an exam, this may have already been calculated for you. The discount factor used, will be the interest rate implicit in the lease, if that can be determined; if not then the lessee can use the incremental borrowing rate. [IFRS 16:26]

Definitions:

Right-of-use asset – **"***An asset that represents a lessee's right to use an underlying asset for the lease term."* [IFRS 16 Appendix A]

Interest rate implicit in the lease – *"The rate of interest that causes the present value of (a) the lease payments and (b) the unguaranteed residual value to equal the sum of (i) the fair value of the underlying asset and (ii) any initial direct costs of the lessor."* [IFRS 16 Appendix A]

Lessee's incremental borrowing rate – *"The rate of interest that a lessee would have to pay to borrow over a similar term, and with a similar security, the fund necessary to obtain an asset of a similar value to the right-of-use asset in a similar economic environment."* [IFRS 16 Appendix A]

Subsequent Measurement

After the commencement date the lessee shall measure the right of use asset at cost less any accumulated depreciation and any impairment. The depreciation period is the useful life of the asset.

If the conditions of the lease transfers ownership of the asset to the lessee by the end of the lease term, the lessee shall depreciate the right-of-use asset from the commencement date to the end of the useful life of the underlying asset.

If the conditions of the lease does not transfer ownership of the asset, the lessee shall depreciate the right-of-use asset from the commencement date to the earlier of the end of the useful life of the right-of-use asset or the end of the lease term.

The depreciation charge will be transferred to the Statement of Profit or Loss each year.

DR Statement of Profit or Loss
CR Depreciation charges

After the commencement date the lessee shall measure the lease liability by:

a) increasing the lease liability to reflect interest on the lease liability;

   DR Finance Costs
   CR Lease Liability

b) reducing the lease liability to reflect the lease payments made.

   DR Lease Liability
   CR Bank

Interest on the lease liability will be at a rate of interest on the remaining balance of the lease liability.

Example 4.6

Zandra Ltd leases a milling machine for use in the business. The milling machine is leased from Westbourne plc from 1 January 20X7. The lease is for a four year period, which is also the estimated useful life of the machine.

The terms of the lease are that Zandra Ltd must pay £4,000 per year (payable at the start of each year in advance). The lease contract also stipulates that Zandra Ltd are responsible for meeting the costs of any necessary repairs or machine servicing and there were no initial direct costs. At the end of the lease term, Zandra Ltd will return the machine to Westbourne plc.

Zandra Ltd depreciates PPE on a straight-line basis.

The interest rate implicit on the lease is 5%.

How should Zandra Ltd account for the lease?

Solution

As the milling machine has been leased and Zandra Ltd has a right to use and control the asset, Zandra Ltd must therefore account for the asset as if they owned it.

First, we will calculate the present value of the lease payments at the interest rate of 5% by multiplying the lease payment by the discount factor:

	20X7	20X8	20X9	20Y0	Total
Lease payment	£4,000	£4,000	£4,000	£4,000	£16,000
Discount factor	1.000	0.952	0.907	0.864	-
Discounted amount	£4,000	£3,808	£3,628	£3,456	£14,892

Note: Over time, the value of money will decrease, by using discount factors we can calculate the value of the lease in terms of today's values (the present value). The present value of the lease is £14,892.

Initial Measurement

The discounted total value will initially be recognised for the lease related asset and liability in the accounts at 1 January 20X7 as:

DR PPE / Right of use assets £14,892

CR Lease Liability £14,892

Subsequent Measurement

The following entries (after the commencement date) would be entered.

At the end of the period, the next step is to calculate the depreciation. This is calculated over four years on a straight-line basis.

£14,892 / 4 years = £3,723

The depreciation charge will be transferred to the Statement of Profit or Loss each year.

DR Statement of Profit or Loss £3,723

CR Depreciation charges £3,723

The lease payment would be recorded in the accounts as:

DR Lease Liability £4,000

CR Bank £4,000

We will now need to calculate the interest expense to be entered into the Statement of Profit or Loss.

Remember that the first payment was made in advance, therefore we need to reduce the lease liability at the start of the year, by the payment that was made, before calculating the interest.

Note: If the payment was made at the end of the year, the interest would be calculated on the lease liability at the start of the year i.e. before the lease payment is deducted.

	20X7	20X8	20X9	20Y0
Lease liability (1 Jan)	£14,892	£11,437	£7,809	£4,000
Lease payment	-£4,000	-£4,000	-£4,000	-£4,000
Sub-total	£10,892	£7,437	£3,809	Nil
Interest (5%)	£545	£372	£191*	-
Lease liability (31 Dec)	£11,437	£7,809	£4,000	-

Round up to balance and make the outstanding total nil.

This interest expense for would be recorded as:

DR Finance Cost **£545**
CR Lease Liability **£545**

The finance cost would then be transferred to the Statement of Profit or Loss at the end of the year.

Presentation in the Financial Statements

The Statement of Profit or Loss of the lessee at the end of the year will show:

- **The depreciation charge for the asset.**
- **Interest on the lease liability (Finance Cost).**

The Statement of Financial Position of the lessee at the end of the year will show:

- **The carrying amount of the right of use asset in the non-current assets.**
- **The amount of lease liability split between non-current liabilities and current liabilities (i.e. those due in less than one year).**

Right of use assets should be presented separately within the Statement of Financial Position under the non-current assets heading. If they are not presented separately, then the assets should be included under the same line item that the asset would be, as if the assets were owned by the company. If this method is taken, then this must be disclosed in the notes.

In the Statement of Profit or Loss, the interest expense on the lease liability should be presented separately from the depreciation charge for the right-of-use asset. Interest expense on the lease liability is a component of finance costs.

Example 4.7

Following on from Example 4.6 we will now look at how these entries for Zandra Ltd would appear in the financial statements.

The entries in the financial statements would then look like this:

Extracts of the Statement of Profit or Loss

31/12/20X7	£	£
PPE Depreciation	3,723	
Finance costs	545	
		4,268
31/12/20X8		
PPE Depreciation	3,723	
Finance costs	372	
		4,095
31/12/20X9		
PPE Depreciation	3,723	
Finance costs	191	
		3,914
31/12/20Y0		
PPE Depreciation	3,723	
		3,723

Extracts of the Statement of Financial Position

31/12/20X7	£	£
Non-current assets		
PPE	14,892	
Less depreciation	3,723	
		11,169
Non-current liabilities		
Lease Liability	7,437	
Current liabilities		
Lease Liability	4,000	
		11,437

31/12/20X8	£	£
Non-current assets		
PPE	14,892	
Less depreciation	7,446	
		7,446
Non-current liabilities		
Lease Liability	3,809	
Current liabilities		
Lease Liability	4,000	
		7,809

31/12/20X9	£	£
Non-current assets		
PPE	14,892	
Less depreciation	11,169	
		3,723
Non-current liabilities		
Lease Liability	-	
Current liabilities		
Lease Liability	4,000	
		4,000

Note: The final entries for lease liability in the last period will all be nil under the non-current liabilities, as the lease term has ended.

You will see from the entries that the total lease liability is split between the non-current and current liabilities. This is because the lease payment for the next period is due in less than one year and is therefore a current liability.

Accounting for leases by the lessor is not part of the AAT syllabus and is outside the scope of your course.

Recognition exceptions - Short-Term Leases / Leases of low value assets.

IFRS 16 allows lessees to use a different accounting treatment for:

- **Short term leases**
- **Leases for which the underlying asset is of low value**

A **short-term lease** is a lease that, at the commencement date, has a lease term of 12 months or less and does not contain a purchase option.

Leases of **low value assets** are leases for items such as small items of office furniture, laptops, personal computers, printers and telephones etc. These items should be assessed by the value of the asset, based on the value of the asset when it is new, regardless of the age of the asset and whether the lease is material to the size, nature or circumstances of the company leasing it.

The accounting treatment for short term leases and low value asset leases is to simply recognise them as an expense in the Statement of Profit or Loss.

DR Lease Expense (SFP)
CR Bank

The lessee shall recognise the lease payments as an expense on either a straight-line basis over the lease term or by the pattern that appropriately represents the lessee's benefit.

Short-term leases shall be made by class of the asset to which the right of use relates. For example, the lease of telephone and printers would most likely relate to administration expenses. If the business chooses the 'leases for which the asset is of low value' then these can be made on a lease-by-lease basis.

Activity 4.2

What is the definition of a lease in accordance with IFRS 16?

What is the definition of a lessor and a lessee?

Activity 4.3

PP Ltd is a sweet manufacturer. In PP Ltd's latest financial year, it undertook a number of lease agreements for assets as below. For each, you should identify whether it should be treated as a **lease, short term lease** or a **lease of a low value asset**.

Description of lease	Lease	Short term lease	Low value asset lease
Leased a machine on a six year contract. At the end of the six year period PP Ltd will own the asset.			
Leased a Vauxhall car on a five year lease for use by a director. The list price of the car at the time of the lease is £25,000. The lease payments are agreed at £420 per month for the duration of the lease.			
Leased a printer. The term of the lease is 3 years and the value of the printer is £2,000.			
Leased an industrial food mixer on a 10 month lease. The value of the mixer is £6,000.			

Activity 4.4

Clayton Engineering Ltd have leased a machine with a lease term of 4 years. The commencement date is 1 January 20X1. Lease payments are £6,000 per year in advance.

The interest rate implicit on the lease is 6%.

Complete the following table to show the present value of the lease payments for each year. The discount factors have been entered.

	20X1	20X2	20X3	20X4	Total
Lease payment					
Discount factor	1.000	0.890	0.840	0.792	-
Discounted amount					

Activity 4.5

Colourscan Ltd have leased an industrial, state of the art, scanner on the 1 January 20X2. The lease term is 4 years. The interest implicit on the lease is 5%. Lease payments are £8,000 per year with the first payment due on the 31 December 20X2. Lease payments will then be made on the 31 December of each year until the lease term ends. The useful life of the asset is equal to the lease term.

The total lease payments have been calculated at a present value of £28,368.

a) Show the entries that will be recorded for the lease in the accounts at 1 January 20X2.

	Account	£
DR		
CR		

b) Calculate the depreciation charge for the year using the straight-line method.

c) You have been asked to calculate the interest expense for each year of the lease, that is to be recorded in the Statement of Profit or Loss. Round your answers to the nearest whole pound.

	20X2	20X3	20X4	20X5
Lease liability (1 Jan)				
Interest (5%)				
Sub-total				
Less Lease payment				
Lease liability (31 Dec)				

d) Show the entries that will be recorded in the accounts at the end of the period for the interest charged.

	Account	£
DR		
CR		

e) Show the entries for the lease payment at the end of the period.

	Account	£
DR		
CR		

f) Calculate the carrying amount of the asset that will be appear in the Statement of Financial Position, at the end of the year.

Activity 4.6

Adient Engineering Ltd have leased a machine with a lease term of 3 years. The commencement date is 1 January 20X3. The asset has a useful life of 6 years. Lease payments are £10,000 per year. With the first payment being due on the 1 January 20X3. The present value has already been calculated as £28,334. Adient Engineering will own the asset at the end of the lease term.

The interest rate implicit on the lease is 6%.

What entries will be entered into the Statement of Profit or Loss at the end of the year. Round your answers to the nearest whole pound.

Entry	£	Workings

What entries will be entered into the Statement of Financial Position at the end of the year.

Entry	£	Workings

How will the lease liability be split between the non-current liabilities and the current liabilities in the Statement of Financial Position?

	£
Non-current Liability	
Current Liability	

Assessment 4.1

You are now required to log-in to your ROGO account to complete your online assessment before progressing on to the part of this chapter.

IAS 36 Impairment of Assets

As we have seen, non-current assets are valued at either their historic cost less accumulated depreciation (**the cost model**) or at their revalued amount less subsequent accumulated depreciation (**the revaluation method**). The annual deduction of the depreciation charge from the carrying value reduces the value of the asset in the accounts of the business; this reduction reflects the fact that a portion of the value of the asset has been used up by the business during that year's operations.

However, sometimes an asset will lose value due to other reasons. These could include:

- Significant decline in the market value of the asset.
- Evidence of obsolescence or physical damage to the asset itself.
- Significant adverse change in the business or market in which the asset is involved – for example, if the asset is used to manufacture a product which is no longer popular with customers.
- Significant changes in the way the asset is used or will be used in the future.
- Evidence the economic performance of the asset is, or will be, worse than expected.

Any of these will lead to a potential reduction in the value of the asset, beyond that caused by depreciation.

Example 4.8

Waterloo Ltd owns a machine which is carried in the statement of financial position (SFP) at 31st December 20X7 at a value of £48,000, representing the historic cost of £80,000, with accumulated depreciation of £32,000.

It has been identified that the machine has become damaged and is no longer operating at full capacity. Furthermore, the product made by the machine has recently been the subject of adverse publicity following a health scare affecting some of the company's customers.

As a result, the directors of Waterloo Ltd have identified that the value of the asset may have become **impaired** – that is, reduced below the carrying value in the accounts.

IAS 36 *Impairment of Assets* requires the directors of an entity to **review** the value of any non-current assets when there is any **indication of a possible impairment** to its value. This indication of possible impairment could be any of the factors listed above, or any other indication which may arise.

Some assets – such as intangible assets with an indefinite useful life, and goodwill acquired in a business combination – must be reviewed for impairment at least annually, even if there is no indication of impairment.

Example 4.9

Blenheim Ltd own an intangible asset valued in the accounts at the year end at £240,000. This intangible asset (a licence to use a particular piece of specialised engineering software) has been central to Blenheim Ltd becoming a market leader in its industry. Even though there is no physical asset to review, the directors must still carry out a review of the asset's value **at least annually** in order to ensure that its value has not fallen below it's carrying value in the Statement of Financial Position.

In particular, the directors of Blenheim Ltd would review the licence to ensure that the software is still current and as useful to the organisation now as it was before, and that competitors are not now using software which makes this licence less valuable or even obsolescent.

IAS 36 *Impairment of Assets* applies to all classes of assets, including investments in other companies, except:

- Inventories (see IAS 2).
- Investment property measured at fair value (covered in IAS 40 – outside the scope of your studies).
- Non-current assets held for sale (covered in IFRS 5 – outside the scope of your studies).

Reviewing and accounting for impairment losses is an application of the **prudence** concept – its aim is to ensure that an organisation **does not overstate the value of its non-current assets in its Statement of Financial Position**. If the value of a non-current asset has been impaired (reduced), the Statement of Financial Position should reflect this.

The Impairment Review Process

Definitions:

The following specific terms are used in impairment reviews:

- **Carrying Amount** – *"the amount at which an asset is recognised after deducting any accumulated depreciation or amortisation and accumulated impairment losses."*
- **Recoverable Amount** – *"the higher of fair value less costs to sell, and value in use."*
- **Fair value less costs to sell** – *"amount obtainable from the sale of an asset at arms' length between knowledgeable, willing parties, less costs of disposal."*
- **Value in use** – *"present value of future cash flows expected to be obtained from an asset as a result of continuing to use it normally in the business."*

The **impairment review process** initially involves the consideration of two different accounting values for the asset – the **fair value less costs to sell**, and the **value in use**. The higher of these two values is called the **recoverable amount**.

The **recoverable amount** is then compared with the current **carrying value**. If the recoverable amount is the higher of these two figures, no impairment has taken place and the carrying value is not adjusted. However, if the recoverable amount is lower than the carrying value, there has been an **impairment loss** and the carrying value of the asset will need to be adjusted.

The process can be seen in the illustration overleaf:

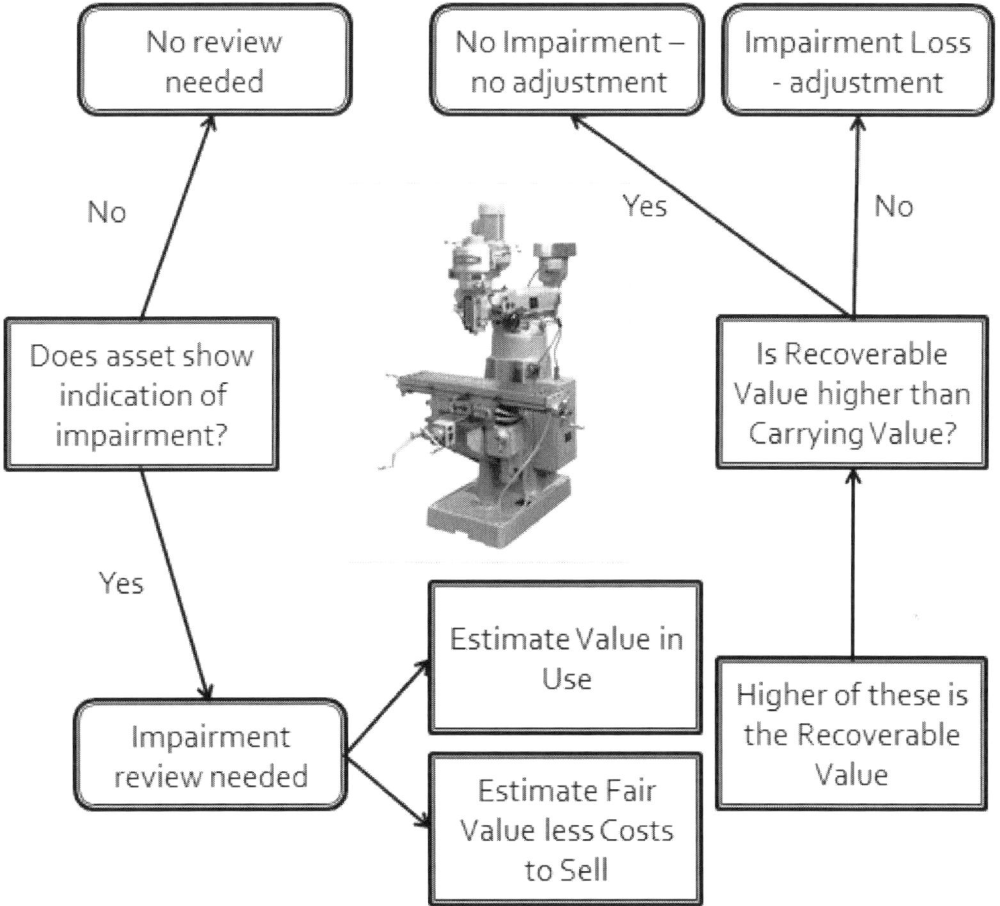

Value in Use represents the expected future cash flows which can be generated by the entity keeping and using the asset over the rest of its useful life. The **value in use**, then, is effectively the expected benefit to the organisation of keeping the asset and continuing to use it.

Fair Value less Costs to Sell represents the amount the organisation could realistically expect to sell the asset for in an open market. It deducts the costs to sell (e.g. repair costs, marketing costs or transportation costs) as these will reduce the net amount which would be received.

The **Recoverable Amount** is the greater of these two values; it represents the value of the asset to the business assuming the business makes the most rational decision about whether to keep or sell the asset.

The **Recoverable Amount** is then compared with the current **Carrying Value** in the Statement of Financial Position. Remember that the prudence concept states that the value of assets should not be over-stated. Therefore, if the Carrying Value is **greater** than the Recoverable Amount, an impairment loss will need to be accounted for.

Both the values for **Fair Value less Costs to Sell** and **Value in Use** are estimates. There are therefore several considerations to be made when making these estimates:

- **Estimating 'Fair value, less costs to sell'**
    - Best evidence is a binding sale agreement, less disposal costs.
    - Market value less disposal costs can be used if there is an active market – guidance can be taken from reputable sources such as estate agents or specialist valuers.
    - Otherwise, estimates of selling price, less disposal costs, will need to be made.
    - Only direct disposal costs (e.g. legal fees, removal fees) are allowed.
- **Estimating 'Value in Use'**
    - The organisation should consider estimated future cash flows from the asset however, it is probable that the amount and timings of future cash flows will be difficult to forecast accurately.
    - The organisation's current cost of capital (for use in calculating discounted cash flows) may change over time.
    - It is difficult to predict future use of assets as there is a degree of inherent uncertainty – the organisation may change its strategic direction, or technological advances may render the asset obsolete.

The **impairment loss** is calculated as the difference between the asset's carrying value and its recoverable value.

Example 4.10

Agincourt Ltd carries out impairment reviews on three of its assets. The carrying value, fair value (less costs to sell) and the value in use for all three assets is shown below.

	Carrying Amount £000	Fair value less costs to sell £000	Value in use £000
Asset A	20	18	25
Asset B	25	20	22
Asset C	30	40	38

Required

For each asset calculate:

(a) The Recoverable Amount.

(b) Whether there has been an impairment loss.

(c) The amount (if any) of that impairment loss.

Answer

(a) The Recoverable Amount is the higher of the Fair Value (less costs to sell) and the Value in Use. Therefore, the Recoverable Amounts are:

Asset A - £25,000 (Value in Use)

Asset B - £22,000 (Value in Use)

Asset C - £40,000 (Fair Value less Costs to Sell)

(b) To identify if the asset is impaired, compare the Carrying Value with the Recoverable Amount. The asset is only impaired if the Carrying Value is **higher** than the recoverable amount:

Asset A: Carrying Value = £20,000, Recoverable Amount = £25,000

Asset B: Carrying Value = £25,000, Recoverable Amount = £22,000

Asset C: Carrying Value = £30,000, Recoverable Amount = £40,000

The only asset which has a higher carrying value than its recoverable value is Asset B; this is the only impaired asset.

(c) The amount of the impairment loss on asset B is £25,000 - £22,000 = £3,000.

The impairment loss is treated as an **expense** in the Statement of Profit or Loss and Other Comprehensive Income. The amount of the impairment loss is also deducted from the carrying value of the asset in the Statement of Financial Position – this will make the new carrying value equal to the recoverable amount.

The double entry is therefore:

Dr Impairment Loss (SPLOCI)

Cr Asset (SFP)

If the asset had previously been revalued upwards, the **debit entry** should instead be made to the **Revaluation Reserve**.

Following an impairment loss, the organisation will also need to recalculate the estimated useful life of the asset, and adjust its depreciation calculations for future period to take account of this.

Disclosure

For each class of assets, the following must be disclosed in the notes to the financial statements:

- The amount of impairment losses recognised in the statement of profit or loss or other comprehensive income for the period.
- Which line item(s) of the statement of profit or loss those impairment losses are recognised – this will help the user reading the statements and notes to identify which class of assets the impairments relate to.

Activity 4.7

Battle-Hastings Ltd have identified a number of assets which may have indications of impairment.

The assets identified are:

a) Machine 765/23 has not been used by the business for a number of years. Its carrying value in the SFP is £32,000 but the machine is now rusty and in need of maintenance. The directors believe the asset could be sold in the open market for £38,000 – but that it would need £5,000 maintenance before it could be sold. The business no longer makes the product which Machine 765/23 was used for, and the directors believe it is unlikely that the machine will ever be used in the production process again. They have therefore estimated its value in use at zero.

b) Number 36 Glade Street is a property owned by the business which they originally used as administrative offices but which is now used for storage of archived records. The building originally cost £180,000 in 20X1 and following a spike in property prices was revalued to £300,000 in 20X5. It's carrying value at 31st December 20X7 was £288,000. The directors recently purchased scanning equipment which means that all records will now be kept electronically and the business will have very little use for the property – its value in use has been estimated at £80,000. Property prices have fallen since the revaluation, and it is estimated that the property could now be sold for £270,000 after incurring costs of £8,000.

c) A Peugeot van has been used by the business as a delivery vehicle. It was bought for £18,000 and it's carrying value at 31st December 20X7 was £4,500. A new van has been bought and the directors plan to keep the Peugeot as a spare. Its value in use is estimated at £3,000. If the directors decide to sell the van it will firstly need some repairs carrying out to its bodywork at an estimated cost of £1,800. It could then be sold for £5,400.

Required

For each asset, determine the recoverable amount and whether any impairment has actually taken place. If impairment **has** occurred, identify the amount of the impairment loss and the correct accounting treatment.

Present your findings in an email to Vidrun Singh, the Managing Director of Battle-Hastings Ltd.

To: Vidrun Singh, MD From: Accounting Technician Subject: Impairment Review

IAS 38 Intangible Assets

We have focussed so far on **tangible assets** such as property, plant and equipment. However, an entity may also have **intangible assets** which have value and which should be recorded in the Statement of Financial Position.

Definitions:

An intangible asset is ***"an identifiable non-monetary asset without physical substance".***

Amortisation is ***"the systematic allocation of the depreciable amount of an intangible asset over its useful life"*** – amortisation is exactly the same as depreciation, but applied to intangible assets.

An intangible asset must be ***identifiable*** (i.e. capable of being sold or transferred, or arising from contractual rights), under the ***control*** of the entity, and likely to generate ***future economic benefits.***

Typical examples of intangible assets include:

- Computer software
- Patents
- Copyrights
- Customer Lists
- Licences
- Marketing Rights

You should note that goodwill is not included within the scope of IAS37 *Intangible Assets*, as it is specifically covered by IFRS 3 *Business Combinations*.

There are two main sources of intangible asset:

- Purchased intangible assets.
- Intangible assets which have been generated internally.

Internally generated assets such as a company's reputation or its brand names, customer lists etc can never be recognised as an asset, as it is impossible to reliably measure the cost of an asset which has been internally generated. Therefore, only intangible assets which have been **purchased** should be recognised in the Statement of Financial Position.

For the same reason, staff are not shown as an intangible asset – their salaries are instead shown as an expense in the Statement of Profit or Loss and Other Comprehensive Income. One exception to this is professional football clubs, who "purchase" players from other clubs for a transfer fee. Players 'acquired' by a club in this way are recorded in the Statement of Financial Position as intangible assets at their initial transfer fee. The value of that intangible asset is then **amortised** (written down) over the life of the initial contract. Players who come through the club's youth system are not recorded as intangible assets, nor are players who extend their contract at the expiry of their original contract term.

Valuation and Amortisation

Intangible assets which meet the recognition criteria should be shown in the Statement of Financial Position at their original **cost** (purchase price plus any other attributable costs).

Any **goodwill** paid by the organisation to acquire the intangible asset (representing the excess payment made over and above the fair value of the assets and liabilities acquired) should be accounted for under the requirements of IFRS 3 (see later in this chapter).

A decision must then be taken by the entity as to the expected useful life of the intangible asset. Some intangible assets (e.g. a software licence) may have a **finite** (limited) life (e.g. five years). Intangible assets with a **finite life** must be **amortised** over that life on a systematic basis (e.g. a straight line basis).

Any intangible assets with an **indefinite life** are those which are expected to generate cash flows for the organisation into the future, and the organisation cannot realistically predict when these cash flows will stop. **Indefinite life intangible assets** are **not** amortised; instead, at the end of each financial year the entity must:

- Review the useful life (to see if a finite life can now be established.
- Carry out an **impairment review** to establish if the value of the intangible asset has reduced.

Research and Development

Many businesses undertake research and development. For some businesses, expenditure on research and development can represent a significant proportion of their overall expenditure in a year.

Example 4.11

In 2020 Glaxo Smithkline (UK) spent a little under £4.6 billion on researching and developing new medicines and treatments for a wide range of medical conditions.

You can read more about the spending on R&D of Glaxo SmithKline using the following link: https://www.gsk.com/en-gb/research-and-development/

Much of this research and development will be on completely new drugs and treatments which will eventually prove to be ineffective, or have unacceptable side-effects, or be too expensive to convert into actual products. Therefore, much of the expenditure on research and development may not result in a product which is ultimately saleable to the public and health services. However, when the research leads to the development of a new drug which **does** make it to the market, the financial rewards to the company can be enormous.

Definitions

Research is *"Original and planned investigation undertaken with the prospect of gaining new scientific or technical knowledge and understanding"*.

Development is *"The application of research findings or other knowledge to a plan or design for the production of new or substantially improved materials, devices, products, processes, systems or services before the start of commercial production or use"*.

So, research is anything which leads to the gaining of **new** knowledge, whereas development is the **application of existing knowledge**. This distinction is extremely important in determining how expenditure on research and development should be accounted for.

Accounting for Research and Development Costs

All revenue expenditure on **research** must be treated as an expense in the Statement of Profit or Loss and Other Comprehensive Income (SPLOCI). This means the cost of research must be written off against profits in the year in which it is incurred. This is because it is far from certain that future economic benefits will flow to the entity at this stage.

Any research-related capital expenditure (e.g. the construction of new research laboratories) should be treated as a normal non-current asset, with the cost being capitalised and then depreciated over its expected useful life.

Revenue expenditure on **development** must also be treated as an expense in the SPLOCI, **unless** it meets **all** of the following criteria:

- It must be **technically feasible** to complete the intangible asset so that it will be available for sale.
- The entity must have the **intention to complete**, and then use or sell, the asset.
- The entity must have sufficient **resources** available to complete the development of the product.
- The entity must have the **ability** to use or sell the asset.
- The entity must be able to demonstrate how the intangible asset will generate **probable** future economic benefits.
- The entity must be able to **measure any expenditure reliably**.

Example 4.12

You work for Sedgefield Chemical Company Ltd. The accounting records show that in 20X3 the company spent £480,000 on research and £630,000 on development.

The research costs were incurred in attempting to create a new type of gloss paint which could be applied by a paint sprayer. Work on this research is continuing into 20X4. The research costs include laboratory rental costs, payroll costs for scientific staff and materials used in the research process.

The development costs have been incurred in respect of a new chemical FD43 which is used in the manufacture of paint stripper. The product development is now complete, and sales of the product are expected to commence in summer 20X4. The company forecasts that the product will become a best-seller and will enhance the company's overall profits.

Required

It is now February 20X4 and you are preparing the company's financial statements for the year ended 31 December 20X3. How will you deal with the research and development expenditure?

Answer

The £480,000 expenditure on research must be shown as an expense in the Statement of Profit or Loss and Other Comprehensive Income.

The £630,000 expenditure on development should also be shown as an expense, **unless** it meets the six criteria for capitalisation.

It seems certain that future economic benefits will flow to the entity, and the costs are measurable. The company has already completed the development and has the ability to use the product. Therefore, the correct treatment for these costs would be to show the £630,000 as an intangible asset in the Statement of Financial Position.

Activity 4.8

For each of the following scenarios, identify whether the asset should be capitalised (shown as an intangible asset in the Statement of Financial Position) or not. For each, justify your reason.

Scenario 1

Bartley Academy is a top-performing college which is consistently ranked in the top 5% of colleges nationwide. The Principal, Dipanwita Singh, regularly praises the quality of her staff, praising them for their professionalism, experience, knowledge and commitment. They are, she says, "the college's greatest asset".

How should the value of the staff be accounted for?

Scenario 2

Gervil Ltd is a manufacturer of dried dog food. Launched in 20X4, it has quickly become a market leader, with excellent brand loyalty. It is instantly recognisable due to its logo, which features "Dexter", a bloodhound dog carrying a magnifying glass – this 'character' has featured heavily in its TV advertising campaigns, is a popular soft toy for children and has even featured in its own TV cartoon series. The popularity of the Dexter character has undoubtedly played a significant role in making the product a market leader. The value of this character is estimated to be around £20 million.

How should the value of Dexter be accounted for?

Scenario 3

Punkguin Ltd manufactures alternative designer clothing which is particularly popular with young people and students. In 20X6, they acquired the rights to use images produced by a popular urban graffiti artist on their clothes. The company paid £8,000,000 for these rights, which last for 4 years. The company expect to make overall profits of £30,000,000 from products bearing these images over the next four years.

How should this be accounted for?

Scenario 4

Hohunku plc is a motor vehicle engine manufacturer. In 20X7 the company spent £400 million on a new research facility in South Wales, creating 300 new jobs. The research facility will be used solely on projects aimed at building on research conducted previously by the company, to develop a new engine which will be powered by energy derived from recycled waste oil. The company is confident that there will be a market for this engine if it can be developed, and that it will have the resources to complete the project within the next four years. All costs incurred are charged to this factory, and so can be accurately recorded. The scientists working on the project have produced an end of year report in which they state they have encountered some unforeseen difficulties which has cast doubt on the technical feasibility of the project – there are now some indicators that, although the concept is technically feasible, the costs which will be incurred in converting the waste material to fuel may be prohibitively expensive. Costs during the first year were £28 million.

How should this be accounted for?

Goodwill

Goodwill is ***"the amount paid over and above the fair value of the identifiable net assets and liabilities acquired".***

When a business entity acquires shares of another business, the price paid may reflect a higher figure than the actual valuation of the net assets and liabilities acquired.

Example 4.13

Groovy Ltd buys all the shares in a competitor, Square Ltd, for £600,000. The fair value of Square Ltd.'s assets and liabilities at the date of acquisition were:

• Property, Plant and Equipment	£400,000
• Net Current Assets	£ 60,000
• Non-Current Liabilities	(£30,000)
Value of the Business	**£430,000**

The **book value** of Square Ltd was therefore £430,000, but Groovy Ltd paid £600,000. The **purchased goodwill** was therefore £170,000.

In this example, Groovy Ltd paid a higher price than the business was actually worth at that date. This could be for a number of reasons; perhaps it forecasts earning higher revenues (future economic benefits) by removing a competitor, or perhaps it anticipates being able to combine the operations to achieve economies of scale.

Whatever the reason for paying the goodwill, this figure (£170,000) can be included in the Statement of Financial Position as an intangible asset, because it has a cost which can be reliably measured.

Purchased goodwill falls outside the scope of IAS 38 *Intangible Assets* and is instead covered by IFRS 3 *Business Combinations*. You should note (as seen previously) that internally generated goodwill (e.g. business reputation) is never included as an intangible asset in the Statement of Financial Position.

IAS 2 *Inventories*

Inventories are items which are held for sale, or held for use in the manufacturing process which will eventually lead to the production of saleable items.

Inventories include:

- Raw materials
- Work in Progress
- Bought in components
- Finished goods ready for resale
- Bought in finished goods ready for resale

Closing inventories can be valued using a range of methods, including:

- Actual cost (where this can be ascertained on an item by item basis)
- Last In First Out (LIFO)
- First In First Out (FIFO)
- Weighted Average Cost (AVCO)

Last In First Out (LIFO) is prohibited by IAS 2, and so if an organisation uses LIFO for costing purposes, an adjustment must be made at the year end to bring the valuation of closing inventory into line with one of the allowable methods.

Under IAS 2, inventories must be valued at:

The lower of Cost and Net Realisable Value.

Cost includes the purchase price plus all attributable costs.

Net Realisable Value includes the selling price less any selling costs which would be incurred to complete the product or to enable it to be sold.

Example 4.14

Paswell Ltd holds four distinct types of inventory at the end of its accounting year. The valuations of these on 31st December 20X5 are:

Inventory Item	Cost £ (AVCO)	Estimated Selling Price £	Costs to Sell £
Arc	4,860	5,440	400
Bin	8,650	9,150	460
Cos	4,760	5,230	610
Dix	6,680	7,240	550

Required

What is the total valuation of closing inventory which should be included in Paswell Ltd.'s financial statements at 31st December 20X5?

Answer

Inventory Item	Cost £ (AVCO)	NRV £	Valuation £
Arc	4,860	5,040	4,860
Bin	8,650	8,690	8,650
Cos	4,760	4,620	4,620
Dix	6,680	6,690	6,680
			24,810

The total valuation of closing stocks is therefore **£24,810**.

Note that each inventory line must be calculated separately; you cannot simply take the lower of the total cost (for all items) and the total NRV.

Activity 4.9

Burghley Ltd holds three distinct types of inventory at the end of its accounting year. The valuations of these on 31st March 20X8 are:

Inventory Item	Cost £ (AVCO)	Estimated Selling Price £	Costs to Sell £
Zed	18,540	21,330	2,080
Wye	21,685	22,950	1,840
Exe	22,470	24,080	1,630
	62,695	68,360	5,550

Required

What is the total valuation of closing inventory which should be included in Burghley Ltd.'s Statement of Financial Position at 31st March 20X8?

Assessment 4.2

You are now required to log-in to your ROGO account to complete your online assessment before progressing on to the next chapter.

Chapter 5: Other Accounting Standards

By the end of this chapter you should:

- Understand the requirements and application of the accounting standards for:
    - Events after the reporting period
    - Tax (under and over provision)
    - Revenue from contracts
    - Provisions for contingent liabilities and assets

Introduction

This chapter considers some of the other International Accounting Standards (IAS) which are included in the syllabus for this unit. Other standards (e.g. IAS7 *Statements of Cash Flows* and IAS3 *Business Combinations)* are considered in later chapters as appropriate.

The accounting standards considered in this Chapter are:

- IAS 10 *Events after the Reporting Period*
- IAS 12 *Income Taxes*
- IFRS 15 *Revenue from Contracts with Customers*
- IAS 37 *Provisions, Contingent Liabilities and Contingent Assets*

IAS 10 Events After the Reporting Period

Entities prepare their financial statements to show the Statement of Financial Position as at their financial year end, and the Statement of Profit or Loss and Other Comprehensive Income for the period to that date. However, it can take a significant period of time for the entity to actually prepare its accounts and publish its statements – the legal requirement is that the financial statements must be published within nine months of the end of the financial accounting period. Therefore, a limited company with a financial year end of 31st December 20X3 will have until 30th September 20X4 to publish its financial statements.

This creates a 'window' of time after the reporting period has ended, to when the financial statements have been finalised and authorised. During this time events could occur that could have an impact on the information contained within those financial statements. IAS 10 provides guidance on when an entity should adjust its financial statements for events after the reporting period.

Events after the reporting period are those events, favourable and unfavourable, that occur between **the end of the reporting period** and **the date when the financial statements are authorised** for issue. [IAS 10 para 3.]

Two types of events can be identified:

An adjusting event *"provides evidence of conditions that existed **at the end** of the reporting period".*

A non-adjusting event *"is indicative of conditions that arose **after** the reporting period".*

Typical adjusting and non-adjusting events include:

Typical Adjusting Events	Typical Non-Adjusting Events
Conclusion of a court case which had been ongoing at the financial year end.	A new business combination – purchase of, or sale to, another entity.
Impairment of assets.	The major purchase of non-current assets.
A reduction in value of inventories where net realisable value falls below cost.	Damage to non-current assets or loss of production capacity to fire or flood.
Insolvency of a major trade customer.	Issue of new share capital.
Discovery of fraud by an employee.	Taking out a new (or increasing an existing) loan.

Material adjusting events are accounted for by altering the amounts shown in the financial statements to reflect the event.

Material non-adjusting events are not included by making amendments to the financial statements; instead, they are included as a note to the accounts giving, where possible, an indication of the likely financial effect of the event.

Example 5.1

Huntsman Ltd prepares its financial statements to 31st December each year. The following events occurred in January 20X6, before the financial statements for the year ended 31st December 20X5 had been authorised.

(a) On 3rd January 20X6, some inventory which had been included in the financial accounts at its cost of £31,000 was found to have been damaged during its delivery in early November 20X5. The company predicts it could sell this inventory for £18,000, but only once a further £3,000 has been spent on it.

(b) A customer sued Huntsman Ltd in July 20X5 after hurting their back using one of Huntsman Ltd.'s products. On 13th January, the court found in favour of the customer, and ordered Huntsman Ltd to pay £85,000 in compensation to the customer.

(c) On 17th January 20X6, there was a flood at a warehouse which led to £45,000 of inventory being damaged beyond repair. The company had failed to insure this inventory against damage by flood.

(d) On 19th January 20X6, the company sold a piece of machinery for £100,000. The carrying value of this asset in the financial statements at 31st December 20X5 was £25,000.

(e) On 27th January 20X6, Snow-wight Ltd, a major customer of Huntsman Ltd announced they were going into liquidation. The outstanding balance on Snow-wight Ltd's account as at the 31st December 20X5 was £15,000.

Required

For each event, identify whether it is an adjusting or a non-adjusting event, and determine the correct accounting treatment.

Answer

(a) This is an adjusting event – the damage to the inventory occurred **before** the financial year end date, and the inventory was included in the current assets at that date. If the reduction in value of the inventory (£31,000 - £18,000 + £3,000 = £16,000) is classed as material, the value of closing inventory in the financial statements should be adjusted.

(b) This is an adjusting event – the court case was in progress at the financial year end date. The expense of £85,000 should be included in the financial statements for the year ended 31st December 20X5.

(c) This is a non-adjusting event – it does not relate to conditions as at the financial year end date. No adjustment should be made to the financial statements as at that date. However, if the value of the lost inventory (£45,000) is considered to be material then a note should be included with the accounts which explains about the loss of inventory due to the flood and the likely financial effect of this.

(d) Again, this is a non-adjusting event – the sale of the piece of machinery took place **after** the financial year end date. A note should be included with the accounts to indicate the sale of the asset and the gain on its disposal – but no adjustment to the financial statements is required.

(e) This is an adjusting event as it relates to conditions in existence at the reporting date. The bankruptcy / liquidation of a customer that occurs after the reporting period usually confirms that the customer was 'credit-impaired' at the end of the reporting period, therefore an adjustment should be made in the accounts as an irrecoverable debt.

Dividends

Dividends are the return to shareholders based (largely) on the level of profits earned during the year.

Dividends are often declared after the reporting period has ended, but before the financial statements are authorised. These are treated as a **non-adjusting event**, because there is no obligation to pay them at the financial reporting date. Any dividends declared after the reporting date are therefore not shown in the financial statements themselves, but are included as a note to the accounts.

Going Concern

The going concern principle is one of the fundamental accounting concepts. All financial statements are prepared on the assumption that the entity will continue in business for at least the next twelve months.

If the directors of the entity decide after the financial year end date that they intend to liquidate the company or cease trading (or that there is no other realistic alternative other than to liquidate the company or cease trading), this will create an **adjusting event**. The financial statements must therefore be amended accordingly.

Date of authorisation for issue

An entity shall disclose the date when the financial statements were authorised for issue and who gave that authorisation. If the entity's owners or others have the power to amend the financial statements after issue, the entity shall disclose that fact. It is important for users to know when the financial statements were authorised for issue, because the financial statements do not reflect events after this date.

IAS 12 Income Taxes

Limited companies in the UK pay Corporation Tax on their profits. Companies will estimate the amount of tax payable on its current year profits – this is because a figure for this year's tax charge needs to be included in the financial statements, but the figure may change as a result of adjusting events or other factors. Corporation Tax is payable 9 months and one day after the end of the financial reporting period, and so the actual tax paid in the accounting period will usually relate to the **previous** year.

The accounting entry for the current year estimate of tax is:

Dr Tax charge (SPLOCI)

Cr Tax liability (SFP)

This establishes a liability at the year-end for the estimated tax payable for that year.

The actual tax liability is usually not agreed until the financial statements are published – hence there will often be an **under-provision** or **over-provision** of taxation in any given financial period. An **under-provision** will occur when the estimate of tax is too low, whilst an **over-provision** arises if the estimate is too high.

Any under- or over-provision for taxation should be adjusted in the following year's financial statements.

Example 5.2

On 1st April 20X2, Babbly Ltd had an estimated tax liability of £170,000 in respect of the financial year ended 31st March 20X2.

In August 20X2, Babbly Ltd paid £166,500 to HMRC in respect of the Corporation Tax liability for the year ended 31st March 20X2.

At 31st March 20X3 Babbly Ltd estimate their tax liability for the financial year 20X2-X3 to be £195,000.

Required

Calculate the tax charge that Babbly Ltd will show in the Statement of Profit or Loss and Other Comprehensive Income for the year ended 31st March 20X3, and the tax liability that will be shown in the Statement of Financial Position at that date.

Answer

There is an **over-provision** in the SPLOCI for the year ended 31st March 20X2 of £3,500 (£170,000 - £166,500).

Therefore, the tax charge that will be shown in the SPLOCI for the year ended 31st March 20X3 will be £195,000 - £3,500 = **£191,500.** The tax liability as at 31st March 20X3 will be **£195,000** – this is the estimate for the year ended 31/3/20X3.

Activity 5.1

On 1st January 20X3, Kickfish Ltd had an estimated tax liability of £225,000 in respect of the financial year ended 31st December 20X2.

In May 20X3, Kickfish Ltd paid £231,400 to HMRC in respect of the Corporation Tax liability for the year ended 31st December 20X2.

At 31st December 20X3 Kickfish Ltd estimate their tax liability for the financial year ended 31st December 20X3 to be £268,000.

Required

Calculate the tax charge that Kickfish Ltd will show in the Statement of Profit or Loss and Other Comprehensive Income for the year ended 31st December 20X3, and the tax liability that will be shown in the Statement of Financial Position at that date.

IFRS 15 *Revenue from Contracts with Customers*

IFRS 15 was incorporated in January 2018. It replaced IAS 18, which previously provided guidance on the recognition of 'Revenue'.

IFRS 15 introduced a new model for revenue recognition that is based on the transfer of control, at what point the transfer takes place and the amount to recognise.

First, we need to look at the definitions of a contract and customer.

A contract is *"an agreement between two or more parties that creates enforceable rights or obligations"*. These can be written, oral or implied.

A customer is *"a party that contracts with an entity to purchase goods or services that are the output of the entity's ordinary activities in exchange for consideration"*.

Now let's look at the definitions and the difference between income and revenue. It is important that we know the difference between these two elements so there is no confusion on what should be included or recognised as revenue.

Income is *"Increases in assets, or decreases in liabilities, that result in increases in equity, other than those relating to contributions from holders of equity claims"*.

Revenue is *"The gross inflow of economic benefits during the period arising in the course of the ordinary activities of the entity, when those inflows result in increases in equity, other than increases relating to the contributions from equity shareholders"*.

The main difference between **income** and **revenue** is that revenue is only derived in the **'course of the ordinary activities of the entity'**.

The main principle of this standard is that **revenue is recognised** by an entity **when (or as)** the promised goods or services **are transferred** to the customers.

The amount recognised should only reflect the consideration given for those goods or services that have been received and to which that entity is entitled to. It focuses on **control** and **when it passes**. It does this by looking at whether the contract's performance obligations are satisfied **over time** or satisfied at **a point in time**.

The Five Step Model

The five-step model is used to decide when to recognise revenue and at what amount.

Step 1. Identify the contract with the customer.

Step 2. Identify the performance obligations in the contract.

Step 3. Determine the transaction price.

Step 4. Allocate the transaction price.

Step 5. Recognise revenue when (or as) a performance obligation is satisfied.

Now let us look at what these mean in more detail.

Step 1. To identify the contract with the customer.

The contract should:

- Be approved by both parties.
- Identify the rights of each party.
- Identify the payment terms.

- Have commercial substance.
- Show that it is probable that the entity will collect the consideration (payment) when it falls due, in exchange for goods and services.

Step 2. Identify the performance obligations in the contract.

Performance obligation is a promise in a contract with the customer to transfer goods or services to the customer. Therefore, the key to this step is to identify the distinct promises made.

A contract may contain more than one promise to transfer distinct goods or services. An example of this may be a mobile phone contract. We pay for the phone along with minutes, texts and data as a complete package together.

Keeping the idea of a mobile phone contract in your mind, step 2 expects us to:

1. Consider if a customer is able to benefit from the goods or services either on their own or together with other resources that are readily available to the customer.
2. This promise is separately identifiable from other promises in the contract.

Step 3. Determine the transaction price.

The transaction price is the amount to which the entity is entitled, in exchange for transferring the provided goods and services. This is the fixed amount specified in the contract. However, this could become quite complex if the contract price was variable, or contains discounts, rebates, refunds, credits, incentives, performance bonuses, penalties and so on.

Variable consideration can only be included in the transaction price if it is highly probable that there will not be a significant reversal of revenue in the future.

Step 4: Allocate the transaction price.

Allocation is based on the relative standalone (separate) selling price of each performance obligation. This means we need to determine what we would normally charge for each individual part. So, if we use the mobile phone contract example again, this would mean we need to distinguish between the amount the entity is receiving from the customer for the phone and the amount they will receive for the calls, texts and data package. Any overall discounts should also be proportioned evenly between each individual part.

Step 5. Recognise revenue when (or as) a performance obligation is satisfied by transferring goods or services to the customer.

Revenue is recognised in financial statements when an entity satisfies a performance obligation by transferring promised goods or services to a customer. This is the point that the control of the goods or services is passed to the customer.

A performance obligation can be satisfied:

- Either '**over time'** (typically for promises to transfer **services** to a customer).
- Or at a '**point in time'** (typically for promises to transfer **goods** to a customer).

For a performance obligation to be satisfied over time, an entity would select an appropriate measure of progress to determine how much revenue should be recognised as the performance obligation is satisfied.

Recognising revenue 'over time' must meet the following criteria:

- The customer simultaneously receives and consumes all the benefits provided by the entity and the entity performs.
- The entity's performance creates or enhances an asset that the customer controls as the asset is created.
- The entity's performance does not create an asset with an alternative use to the entity, and the entity has an enforceable right to the payment for performance completed to date.

If that entity does not satisfy its performance obligation over time then it satisfies it at a point in time. The revenue is recognised when control is passed.

To consider whether control passes at a point in time some of these factors may apply:

- The customer has legal entitlement to the asset.
- The customer has physical possession and has accepted the asset.
- The significant risks and rewards have passed to the customer.
- The entity has a present right to payment for the asset.

Look at the table for an overview of the steps and to help consolidate all that information.

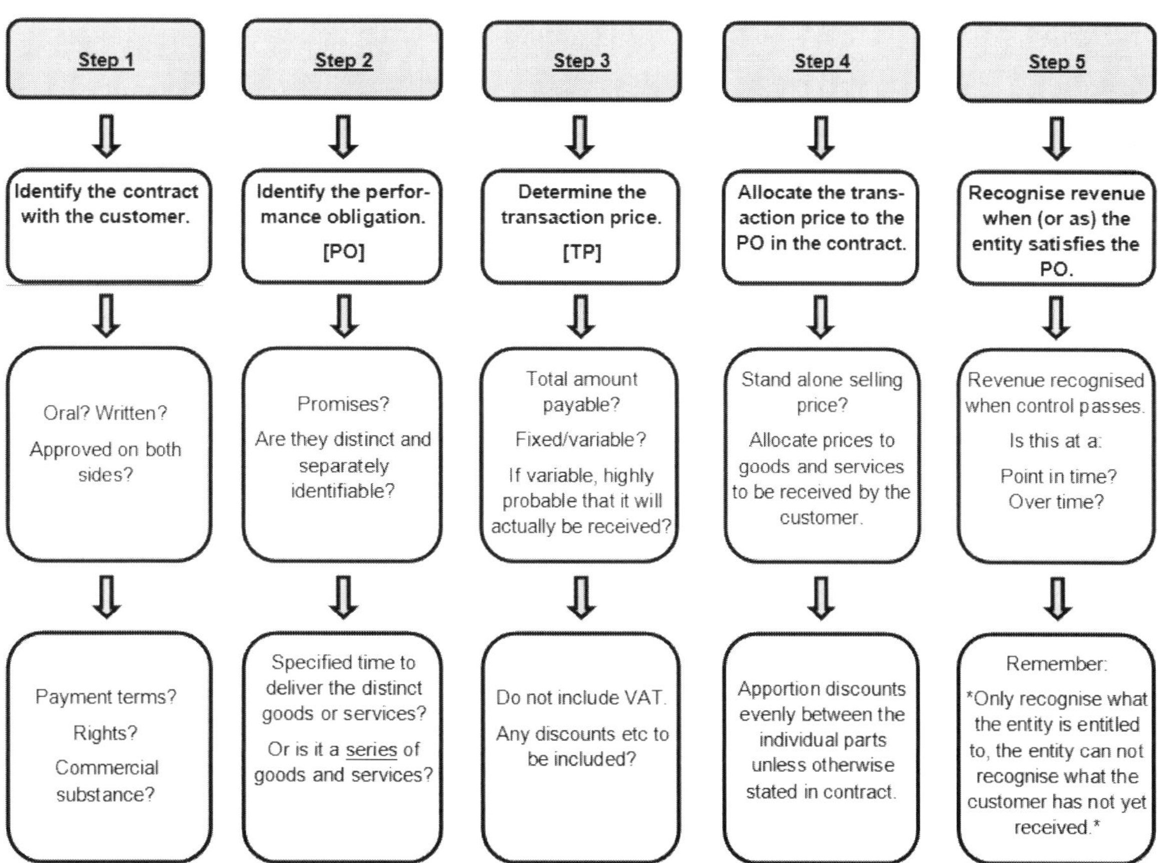

Step 1
Identify the contract with the customer.
Oral? Written?
Approved on both sides?
Payment terms?
Rights?
Commercial substance?
Step 2
Identify the performance obligation.
[PO]
Promises?
Are they distinct and separately identifiable?
Specified time to deliver the distinct goods or services?
Or is it a series of goods and services?
Step 3
Determine the transaction price.
[TP]
Total amount payable?
Fixed/variable?
If variable, highly probable that it will actually be received?
Do not include VAT.
Any discounts etc to be included?
Step 4
Allocate the transaction price to the PO in the contract.
Stand alone selling price?
Allocate prices to goods and services to be received by the customer.
Apportion discounts evenly between the individual parts unless otherwise stated in contract.
Step 5
Recognise revenue when (or as) the entity satisfies the PO.
Revenue recognised when control passes.
Is this at a:
Point in time?
Over time?
Remember:
Only recognise what the entity is entitled to, the entity can not recognise what the customer has not yet received.

Example 5.4

Roda-phone Ltd supplies mobile phone services to its customers. The mobile phone contract it supplies to Mr Blackberry started on the 1 July 20X1.

The contract is for 12 months with unlimited calls, texts, 100GB of data, and a free handset. The monthly fee is £80 per month and the free handset is received immediately. The handset normally costs £360 and the same contract but without the phone normally costs £50 per month.

Roda-phone Ltd has a year end of 31 December 20X1.

So now we apply the 5 Step Model to the scenario.

1. There is a contract. It is identifiable, payment terms are defined, commercial substance etc.
2. What is the performance obligation or distinct promises? There are two distinct promises, one being the supply of the handset and the other being the on-going supply of the calls, texts and data.
3. What is the transaction price? This is the full price we expect the entity to be entitled to in exchange for the goods and services we provide. This would be the total amount over the whole contract.

   The transaction price would be £80 x 12 months = £960
4. Allocate the transaction price to the performance obligations in the contract.

   What are the stand-alone prices of the performance obligations? The normal selling price of the handset is £360 and £50 per month for the calls, texts and data package.

£50 x 12	=	£600	£960
£360	=	£360	

5. Recognise the revenue when or as a performance obligation is performed.

   Mr Blackberry has received the benefit of July to December of calls, texts and data and he received the phone immediately. The performance obligation has been fulfilled for July to December, the handset has been received, therefore, control has been passed to the customer.

   The handset satisfies the point in time criteria and the calls, texts and data satisfy the criteria for the over time.

Now we need to calculate what revenue will be recognised for the financial statements.

July to December of calls etc	£50 x 6	=	£300
Handset price	£360	=	£360
			£660

Therefore, the amount to be recognised is £660 because this is what has passed to the customer and we are entitled to the payment for what the customer has received.

Example 5.5

Furniture King Ltd has a financial year ending on 31 December.

On the 1 August 20X5 Furniture King Ltd enters a contract to supply Glamorous Interiors UK Ltd with premium range white high gloss sideboards as part of a show-home project all over the country for new homes.

The contract states a sale price of £1,000 per sideboard. However, if Glamorous Interiors Ltd purchases more than 200 sideboards during the first year of the contract a 20% discount will be applied on all sideboards supplied under the contract.

On the 31 December 20X5, Glamorous Interiors UK Ltd had only bought 150 sideboards.

By applying and complying with IFRS 15 Revenue from Contracts with Customers, what should the amount be that Furniture King Ltd records as revenue from the contract for the year ending 31 December 20X5.

Answer:

150 sideboards at £1,000 less the 20% discount = £120,000

£1,000 x 20% = £800 per sideboard.

150 x £800 = £120,000

This is the amount of consideration, based on Furniture King Ltd expecting to sell more than 200 sideboards to Glamorous Interiors Ltd. This means that it is very probable that the discount of 20% will apply to all the sideboards sold to Glamorous Interiors Ltd and that there is unlikely to be a reversal of the discount allowed.

Example 5.6

Community Ltd entered into a contract with Bricks and Mortar Ltd to construct a building. The construction commenced on 1 November 20X1. The contract price was £400,000. The building was especially designed for Community Ltd and therefore could not be sold to anyone else without significant modifications.

It was specified in the contract that Community Ltd would pay Bricks and Mortar Ltd within thirty days of the end of each 90 day period. The contract stated that this would be based on the progress of the building at the end of each quarter.

Bricks and Mortar Ltd assess the progress by using the costs incurred so far, compared to the total costs of the contract.

The total cost of the contract is expected to be £200,000. On the 31 January 20X2 Bricks and Mortar Ltd calculated they had incurred costs of £50,000.

Required:

Explain how this should be accounted for in the financial statements of Bricks and Mortar Ltd for the year ended 31 January 20X2 in accordance with IFRS 15 *Revenue from Contracts with Customers*.

Answer:

The performance obligation (PO) is a single PO which is to construct the building.

Revenue should only be recognised as or when the PO is satisfied. On this basis, Bricks and Mortar Ltd need to decide whether it satisfies the PO over time or at a specific point in time.

The building is specifically designed and has no alternative use. This means that Bricks and Mortar Ltd has a right to payment for its performance to date. Therefore, this means that the PO is satisfied over time.

For a PO satisfied over time the revenue should be recognised based on the performance of Bricks and Mortar Ltd so far.

Based on the costs incurred the construction is 25% complete. (£50,000 / £200,000 = 25%). Therefore, the revenue that should be recognised in is £100,000. (£400,000 x 25%)

The appropriate accounting entries would be:

DR: SFP Receivables £100,000

CR: SPL Revenue £100,000

Activity 5.2

What are the steps of the 5 Step Model for IFRS 15 *Revenue from Contracts with Customers*?

Step 1:	
Step 2:	
Step 3:	
Step 4:	
Step 5:	

Activity 5.3

Hoovers R Us Ltd is a wholesaler and signed a contract with Clenzit Ltd to supply them with hoovers for their online retail store on the 1 January 20X8.

It was agreed that each hoover would cost £100 but if Clenzit Ltd bought more than 1000 hoovers in the first year of the contract then the price would be reduced by 25% on all hoovers supplied under the contract.

By 31 August 20X8 Clenzit Ltd has only bought 850 hoovers.

On the 31 August 20X8 Hoovers R Us Ltd prepared their financial statements. You have been asked by your manager to calculate what revenue should be recognised in the financial statements in relation to this contract.

What is the amount of revenue to be recognised?

Activity 5.4

Magazine World Ltd is a magazine publisher with a year end of 31 March 20X5.

During the year Magazine World Ltd received 3,000 annual subscriptions of £50 each for a new magazine called 'Cute Dogs'. The magazine will be received monthly.

The first edition is due to be published and sent out in May 20X5. What is the amount of revenue that should be recognised in the financial statements in accordance with IFRS 15 *Revenue from Contracts with Customers?* Explain your answer.

IAS 37 Provisions, Contingent Liabilities and Contingent Assets

When an entity prepares its financial statements, there may be some items about which it is uncertain. It may be that the company believes an event may happen in the future which would have an impact on its financial position, or that an event has happened but the organisation is uncertain exactly how much impact it will have on its financial position.

IAS 37 identifies three such types of uncertain events:

- Provisions
- Contingent Liability
- Contingent Asset

PROVISION

A provision is ***"a liability of uncertain timing or amount".***

You should recall that a liability is defined as ***"a present obligation of the entity arising from past events, the settlement of which is expected to result in an outflow from the entity of resources embodying economic benefits".***

So, a provision is a liability which has arisen as a result of something which has already happened, but about which there is uncertainty concerning either:

- The amount of the liability
- The timing of the liability (i.e. when it will become payable)

A provision should be recognised in the Statement of Financial Position only when the following criteria are met:

- The company has a **present obligation** as a result of a **past event**;
- It is **probable** that there will be an outflow of economic resources required to settle the liability;
- A **reliable estimate** of the liability can be made.

The present obligation arises once an **obligating event** (either a legal obligation or an obligation derived from the company's actions) has occurred.

The double entry for recording a provision is:

Dr Expense (SPLOCI)

Cr Liabilities (SFP)

The value of all provisions should be re-assessed at the end of each financial year, and adjusted if necessary. If a provision is no longer required, it should be reversed and removed from the Statement of Financial Position.

CONTINGENT LIABILITY

A contingent liability is defined as either a:

"Possible obligation arising from past events whose existence will only be confirmed by one or more uncertain future events not entirely within the entity's control."

or ***"A present obligation that arises from past events, but which is not recognised because it is not probable that an outflow of economic benefits will be required, or that obligation cannot be measured with sufficient reliability."***

The main difference between a contingent liability and a provision is therefore the **degree of certainty** that the event will happen.

A **provision** is established when it is **probable** that the event will occur. In reality, this means that it is **more than 50% likely to happen.**

A **contingent liability** occurs when the event is **possible** but not probable. In reality, this means that it is less than 50% likely to happen. Where the likelihood is less than 20% likely to happen, it is called a **remote contingent liability.**

Unlike provisions, which are shown in the financial statements (if material), contingent liabilities are never shown in the financial statements. Instead, a contingent liability should be **disclosed as a note to the accounts** with details of the possible liability and the likely financial effect.

A **remote contingent liability** should not be disclosed at all, either in the financial statements or the notes.

CONTINGENT ASSET

A contingent asset is defined as ***"A possible asset arising from past events which will only be confirmed by uncertain future events not wholly within the entity's control".***

A contingent asset is **never** shown in the financial statements – this is an application of the prudence concept. However, when the inflow of benefits is virtually certain an asset is recognised, because that asset is no longer considered to be contingent.

If a contingent asset is **probable** (i.e. more than 50% likely to happen) then it should be shown in the notes to the accounts only. If it is only **possible** (or even **remote**) then no disclosure should take place at all.

The following table shows the accounting treatment for each type of provision / contingent liability / contingent asset.

	Almost Certain	**Probable**	**Possible**	**Remote**
Contingent Liabilities	*Make Provision*	*Make Provision*	*Disclose in Notes*	*Ignore*
Contingent Assets	*Recognise*	*Disclose in Notes*	*Ignore*	*Ignore*

Assessment 5

You are now required to log-in to your ROGO account to complete your online assessment and midpoint assessment before progressing on to the next chapter.

Chapter 6: Statement of Cash Flows

By the end of this chapter you should:

- Be able to make appropriate entries in the statement, using the indirect method, in respect of information extracted from:

  - a statement of profit or loss and other comprehensive income for a single year

  - statements of financial position for two years, and

  - any additional information provided

Introduction

The performance of a business can be measured in many ways. So far, we have focussed on showing the **PROFITABILITY** of the business (shown through the Statement of Profit or Loss) and the **FINANCIAL STRENGTH** of the business (shown through the Statement of Financial Position). Both of these are, of course, key measures of success in the past and future viability.

PROFITABILITY – whether or not the business makes an excess of money from carrying on its trade over a given period.

FINANCIAL STRENGTH – the net value of the business in terms of assets and liabilities.

Some investors of limited companies may ask why the company is in its overdraft, or why there is not enough cash to pay a dividend when they have made a large profit. Therefore, to answer these questions and help investors understand that profit does not necessarily mean cash, limited companies are required under IAS 7 to prepare a statement of cash flows.

Therefore, this third indicator (statement of cash flows) is something that the users of financial statements will be desperately keen to analyse – this will show how well the business has managed its cash resources over the period. In particular, we will look at how much cash the business was able to generate from its day-to-day activities, how it invested its surplus cash and how any changes in the way the business is financed have affected the cash position.

The Importance of Being Liquid

Liquidity is all-important for a business; it must be able to pay any upcoming liabilities otherwise its very existence as a business could be at risk. Many strong, profitable businesses have gone into liquidation because they ran out of cash.

Example 6.1

MFI was a successful furniture retailer which was formed in the 1960's and continued to expand into the 21st Century. However, an increasingly competitive market (with competitors such as IKEA and Argos) and the recession and so-called 'credit crunch' of 2008 led to the business being placed into administration. It later ceased to trade when the administrator failed to find a buyer.

One of the major reasons cited for this was the cash flow problems it was encountering due to the '*buy now, pay later*' business model and the withdrawal of credit facilities by banks and suppliers.

Having enough cash is essential for any business – there is a well-known business saying which describes this:

"Turnover is for vanity

Profit is for sanity

But cash is king"

In other words, too many businesses focus on sales turnover, believing that the more they sell the bigger and better they are. A more logical approach is to focus on profit (it is better to make a £20,000 profit on sales of £100,000 than a £15,000 profit on sales of £140,000). However, the key measure is ensuring that the business has sufficient cash to pay its way – a business may make profitable sales but if it doesn't get paid for them quickly enough by its customers it may well face trading difficulties.

Cash Inflows and Cash Outflows

Let's think about how a business can generate cash. The most obvious source of cash is from sales – either cash sales or receipts from debtors in relation to credit sales. Other sources of cash are likely to be irregular – receipts of bank loans, tax rebates, interest or dividends received, proceeds from the sale of non-current assets and so on.

Similarly, businesses will need to spend cash on a variety of items – day to day items such as paying suppliers, paying wages, and meeting necessary expenditure such as utility bills, insurance and so on. There will also be less regular uses of cash, such as purchasing non-current assets, paying tax liabilities, paying dividends to investors and repaying loans.

The important thing to remember here is that in preparing a Statement of Cash Flows, the only thing we are interested in is the actual flow of cash – the amounts of money actually received and spent by the business. The Statement of Cash Flows is therefore prepared on the **CASH** basis. This is, of course, a totally different approach to the other financial statements which are prepared on the **ACCRUALS** basis.

We can see in the diagram below, the cash *inflows* and cash *outflows* of a business.

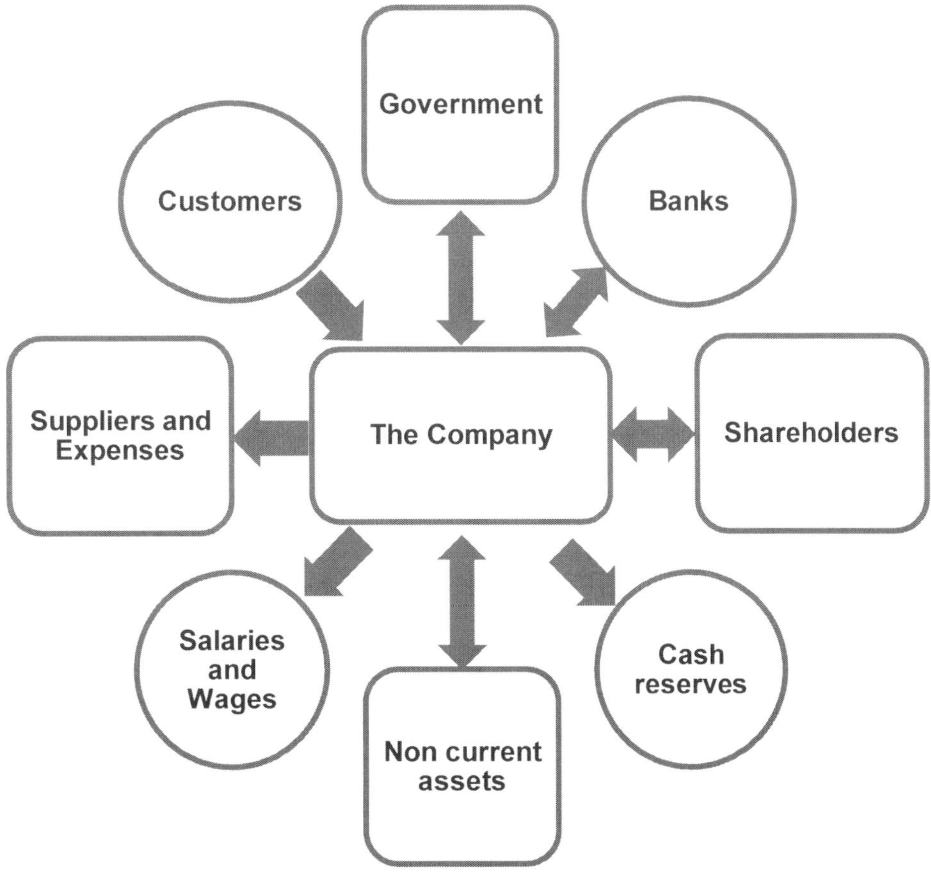

The company's cash reserves increase through positive cash flows from day to day trading (receipts from customers) and other irregular positive cash flows (new bank loans, new share issues, government grants and subsidies, sale of non-current assets). The cash reserves reduce through regular outflows (payments to trade and other suppliers, wages and other expenses) and irregular outflows (payment of tax liabilities, repayment of bank loans, purchase of non-current assets and payment of dividends to shareholders).

Why Profit and Cash are not the Same

As you will be aware, financial statements are prepared on the accruals basis – this is one of the fundamental accounting concepts. This means that credit sales are recorded in the Statement of Profit or Loss before any cash has actually been received by the business; similarly, it will record its purchases and expenditure when it becomes a liability, rather than when the cash is actually paid. This means there is a timing difference between the profit that a business makes and the cash it actually receives and pays out.

Similarly, when a business purchases a non-current asset such as a new machine, it will perhaps pay cash for the machine today, but will record it in the accounts as a non-current asset and write off the cost of the asset against profits over the estimated useful life of the asset.

Example 6.2

Imagine a business, B Ltd, has the following results for the year ended 31st December 20X3.

	B Ltd
Revenue	£800,000
Less Cost of Sales	£200,000
Gross Profit	£600,000
Less Expenses	£250,000
Operating Profit	£350,000

If we are now told that B Ltd purchased a piece of machinery for £80,000 during the year, then this would only impact on the profit by the depreciation charge for the year. If the machine is being depreciated over twenty years on the straight line basis, expenses would increase by (£80,000 / 20 years) = £4,000.

So, the profit would now fall by £4,000 to £346,000 – but the company's bank balance will have been reduced by the full £80,000.

Depreciation

One major difference between profit and cash is depreciation. You should be aware that depreciation is charged against profit each year to take into account the estimated usage of the non-current assets – again, this is an example of the accruals concept.

However, this depreciation adjustment is only an accounting adjustment – it is not a **real** payment. The business does not physically make a payment to anybody, and no money leaves the bank – although the profit for the year is reduced.

Example 6.3

Grubbles Ltd had an Operating Profit for the year ended 31st December 20X1 of £350,000. This was after charging depreciation of £28,000 for the year.

The Operating Profit is understated in cash terms because the £28,000 which has been deducted is not a cash item. Therefore, in calculating the cash position we would need to **add back** the £28,000 to give a figure of £378,000.

As we shall see, depreciation is a required adjustment in every cash flow calculation; however, we shall also see there are others as well.

Reconciling Profit and Cash

You should now understand that profit and cash is not the same thing – although there is clearly a link between them. Intuitively, we would expect a profitable business to generate more cash over a year than a loss-making company.

The starting point of producing a Statement of Cash Flows is to reconcile the profit for the year to the net cash that has been generated during the year. We will look at some other factors which affect the cash balance shortly, but for now we are only concerned with the regular, day-to-day transactions which the business has had (operating activities).

Reconciliation of Net Cash from Operating Activities

The **Reconciliation of the Profit to the Net Cash from Operating Activities** forms the top section of the Statement of Cash Flows.

There are two methods of reconciling the profit for the purpose of the Statement of Cash Flows. These are:

- The **Direct** method
- The **Indirect** method

The AAT exam will only test the **indirect method** and it is this method which uses the **'Reconciliation of Net Cash from Operating Activities'**. You are only expected to be aware that there are two methods of presenting this therefore the rest of this chapter will concentrate on the indirect method.

The Reconciliation of Net Cash from Operating Activities can be done in one of two ways. It can be started from the **Profit before Tax** figure or the **Profit from Operations** figure, both are found in the SPL.

Reconciliation of Profit Before Taxation to Net Cash from Operating Activities	**£000**
Profit before taxation	
Adjustments For:	
Depreciation	
Finance Costs	
Gain on disposal of PPE	
Dividends received	
Adjustment in respect of inventories	
Adjustment in respect of trade receivables	
Adjustment in respect of trade payables	
Cash Generated by Operations	
Interest Paid	
Taxation Paid	
Net Cash from Operating Activities	

Reconciliation of Profit from Operations to Net Cash from Operating Activities	**£000**
Profit from Operations	
Adjustments For:	
Depreciation	
Gain on disposal of PPE	
Dividends received	
Adjustment in respect of inventories	
Adjustment in respect of trade receivables	
Adjustment in respect of trade payables	
Cash Generated by Operations	
Interest Paid	
Taxation Paid	
Net Cash from Operating Activities	

In the exam, you may be asked to draft a reconciliation of profit to net cash from operating activities. The first thing to do is to make sure you start with the right profit figure!

You will notice that the reconciliations are very much the same, the only difference between the reconciliations is the adjustment for the finance cost.

When starting from the **profit before tax** figure, it may well include some items which do not actually represent normal day-to-day trading activities, and these will need to be added back to the profit (if they have been deducted) or deducted from the Profit from Operations if they represent additional income. This is to ensure that the profit figure we are working with is the **TRADING PROFIT** of the business. This is the profit we have made through the ordinary course of business from the selling of goods or services.

When starting from the **profit from operations** figure, we will need to adjust the reconciliation to not include the finance costs. This is because the profit from operations figure does not include the finance costs (this is deducted after the 'Profit from Operations' in the ordinary SPL), so there would be no need to make any adjustment for it.

Example 6.3

The Statement of Profit or Loss and Other Comprehensive Income for Strubin Ltd for the year ended 31st July 20X7 is shown on the following page.

Strubin Ltd – Statement of Profit or Loss for the year ended 31/07/20X7	
	£
Revenue	401,354
Cost of Sales	(185,967)
Gross Profit	215,387
Loss on Disposal of PPE	(44)
Dividends Received	89
	215,432
Distribution Costs	(96,741)
Administrative Expenses	(64,513)
Profit from Operations	**54,178**
Finance Costs	(85)
Profit Before Taxation	**54,093**
Taxation	(1,794)
Profit from Continuing Operations	**52,299**

Which is the correct figure? – Always check what the question asks you to start with.

We are also told that Distribution Costs include this year's depreciation charge of £209.

Therefore, to calculate the **Trading Profit** (profit from the ordinary course of business) from '**profit before tax**' for inclusion in the Statement of Cash Flows we must make the following adjustments:

Profit before tax	**£54,093**
***Add* Finance costs**	**£ 85**
***Add* Depreciation**	**£ 209**
***Add* Loss on Disposal of PPE**	**£ 44**
***Less* Dividends Received**	**£ (89)**
TRADING PROFIT	**£54,342**

If we are asked to calculate the **Trading Profit** from **'profit from operations'** for inclusion in the Statement of Cash Flows we will simply not include the finance costs because these are already included in the trading profit from the SPL.

Profit from Operations	**£54,178**
***Add* Depreciation**	**£ 209**
***Add* Loss on Disposal of PPE**	**£ 44**
***Less* Dividends Received**	**£ (89)**
TRADING PROFIT	**£54,342**

We can now see that both methods give the same trading profit figure.

Now to Adjust

Once you have identified the correct profit figure to start with, you will need to make a number of adjustments to complete the reconciliation.

We will now look at the adjustments in more detail:

	DEPRECIATION Identify the depreciation charge for the year – often this is given to you in the scenario. It is a non-cash item that has decreased our profit and is not part of our ordinary trade, so we will need to add it back to our profit.	**Deduct** – Never	**Add** – Always
	DIVIDENDS RECEIVED Dividends received are not part of *profit from operations* – they will be dealt with later under investing activities.	**Deduct** – Always	**Add** – Never
	GAIN/LOSS ON DISPOSAL OF PPE Again, if there is a gain or loss arising from the sale or other disposal of a non-current asset, this should not be included in the profit from normal trading/operations.	**Deduct** – Any gains on disposal	**Add** – Any losses on disposal

	FINANCE COSTS. We add it back (not ordinary trade) and is deducted after in the second part of the reconciliation with Tax.	**Deduct –** After: only in second part.	**Add –** Always
	INVENTORY Calculate the difference between the inventory at the start of the year and the end (you get the figures from the Current Assets section of the SFP).	**Deduct** – if Inventories have **increased**	**Add** if Inventories have **decreased**
	RECEIVABLES Calculate the difference between the receivables at the start of the year and the end (the figures are from the Current Assets section of the SFP).	**Deduct** if Receivables have **increased**	**Add** if Receivables have **decreased**
	PAYABLES Calculate the difference between the payables at the start of the year and the end (you get the figures from the Current Liabilities section of the SFP).	**Deduct** if Payables have **decreased**	**Add** if Payables have **increased**

If you get a question in your exam which asks you to prepare a Statement of Cash Flows, you will need to watch out for all of these adjustments – they are all extremely common.

You need to learn which adjustments are **added back** to the profit from operations, and which are **deducted**.

For the increase or decrease in inventories, trade receivables and payables, think about whether the increase or decrease will cause an inflow or outflow of cash.

For example, if trade receivables decrease, this means that our credit customers have paid us which means an increase in cash. If trade receivables increase, we have less cash because even though our sales have increased, they are on credit and we have not received the payment yet.

Finance Costs (Interest) and Taxation

The Statement of Cash Flows should only include payments actually made during the year – this means that the figures included in the Statement of Profit or Loss for Finance Costs (interest) and Tax will not necessarily be the figures that you need to include in the Statement of Cash Flows.

The amount of tax or interest actually paid during the period can be calculated from:

Balance at start of year + Charge for this year – Balance at end of year = Amount Paid

Example 6.4

Campbell Ltd is preparing its Statement of Cash Flows for the year ended 31st December 20X5.

The following balances have been extracted from the Statements of Financial Position as at 31st December 20X4 and 31st December 20X5:

	As at 31st December 20X5	As at 31st December 20X4
Tax Payable	£8,905	£9,650
Finance Costs (Interest) Payable	£1,862	£1,648

The extract from the Statement of Profit or Loss for the year ended 31st December 20X5 shows:

Profit from Operations	**£109,354**
Finance Costs	(£1,862)
Profit Before Taxation	**£107,492**
Taxation	(£7,910)
Profit from Continuing Operations	**£99,582**

Required

Calculate how much Campbell Ltd have **actually paid** in regard to tax and interest during the year.

Answer

	Taxation	Interest
Balance at start of year	£9,650	£1,648
Charge for year (from P&L)	£7,910	£1,862
Balance at end of year	(£8,905)	(£1,862)
Amount Paid	**£8,655**	**£1,648**

Let us look at the tax in a T-account to see why we take the start of the year balance, add the current year's charge and take off the end of year balance.

First, we would enter the balance at the start of the year as the brought down figure and then add the charge for the year (again, credit side as tax payable is a liability). We have the carried down figure for the end of the year, we would enter this on the debit side. Therefore, we have a missing figure to make the account balance. This will be the amount of tax that was paid during the year. So, to calculate the amount of tax paid, all we need to do is balance off the account and find the missing or balancing figure. We would total the credit side and deduct the debit side (9,650 + 7,910 – 8,905 = 8,655).

Dr			Cr
(Tax paid during the year)	***8,655* (Balancing figure)**	01/01/20X7 b/d	9,650
31/12/20X7 c/d	8,905	(Charge for the year)	7,910 (SPL)
Total	**17,560**	**Total**	**17,560**

Activity 6.1

You have been asked to prepare a **Reconciliation of Profit Before Taxation to Net Cash from Operating Activities** for Walton Ltd for the year ended 31st July 20X4. The most recent Statement of Profit or Loss and Statement of Financial Position (with comparatives for the previous year) of Walton Ltd can be seen below.

Walton Ltd – Statement of Profit or Loss for the year ended 31/07/20X4	
	£000
Revenue	204,164
Cost of Sales	(105,895)
Gross Profit	98,269
Gain on Disposal of PPE	56
Dividends Received	42
	98,367
Distribution Costs	(27,451)
Administrative Expenses	(19,663)
Profit from Operations	51,253
Finance Costs	(104)
Profit Before Taxation	51,149
Taxation	(3,846)
Profit from Continuing Operations	47,303

Additional Information:

- The total depreciation charge for the year was £12,560,000.
- PPE with a carrying value of £2,120,000 was sold during the year.
- All sales and purchases were made on credit. All expenses were paid for in cash.
- A dividend of £2,575,000 was paid during the year, and a further dividend of £1,080,000 was declared on 12th September 20X4 before the financial statements were authorised for issue.

Walton Ltd – Statement of Financial Position as at…		
	31/07/20X4 £000	**31/7/20X3 £000**
ASSETS		
Non-Current Assets		
Property Plant and Equipment	294,270	234,854
Investments at cost	18,000	18,000
	312,270	**252,854**
Current Assets		
Inventories	19,684	15,483
Trade Receivables	27,956	22,188
Cash and Cash Equivalents	3,684	452
	51,324	**38,123**
TOTAL ASSETS	**363,594**	**290,977**
EQUITY AND LIABILITIES		
Equity		
Share Capital	190,000	155,000
Share Premium	25,000	18,000
Retained Earnings	107,302	79,974
Total Equity	**322,302**	**252,974**
Non-Current Liabilities		
Bank Loans	19,600	17,400
	19,600	**17,400**
Current Liabilities		
Trade Payables	17,846	18,447
Tax Liabilities	3,846	2,156
	21,692	**20,603**
Total Liabilities	**41,292**	**38,003**
TOTAL EQUITY AND LIABILITIES	**363,594**	**290,977**

Required

Produce the **Reconciliation of Profit Before Taxation to Net Cash from Operating Activities** using the following table.

Reconciliation of Profit Before Taxation to Net Cash from Operating Activities	**£000**
Profit before taxation	
Adjustments For:	
Depreciation	
Gain on disposal of PPE	
Dividends received	
Finance Costs	
Adjustment in respect of inventories	
Adjustment in respect of trade receivables	
Adjustment in respect of trade payables	
Cash Generated by Operations	
Interest Paid	
Taxation Paid	
Net Cash from Operating Activities	

The Statement of Cash Flows

The requirement for companies to produce a Statement of Cash Flows is contained within IAS 7 *Statement of Cash Flows.*

The Statement of Cash Flows summarises the cash and cash equivalents that have entered and left the business throughout the period and supplements the information provided in the SPL and SFP. The correct layout is shown on the following page.

Statement of Cash Flows – Pro-Forma

Statement of Cash Flow	£000
Net Cash from Operating Activities	**XXXXX**
Investing Activities	
Purchases of PPE	**XXXXX**
Proceeds on Disposal of PPE	**XXX**
Dividends Received	**XXX**
Net Cash Used in Investing Activities	**XXXXX**
Financing Activities	
Increase /(Decrease) in share capital	**XXX**
Increase /(Decrease) in loan	**XXX**
Dividends paid	**XXX**
Net Cash From Financing Activities	**XXXXX**
Net increase / (decrease) in cash and cash equivalents	**XXXXX**
Cash and cash equivalents at beginning of year	**XXXX**
Cash and cash equivalents at end of year	**XXXX**

All cash *inflows* are shown as positive figures, and all cash *outflows* are shown as negative figures.

Investing Activities and Financing Activities

Once we have reconciled the Profit to the Net Cash Flow from Operations, we then need to consider two further ways in which businesses can generate or spend cash.

These are:

- Investing Activities
- Financing Activities

Investing Activities

This section considers any cash generated from investments – including:

- Purchase of non-current assets (*a cash outflow*)
- Disposal of non-current assets (a *cash inflow*)
- Receipt of dividends (a *cash inflow*)

Financing Activities

This section considers any cash generated from the financing of the business – including:

- Repayment of bank loans (*a cash outflow*)
- Taking out new bank loans (a *cash inflow*)
- Issue of new share capital – including share premium (a *cash inflow*)
- Payment of dividends (a *cash outflow*)

We will now look at these in more depth.

Investing Activities

The main difficulties students face in this section are calculating the cash generated by the disposal of non-current assets (PPE) and the amount spent on purchasing new PPE.

Disposals of Property, Plant and Equipment

The profit or loss on the disposal will appear in the Statement of Profit or Loss for the year, and, as we have seen, must be added back to the profit figure (if it is a loss) or deducted (if it is a profit). Remember the statement of cash flows deals **only** with actual cash flows in and out of the business. The working to calculate the disposal is:

Proceeds on Disposal of PPE – WORKINGS	
	£000
Carrying amount of PPE sold	XXX
Loss on disposal of PPE	-XX
	XXX

Example 6.5

Golightly Ltd sells a piece of machinery in August 20X8. The asset originally cost £50,000 when it was purchased in December 20X5, and it has been depreciated on the straight line basis over five years (assuming no residual value). Golightly Ltd prepares accounts to 31st March each year, and a full year's depreciation is charged in the year of purchase, with none in the year of disposal. The Statement of Profit or Loss and Other Comprehensive Income for the current year ending 31st March 20X9 shows a loss on the disposal of £2,000.

Let's think about the carrying value of the asset when it was sold. The asset was originally bought in December 20X5 (the 20X5-X6 financial year) and will have been depreciated as follows:

y/e 31/3/20X6 £50,000 - £10,000 depreciation = £40,000 carrying value.

y/e 31/3/20X7 £40,000 - £10,000 depreciation = £30,000 carrying value.

y/e 31/3/20X8 £30,000 - £10,000 depreciation = £20,000 carrying value.

No depreciation is charged in the year of disposal – year ending 31st March 20X9.

So, an asset that was showing in the accounts at a carrying value of £20,000 was sold during the year for a loss of £2,000. The disposal proceeds (the amount the asset was actually sold for) must therefore have been £18,000, and this would appear in the Investing Section of the Statement of Cash Flows as a **CASH INFLOW**.

The workings for this can be seen below:

Proceeds on Disposal of PPE – WORKINGS	
	£000
Carrying amount of PPE sold	20
Loss on disposal of PPE	-2
	18

Of course, if the asset had been sold for a gain, the gain would need to be added to the carrying amount to calculate the proceeds. In the above example, if the same asset had been sold for a £7,000 gain the proceeds would be:

Proceeds on Disposal of PPE – WORKINGS	
	£000
Carrying amount of PPE sold	20
Loss on disposal of PPE	7
	27

Purchases of Property, Plant and Equipment

If an organisation purchases Property, Plant and Equipment (PPE) the amount paid will represent a cash outflow from the business. Often in exam questions you will not be told the value of purchases; instead, you will be required to calculate the value from other information that is provided.

So long as you have the following key pieces of information (which will either be provided or can be ascertained from the financial statements) you will be able to calculate the purchases made during the year.

The information you will require is:

- **The carrying value of Non-Current Assets at the start and end of the year (*available from the Statements of Financial Position for this year and last*).**
- **The Depreciation charge for the year (*given in the question or found in the Statement of Profit or Loss*).**
- **The carrying value of any Non-Current Assets disposed of during the year (*usually provided in the question*).**

The workings to calculate the cash outflow is then as follows:

Purchases of PPE – WORKINGS	
	£000
PPE at start of year	XXXX
Depreciation Charge	-XXX
Carrying amount of PPE sold	-XXX
PPE at end of year	-XXX
Total PPE additions	-XXXX

Example 6.5 continued …

You are now told that Golightly Ltd also made a number of acquisitions of PPE during the year ended 31st March 20X9. An extract of the Statements of Financial Position is shown below:

Golightly Ltd – Statement of Financial Position as at…		
	31/3/20X9 £000	**31/3/20X8 £000**
ASSETS		
Non-Current Assets		
Property Plant and Equipment	46,480	37,280
Investments at cost	6,000	6,000
	52,480	**43,280**

You are also told that the depreciation charge for the year ended 31st March 20X9 was £8,350,000.

The amount paid for purchases of PPE during the year was therefore:

Purchases of PPE – WORKINGS		
	£000	**Notes**
PPE at start of year	37,280	*SFP as at 31/3/20X8*
Depreciation Charge	-8,350	*From information given*
Carrying amount of PP sold	-20	*From earlier example*
PPE at end of year	-46,480	*SFP as at 31/3/20X8*
Total PPE additions	-17,570	*Calculated*

You should note that this is a negative figure because it represents the purchase of PPE – this leads to an OUTFLOW of cash from the business.

Sometimes the depreciation charge for the year will not be given to you in a question; instead, this must be calculated by deducting the accumulated depreciation at the start of the year from the accumulated depreciation at the end of the year. This will give the increase in accumulated depreciation throughout the year, however it will not include any accumulated depreciation on any disposed during the year. When the assets were disposed of, any accumulated depreciation relating to them will have been removed from the account as part of the disposal process. This will therefore need to be **added** to the difference between the accumulated depreciation balances at the start and end of the year.

Depreciation Charge = (Acc. Dep at End – Acc. Dep at Start) + Acc. Dep on Disposals

Example 6.6

Bishopric Ltd has the following extracts for its Property, Plant and Equipment at the 31st December 20X1 and 31st December 20X2.

	20X1 £000	20X2 £000
Cost	4,188	4,653
Accumulated Depreciation	(1,052)	(1,245)
Carrying Value (31st December)	3,136	3,408

During the year ended 31st December 20X2 a property which had originally cost £152,000 and had a carrying value of £116,000 was sold for £195,000.

Required

Calculate:

(a) The figure to be included for Proceeds from Sale of PPE in the Statement of Cash Flows under the heading "Investing Activities" for the year ended 31st December 20X2.

(b) The figure for depreciation which should be added back to profit before tax in the reconciliation of profit before tax to net cash from operating activities.

(c) The figure to be included for Purchases of PPE in the Statement of Cash Flows under the heading "Investing Activities" for the year ended 31st December 20X2.

Answer

(a) The figure to be included for Proceeds from Sale of PPE in the Statement of Cash Flows under the heading "Investing Activities" for the year ended 31st December 20X2.

Proceeds from Sale of PPE = **£195,000**

(b) The figure for depreciation which should be added back to profit before tax in the reconciliation of profit before tax to net cash from operating activities.

Accumulated Depreciation at 31/12/20X2	£1,245,000
Less Accumulated Depreciation at 31/12/20X1	£1,052,000
Add Accumulated Depreciation on Disposed Assets	£ 36,000*
Depreciation charge for the year	**£ 229,000**

*£36,000 depreciation = £152,000 (at cost) – £116,000 (carrying amount)

(c) The figure to be included for Purchases of PPE in the Statement of Cash Flows under the heading "Investing Activities" for the year ended 31st December 20X2.

Purchases of PPE – WORKINGS		
	£000	**Notes**
PPE at start of year	3,136	*SFP as at 31/12/20X7*
Depreciation Charge	-229	*See working for (b)*
Carrying amount of PPE sold	-116	*See working for (a)*
PPE at end of year	-3,408	*SFP as at 31/12/20X8*
Total PPE additions	**-617**	*Calculated*

Receipt of Dividends

These are classed as cash inflows from investing activities because they arise when the company has invested in shares in other companies.

Financing Activities

Companies need to obtain finance in order to go about their day-to-day business and to grow. There are generally two sources of finance for limited companies:

- **Investor Finance**: receipts from share issues (including any share premiums paid by investors).
- **Loan Finance**: receipts from new bank loans, debentures etc.

Any increase in either of these during the year will be a positive cash flow; any reductions (e.g. repayment of loans) will be a cash outflow.

You can calculate the financing activities of the company by comparing the balances in the Statements of Financial Position at the start and the end of the year.

Another cash outflow to consider in the Financing Activities section of the Statement of Cash Flows is Dividends paid by the company to its shareholders during the year.

Be careful to understand the difference between dividends received and dividends paid:

Dividends Received are only received if we have invested in shares of other companies - and so are dealt with in the 'Investing Activities' section.

Dividends Paid are paid by limited companies as the return to their shareholders for holding shares in the company – and so are dealt with in the Financing Activities section.

Also note that the dividends paid during a financial year are usually the **FINAL** dividend for the previous year and the **INTERIM** dividend for the current year.

Example 6.7

This example continues from Example 6.5. Looking at the extracts from the Statements of Profit or Loss and Statement of Financial Position for Golightly Ltd, we can calculate the net cash flows from Financing Activities:

Golightly Ltd – Statement of Financial Position as at…*(EXTRACT)*		
	31/3/20X9 £000	**31/3/20X8 £000**
EQUITY AND LIABILITIES		
Equity		
Share Capital	22,400	19,500
Share Premium	8,450	6,730
Retained Earnings	29,845	22,768
Total Equity	**60,695**	**48,998**
Non-Current Liabilities		
Bank Loans	8,740	4,960
	8,740	**4,960**

You are also told that during the year ended 31st March 20X9 Golightly Ltd paid final dividends relating to 20X7-X8 of £120,000, and an interim dividend for 20X8-X9 of £85,000. A final dividend for 20X8-X9 of £98,000 was paid in July 20X9.

Net Cash Flows from Financing Activities

	£000	
Increase in Share Capital	2,900	*(22,400 – 19,500)*
Increase in Share Premium	1,720	*(8,450 – 6,730)*
Increase in Bank Loan	3,780	*(8,740 – 4,960)*
Less Dividends Paid	205	*(120 + 85)*
Net Cash Inflow	**8,195**	

Note that the final dividend for 20X8-X9 is not paid until the following year, and so is not included in this year's Statement of Cash Flows.

The following table is a helpful reminder of what items go where in the Statement of Cash Flows.

Operating Activities	Investing Activities	Financing Activities
• Profit before tax • Add depreciation • Less investment income • Changes in inventories, receivables and payables • Less interest paid • Less taxes on income	**Inflows:** • Sale proceeds from sale of PPE and other non-current assets. • Interest and dividends received **Outflows:** • Purchases of PPE and other non-current assets	**Inflows:** • Receipts from increases in share capital • Increases in long-term loans **Outflows:** • Repayment of share capital / loans • Dividends paid

Pulling it all together

We have seen that the Statement of Cash Flows contains three 'sections':

- A reconciliation of the Profit before tax to the Net Cash from Operating Activities.
- A calculation of the Net Cash Flows in / out from Investing Activities.
- A calculation of the Net Cash Flows in / out from Financing Activities.

These three 'sections' account for **all** cash flows into and out of the organisation over the year. We add the three sections together to establish whether there was an increase or decrease in cash flow.

Therefore, if there is an overall **positive** cash flow this should be reflected in an **increase** in the company's Cash and Cash Equivalents balance at the beginning of the year to the end of the year. Similarly, an overall **negative** cash flow must result in a **decrease** in the company's balance for Cash and Cash Equivalents at the beginning of the year to the end of the year.

This allows us to double-check the figures in the Statement of Cash Flow are correct because the difference between the cash and cash equivalents in the SFP should equal the Net increase/decrease in cash and cash equivalents in the Statement of Cash Flows.

Example 6.8

Fergus Ltd has produced its Statement of Cash Flows for the year ended 31st March 20X2. It has calculated the following figures:

Net Cash from Operating Activities	£387,600
Net Cash to Investing Activities	(£107,400)
Net Cash from Financing Activities	£28,200
Net increase / decrease in cash and cash equivalents	£308,400

Required

If the value of Cash and Cash Equivalents at 1st April 20X1 (the start of the year) was £44,900, calculate what it should be at 31st March 20X2 (the end of the year).

Answer

Cash and Cash Equivalents at start of year	£ 44,900
Net Increase in Cash during year	+ £308,400
Cash and Cash Equivalents at end of year	**£353,300**

The figures for Cash and Cash Equivalents at the start and end of the year can be found in the Current Assets section of the Statement of Financial Position.

The Statement of Cash Flows should show the reconciliation between Cash and Cash Equivalents at the start and end of the year as shown above. This is shown at the bottom of the Statement of Cash Flows.

Activity 6.2

You have been asked to prepare the Statement of Cash Flows for Sadler Ltd for the year ended 31st December 20X9.

The most recent Statement of Profit or Loss and Statement of Financial Position (with comparatives for the previous year) of Sadler Ltd can be seen below.

Sadler Ltd – **Statement of Profit or Loss for the year ended 31/12/20X9**	
	£000
Revenue	90,413
Cost of Sales	(45,108)
Gross Profit	45,305
Loss on Disposal of PPE	(29)
Dividends Received	77
	45,353
Distribution Costs	(16,504)
Administrative Expenses	(7,580)
Profit from Operations	21,269
Finance Costs	(34)
Profit Before Taxation	21,235
Taxation	(979)
Profit from Continuing Operations	20,256

Additional Information:

- The total depreciation charge for the year was £2,405,000.
- PPE with a carrying value of £360,000 was sold during the year.
- All sales and purchases were made on credit. All expenses were paid for in cash.

- A dividend of £965,000 was paid during the year, and a further dividend of £640,000 was declared on 18th January 20X0 before the financial statements were authorised for issue.

Sadler Ltd – Statement of Financial Position as at...		
	31/12/20X9 £000	31/12/20X8 £000
ASSETS		
Non-Current Assets		
Property Plant and Equipment	47,850	28,472
Investments at cost	8,000	8,000
	55,850	**36,472**
Current Assets		
Inventories	6,054	5,810
Trade Receivables	4,689	5,964
Cash and Cash Equivalents	596	2,476
	11,339	**14,250**
TOTAL ASSETS	**67,189**	**50,722**
EQUITY AND LIABILITIES		
Equity		
Share Capital	18,500	16,300
Share Premium	3,600	2,800
Retained Earnings	33,478	14,187
Total Equity	**55,578**	**33,287**
Non-Current Liabilities		
Bank Loans	3,700	5,100
	3,700	**5,100**
Current Liabilities		
Trade Payables	6,932	11,275
Tax Liabilities	979	1,060
	7,911	12,335
Total Liabilities	**11,611**	**17,435**
TOTAL EQUITY AND LIABILITIES	**67,189**	**50,722**

Answer Template – Sadler Ltd

Proceeds on Disposal of PPE – WORKINGS W1	
	£000
Carrying amount of PPE sold	
Loss on disposal of PPE	

Purchases of PPE – WORKINGS W2	
	£000
PPE at start of year	
Depreciation Charge	
Carrying amount of PPE sold	
PPE at end of year	
Total PPE additions	

Reconciliation of Profit Before Tax to Net Cash from Operating Activities	£000	Notes / Workings
Profit Before Tax		
Adjustments For:		
Depreciation		
Finance Costs		
Loss on disposal of PPE		
Dividends received		
Adjustment in respect of inventories		
Adjustment in respect of trade receivables		
Adjustment in respect of trade payables		
Cash Generated by Operations		
Interest Paid		
Taxation Paid		
Net Cash from Operating Activities		
Investing Activities		
Purchases of PPE		
Proceeds on Disposal of PPE		
Dividends Received		
Net Cash Used in Investing Activities		
Financing Activities		
Increase in share capital & share premium		
Decrease in loan		
Dividends paid		
Net Cash From Financing Activities		
Net increase / (decrease) in cash and cash equivalents		
Cash and cash equivalents at beginning of year		
Cash and cash equivalents at end of year		

Activity 6.3

You have been asked to prepare the Statement of Cash Flows for Robson Ltd for the year ended 31st May 20X8.

The most recent Statement of Profit or Loss and Statement of Financial Position (with comparatives for the previous year) of Robson Ltd can be seen below.

Robson Ltd – Statement of Profit or Loss for the year ended 31/05/20X8	
	£000
Revenue	109,265
Cost of Sales	(53,204)
Gross Profit	56,061
Gain on Disposal of PPE	95
Dividends Received	195
	56,351
Distribution Costs	(29,160)
Administrative Expenses	(16,894)
Profit from Operations	10,297
Finance Costs	(68)
Profit Before Taxation	10,229
Taxation	(1,038)
Profit from Continuing Operations	9,191

Additional Information:

- The total depreciation charge for the year was £1,398,000.
- PPE with a carrying value of £475,000 was sold during the year.
- All sales and purchases were made on credit. All expenses were paid for in cash.
- A dividend of £820,000 was paid during the year, and a further dividend of £300,000 was declared on 7th August 20X8 before the financial statements were authorised for issue.

Robson Ltd – Statement of Financial Position as at…		
	31/05/20X8 £000	**31/05/20X7 £000**
ASSETS		
Non-Current Assets		
Property Plant and Equipment	62,124	53,058
Investments at cost	4,500	4,500
	66,624	**57,558**
Current Assets		
Inventories	9,042	7,684
Trade Receivables	6,957	5,810
Cash and Cash Equivalents	0	486
	15,999	**13,980**
TOTAL ASSETS	**82,623**	**71,538**
EQUITY AND LIABILITIES		
Equity		
Share Capital	28,470	22,300
Share Premium	2,139	1,890
Retained Earnings	35,416	27,045
Total Equity	**66,025**	**51,235**
Non-Current Liabilities		
Bank Loans	6,140	8,000
	6,140	**8,000**
Current Liabilities		
Trade Payables	8,053	11,338
Tax Liabilities	1,038	965
Bank Overdraft	1,367	0
	10,458	12,303
Total Liabilities	**16,598**	**20,303**
TOTAL EQUITY AND LIABILITIES	**82,623**	**71,538**

Answer Template – Robson Ltd

Proceeds on Disposal of PPE – WORKINGS W1	
	£000
Carrying amount of PPE sold	
Gain on disposal of PPE	

Purchases of PPE – WORKINGS W2	
	£000
PPE at start of year	
Depreciation Charge	
Carrying amount of PPE sold	
PPE at end of year	
Total PPE additions	

Reconciliation of Profit Before Tax to Net Cash from Operating Activities	£000	Notes / Workings
Profit Before Tax		
Adjustments For:		
Depreciation		
Gain on disposal of PPE		
Dividends received		
Finance Costs		
Adjustment in respect of inventories		
Adjustment in respect of trade receivables		
Adjustment in respect of trade payables		
Cash Generated by Operations		
Interest Paid		
Taxation Paid		
Net Cash from Operating Activities		
Investing Activities		
Purchases of PPE		
Proceeds on Disposal of PPE		
Dividends Received		
Net Cash Used in Investing Activities		
Financing Activities		
Increase in share capital & share premium		
Decrease in loan		
Dividends paid		
Net Cash From Financing Activities		
Net inc / (dec) in cash and cash equivalents		
Cash and cash equivalents at beginning of year		
Cash and cash equivalents at end of year		

Assessment 6

You are now required to log-in to your ROGO account to complete your online assessment before progressing on to the next chapter.

Chapter 7: Consolidated Accounts

By the end of this chapter you should:

- Understand the requirements for reporting as a group.
- Be able to consolidate each line item in the consolidated statement of profit or loss and statement of financial position for a parent company with one partly owned subsidiary.
- Be able to make adjustments in respect of intercompany sales and other intercompany items, impairment losses on goodwill and dividends paid by a subsidiary company to its parent company.
- Be able to calculate goodwill, non-controlling interest, pre- and post-acquisition profits, equity and unrealised profit on inventories.
- Be able to make adjustments in respect of goodwill, non-controlling interest, pre- and post-acquisition profits, equity and unrealised profit on inventories.
- Be able to make adjustments in respect of fair value, impairment of goodwill and intercompany balances.

Introduction

Until this point in your studies you have focussed on preparing financial statements for sole traders and partnerships (at Level 3) and Limited Companies (in this unit at Level 4). Such financial statements are known as **unitary** financial statements, because they are prepared for a single individual organisation.

Modern commerce is generally more complex, and many limited companies do not operate in isolation; instead, they form part of a **group.** In a group of companies, the ownership of individual companies can become very complex but at this stage of your studies the relationships will be kept quite straightforward.

Each company within a group structure retains its separate legal identity, and is therefore responsible for producing and issuing its own sets of financial statements.

However, the group itself must also prepare a set of **consolidated** financial statements, in accordance with the following international Accounting Standards:

- **IFRS 3** ***Business Combinations***
- **IFRS 10** ***Consolidated Financial Statements***

To start with we will consider the simplest form of group structure – where one company (***the parent***) owns all of the shares of another company (***the subsidiary***).

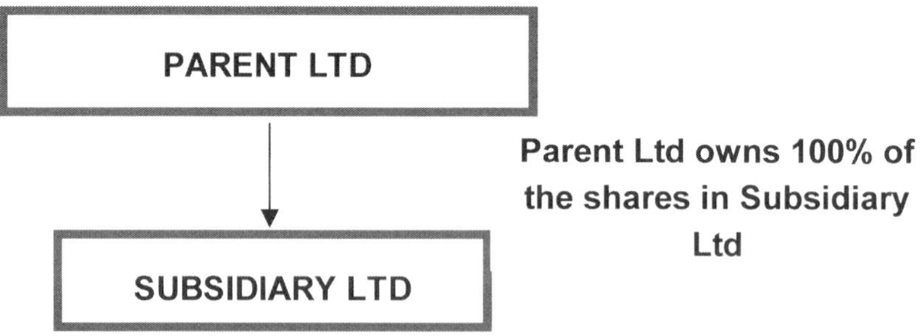

This structure could have come about in two ways:

1. Subsidiary Ltd was an existing company, and Parent Ltd bought 100% of the shares in it.

2. Parent Ltd set up Subsidiary Ltd itself as a new company, and therefore owns 100% of the shares.

However, the relationship arises, a **group** exists where one entity **controls** another – note that the key issue is control, rather than share ownership. However, in most cases, owning more than 50% of the ordinary shares in another entity produces a controlling relationship (although we will look at some other situations later).

What IFRS 10 says...

IFRS 10 Consolidated Financial Accounts contains the following definitions:

A Parent Company is ***"an entity that controls one or more entities".***

A Subsidiary is ***"an entity that is controlled by another entity".***

A Group is ***"a parent company and its subsidiaries".***

IFRS 10 *Consolidated Financial Accounts* also requires that a set of consolidated (group) financial statements are prepared for a group – in addition to the requirement that each entity within the group must also prepare its own individual financial statements.

This chapter will develop the skills required to produce the following consolidated financial statements:

- **Consolidated Statement of Financial Position**
- **Consolidated Statement of Profit or Loss**

The Consolidated Statement of Financial Position

The consolidated financial statements portray:

- the assets, liabilities and equity of the group (in the Consolidated Statement of Financial Position)
- the income, expenses and profit of the group (in the Consolidated Statement of Profit or Loss).

When preparing the consolidated financial statements, some of the calculations are extremely straightforward. For example, if the Parent Company (P Ltd) has £500,000 in the bank, and the Subsidiary (S Ltd) has £200,000 in the bank, then the group has £700,000.

P LTD + **S LTD** = **GROUP**

Whilst this basic addition is true for many aspects of the consolidated accounts, there are a number of adjustments which must be made.

The following examples will build up the skills and techniques required, from the simplest situation (a 100% relationship) to more complex scenarios.

Example 7.1

P Ltd owns 100% of the share capital in S Ltd, having acquired them on 31st March 20X8. The summary financial statements for the two companies as at 31st March 20X8 are shown below.

STATEMENT OF FINANCIAL POSITION	P LTD	S LTD
Non-Current Assets	£	£
Investment in S Ltd	60,000	-
Property, Plant and Equipment	45,000	37,000
	105,000	**37,000**
Current Assets		
Inventories	18,000	16,000
Receivables	26,000	22,500
Cash & Cash Equivalents	15,000	19,800
	59,000	**58,300**
Total Assets	**164,000**	**95,300**
Equity		
Ordinary Share Capital	90,000	35,000
Retained Earnings	50,000	25,000
	140,000	**60,000**
Non-Current Liabilities		
Bank Loan	18,000	20,000
Current Liabilities		
Trade and Other Payables	6,000	15,300
Total Equity and Liabilities	**164,000**	**95,300**

The Consolidated Statement of Financial Position at 31st March 20X8 is shown below, along with notes to explain each of the entries.

STATEMENT OF FINANCIAL POSITION	P LTD	S LTD	CONSOLIDATED	NOTES
Non-Current Assets	**£**	**£**	**£**	
Investment in S Ltd	60,000	-	-	1
Property, Plant and Equipment	45,000	37,000	82,000	2
	105,000	**37,000**	**82,000**	
Current Assets				
Inventories	18,000	16,000	34,000	3
Receivables	26,000	22,500	48,500	3
Cash & Cash Equivalents	15,000	19,800	34,800	3
	59,000	**58,300**	**117,300**	
Total Assets	**164,000**	**95,300**	**199,300**	
Equity				
Ordinary Share Capital	90,000	35,000	90,000	4
Retained Earnings	50,000	25,000	50,000	5
	140,000	**60,000**	**140,000**	
Non-Current Liabilities				
Bank Loan	18,000	20,000	38,000	6
Current Liabilities				
Trade and Other Payables	6,000	15,300	21,300	7
Total Equity and Liabilities	**164,000**	**95,300**	**199,300**	

There is a Non-Current Asset showing in the Statement of Financial Position of P Ltd for the value of £60,000. This investment refers to the purchase on 31st March 20X8 of 100% of the shares in S Ltd; the value of S Ltd on this day is the equity, made up of:

Ordinary Shares (at nominal value)	£35,000
Retained Profit	£25,000
	£60,000

Because the amount paid by P Ltd (£60,000) is the same as the value of the investment, there is no goodwill attached to this investment. We will look at goodwill in later scenarios.

NOTES

1. The Parent's investment in the Subsidiary is not shown in the Consolidated SFP. We are showing the position of the group as a whole, as a single entity. Because P Ltd own 100% of the shares in S Ltd, there are no external shareholders (in later examples we will look at situations where the parent doesn't own the full 100% of the shares).

2. Other non-current assets – Property, Plant and Equipment – are simply added together.

3. Similarly, the current assets of the two businesses are just added together. We will look later at a situation where the two companies trade with each other, which will affect this, but for now we will just calculate the totals.

4. As with Note 1, because the ordinary share capital of S Ltd is fully owned by P Ltd, it is ignored in looking at the group's financial position. Therefore, only the parent company's Ordinary Share Capital is included.

5. Similarly, as with note 4, when preparing the group's consolidated retained profit, we only take the parent company's retained profit.

   This is because on the date of purchase (in this example 31st March 20X8) P Ltd bought 100% of the shares in a company whose total equity was:

Ordinary Shares	£35,000
Retained profit	£25,000
	£60,000

   P Ltd.'s investment is effectively cancelled out by the total of the ordinary shares and the retained profits at the date of acquisition.

6. Non-current liabilities are added together.

7. Current liabilities are also simply added together (as mentioned in Note 3 we will consider the situation of inter-company trading later).

Activity 7.1

Dad Ltd owns 100% of the share capital in Son Ltd, having acquired them on 31st December 20X4. The summary financial statements for the two companies as at 31st December 20X5 are shown below:

STATEMENT OF FINANCIAL POSITION	Dad Ltd	Son Ltd
Non-Current Assets	£	£
Investment in Son Ltd	40,000	-
Property, Plant and Equipment	58,000	46,000
	98,000	**46,000**
Current Assets		
Inventories	13,250	9,450
Receivables	18,400	16,980
Cash & Cash Equivalents	6,700	9,520
	38,350	**35,950**
Total Assets	**136,350**	**81,950**
Equity		
Ordinary Share Capital	75,000	27,100
Retained Earnings	30,250	12,900
	105,250	**40,000**
Non-Current Liabilities		
Bank Loan	22,500	26,000
Current Liabilities		
Trade and Other Payables	8,600	15,950
Total Equity and Liabilities	**136,350**	**81,950**

You are required to produce the Consolidated Statement of Financial Position for the group as at 31st December 20X5.

CONSOLIDATED STATEMENT OF FINANCIAL POSITION as at 31st December 20X5	
Non-Current Assets	**£**
Investment in Son Ltd	
Property, Plant and Equipment	
Current Assets	
Inventories	
Receivables	
Cash & Cash Equivalents	
Total Assets	
Equity	
Ordinary Share Capital	
Retained Earnings	
Non-Current Liabilities	
Bank Loan	
Current Liabilities	
Trade and Other Payables	
Total Equity and Liabilities	

Goodwill

In the earlier scenario, we assumed that the Parent company paid the exact value of the Subsidiary's total equity – in other words the total of the Subsidiary's Ordinary Share Capital and Retained Profit at that date.

However, it is very common for a company to actually pay more (or occasionally less) than the 'book value' of the subsidiary. This situation leads to the establishment of a value for **goodwill**, which must be reflected in the consolidated accounts.

Goodwill is "***the difference between the amount paid by the Parent for the shares in the Subsidiary, and the value that has been acquired***".

The easiest way to measure the value acquired is to add together:

Share Capital in Subsidiary

\+ Other Reserves in Subsidiary

\+ Retained Profit in Subsidiary at the date of acquisition

If the Parent pays **more** than the value it has acquired, the difference is **positive goodwill**. Alternatively (and perhaps less commonly) if the Parent pays **less** than the value acquired, there will be **negative goodwill.**

Positive goodwill is treated as a non-current asset in the consolidated Statement of Financial Position. **Negative goodwill** is added to the Retained Earnings figure in the Statement of Comprehensive Income.

Positive goodwill must also be subject to an impairment review *at least annually* under IAS 36 *Impairment of Assets.*

Example 7.2

H Ltd owns 100% of the share capital in G Ltd, having acquired them on 31st March 20X8. The summary financial statements for the two companies as at 31st March 20X8 are shown below:

STATEMENT OF FINANCIAL POSITION	H LTD	G LTD
Non-Current Assets	**£**	**£**
Investment in G Ltd	90,000	-
Property, Plant and Equipment	45,000	37,000
	135,000	**37,000**
Current Assets		
Inventories	18,000	16,000
Receivables	26,000	22,500
Cash & Cash Equivalents	15,000	19,800
	59,000	**58,300**
Total Assets	**194,000**	**95,300**
Equity		
Ordinary Share Capital	90,000	35,000
Retained Earnings	80,000	25,000
	170,000	**60,000**
Non-Current Liabilities		
Bank Loan	18,000	20,000
Current Liabilities		
Trade and Other Payables	6,000	15,300
Total Equity and Liabilities	**194,000**	**95,300**

The Consolidated Statement of Financial Position at 31st March 20X8 is shown below, along with notes to explain each of the entries.

STATEMENT OF FINANCIAL POSITION	H LTD	G LTD	CONSOLIDATED	NOTES
Non-Current Assets	**£**	**£**	**£**	
Goodwill			30,000	1
Investment in Ltd	90,000	-	-	2
Property, Plant and Equipment	45,000	37,000	82,000	
	135,000	**37,000**	**112,000**	
Current Assets				
Inventories	18,000	16,000	34,000	
Receivables	26,000	22,500	48,500	
Cash & Cash Equivalents	15,000	19,800	34,800	
	59,000	**58,300**	**117,300**	
Total Assets	**194,000**	**95,300**	**229,300**	
Equity				
Ordinary Share Capital	90,000	35,000	90,000	3
Retained Earnings	80,000	25,000	80,000	4
	170,000	**60,000**	**170,000**	
Non-Current Liabilities				
Bank Loan	18,000	20,000	38,000	
Current Liabilities				
Trade and Other Payables	6,000	15,300	21,300	
Total Equity and Liabilities	**194,000**	**95,300**	**229,300**	

NOTES

1. Because the amount paid by H Ltd (£90,000) is more than the value of the investment, there is £30,000 goodwill attached to this investment.

   Goodwill Calculation:

Consideration (amount paid)	*£90,000*
Value of Net Assets Acquired	*£60,000 (£35,000 + £ 25,000)*
Goodwill	*£30,000*

   This is shown as a non-current asset in the Consolidated Statement of Financial Position.

2. The Parent's investment in the Subsidiary is not shown in the Consolidated SFP. We are showing the position of the group as a whole, as a single entity. Because H Ltd own 100% of the shares in G Ltd, there are no external shareholders (in later examples we will look at situations where the parent doesn't own the full 100% of the shares).

3. As with Note 1, because the ordinary share capital of G Ltd is fully owned by H Ltd, it is ignored in looking at the group's financial position. Therefore, only the parent company's Ordinary Share Capital is included.

4. Similarly, as with note 4, when preparing the group's consolidated retained profit, we only take the parent company's retained profit.

   This is because on the date of purchase (in this example 31st March 20X8) H Ltd bought 100% of the shares in a company whose total equity was:

Ordinary Shares	£35,000
Retained profit	£25,000
	£60,000

   G Ltd.'s investment of £90,000 is effectively cancelled out by the total of the ordinary shares and the retained profits at the date of acquisition (£60,000), plus the goodwill calculated earlier (£30,000).

Activity 7.2

Pop Ltd owns 100% of the share capital in Kid Ltd, having acquired them on 1st January 20X8. The summary financial statements for the two companies as at 31st December 20X8 are shown below:

STATEMENT OF FINANCIAL POSITION	Pop Ltd	Kid Ltd
Non-Current Assets	£	£
Investment in Kid Ltd	88,000	-
Property, Plant and Equipment	61,000	69,500
	149,000	**69,500**
Current Assets		
Inventories	18,140	6,890
Receivables	6,550	2,800
Cash & Cash Equivalents	3,890	3,010
	28,580	**12,700**
Total Assets	**177,580**	**82,200**
Equity		
Ordinary Share Capital	90,000	40,000
Retained Profit	53,660	25,600
	143,660	**65,600**
Non-Current Liabilities		
Bank Loan	28,000	8,000
Current Liabilities		
Trade and Other Payables	5,920	8,600
Total Equity and Liabilities	**177,580**	**82,200**

You are required to produce the Consolidated Statement of Financial Position for the group as at 31st December 20X8.

Working – Goodwill Calculation

Consideration (amount paid)	
Value of Net Assets Acquired	
Goodwill	

CONSOLIDATED STATEMENT OF FINANCIAL POSITION as at 31st December 20X8	
Non-Current Assets	**£**
Goodwill	
Investment in Kid Ltd	
Property, Plant and Equipment	
Current Assets	
Inventories	
Receivables	
Cash & Cash Equivalents	
Total Assets	
Equity	
Ordinary Share Capital	
Retained Earnings	
Non-Current Liabilities	
Bank Loan	
Current Liabilities	
Trade and Other Payables	
Total Equity and Liabilities	

Pre-Acquisition and Post-Acquisition Profits

In the scenarios, we have looked at so far, we have assumed that we are preparing the Consolidated Statement of Financial Position immediately after the acquisition of the subsidiary by the parent. This means that the subsidiary's Retained Earnings Reserve will **only** consist of those profits it has made **BEFORE** it was taken over – called **PRE-ACQUISITION PROFITS**. Effectively the parent "bought" those profits as part of the purchase price at the acquisition date.

Of course, as time goes by the subsidiary company will (hopefully) continue to make profits, and will see its Retained Earnings Reserve increase each year. However, from the date of the acquisition onwards the subsidiary is owned by the parent, and so the **POST-ACQUISITION PROFITS** belong not only to the subsidiary, but also to the group.

We must therefore include these **post acquisition profits** in the **consolidated retained earnings reserve.** These will be added to the parent company's Retained Earnings.

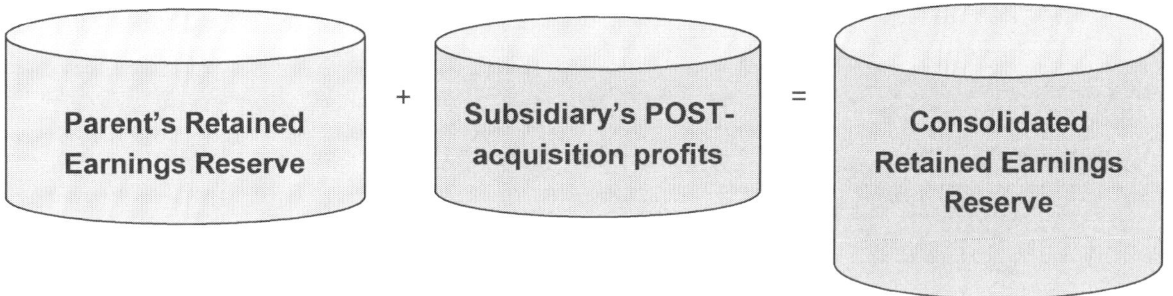

Example 7.3

Tom Ltd purchased 100% of the shares of Jerry Ltd for £135,000 on 1st April 20X3 when the retained earnings reserve of Jerry Ltd was £60,000 and its Ordinary Share Capital was £50,000. At 31st March 20X4, the Retained Earnings Reserve of Tom Ltd was £450,000 and the Retained Earnings Reserve of Jerry Ltd was £95,000.

Calculate the Consolidated Retained Earnings reserve of the group as at 31st March 20X4.

Parent's (Tom Ltd) Retained Earnings	£450,000
Subsidiary's (Jerry Ltd) **Post-acquisition** Profits	£ 35,000 *
Consolidated Retained Earnings Reserve	£485,000

* Jerry Ltd.'s Post Acquisition Profits are £95,000 - £60,000 = £35,000.

Example 7.4

B Ltd owns 100% of the share capital in C Ltd, having acquired them on 1st April 20X7 when C Ltd.'s Retained Earnings were £16,000.

The summary financial statements for the two companies as at 31st March 20X8 are shown below:

STATEMENT OF FINANCIAL POSITION	B LTD	C LTD
Non-Current Assets	£	£
Investment in C Ltd	100,000	-
Property, Plant and Equipment	280,000	140,000
	380,000	**140,000**
Current Assets		
Inventories	46,000	22,000
Receivables	38,000	18,000
Cash & Cash Equivalents	12,000	6,000
	96,000	**46,000**
Total Assets	**476,000**	**186,000**
Equity		
Ordinary Share Capital	200,000	80,000
Retained Earnings	140,000	48,000
	340,000	**128,000**
Non-Current Liabilities		
Bank Loan	100,000	38,000
Current Liabilities		
Trade and Other Payables	36,000	20,000
Total Equity and Liabilities	**476,000**	**186,000**

The Consolidated Statement of Financial Position at 31st March 20X8 is shown below, along with notes to explain each of the entries.

STATEMENT OF FINANCIAL POSITION	CONSOLIDATED	NOTES
Non-Current Assets	**£**	
Goodwill	4,000	1
Investment in C Ltd		
Property, Plant and Equipment	420,000	
	424,000	
Current Assets		
Inventories	68,000	
Receivables	56,000	
Cash & Cash Equivalents	18,000	
	142,000	
Total Assets	**566,000**	
Equity		
Ordinary Share Capital	200,000	
Retained Earnings	172,000	2
	372,000	
Non-Current Liabilities		
Bank Loan	138,000	
Current Liabilities		
Trade and Other Payables	56,000	
Total Equity and Liabilities	**566,000**	

NOTES

1. Because the amount paid by B Ltd (£100,000) is more than the value of the investment, there is £4,000 goodwill attached to this investment. This is shown as a non-current asset in the Consolidated Statement of Financial Position.

Ordinary Shares (at nominal value)	£80,000	
+ Retained Profit	£16,000	*PRE-acquisition reserves*
	£96,000	
Goodwill (£100,000 - £96,000)	£ 4,000	

2. When calculating the group's Retained Earnings reserve, we take the parent company's Reserves (B Ltd) plus the subsidiary company's post-acquisition reserves; these are the profits made **since** the acquisition, calculated as:

Subsidiary's Retained Earnings at 31st March 20X8	£ 48,000
Subsidiary's Retained Earnings at 1st April 20X7	£ 16,000
Subsidiary's Post-Acquisition Reserves	**£ 32,000**
Plus Parent Company's Reserves	£140,000
	£172,000

Activity 7.3

Pater Ltd owns 100% of the share capital in Child Ltd, having acquired them on 31st December 20X2 when the retained earnings of Child Ltd were £80,000. The summary financial statements for the two companies as at 31st December 20X3 are shown below:

STATEMENT OF FINANCIAL POSITION	Pater Ltd	Child Ltd
Non-Current Assets	£	£
Investment in Child Ltd	140,000	-
Property, Plant and Equipment	380,000	158,600
	520,000	**158,600**
Current Assets		
Inventories	22,580	13,950
Receivables	26,850	12,680
Cash & Cash Equivalents	14,150	12,460
	63,580	**39,090**
Total Assets	**583,580**	**197,690**
Equity		
Ordinary Share Capital	400,000	50,000
Retained Earnings	140,000	114,900
	540,000	**164,900**
Non-Current Liabilities		
Bank Loan	30,000	18,500
Current Liabilities		
Trade and Other Payables	13,580	14,290
Total Equity and Liabilities	**583,580**	**197,690**

You are required to produce the Consolidated Statement of Financial Position for the group as at 31st December 20X3.

CONSOLIDATED STATEMENT OF FINANCIAL POSITION as at 31st December 20X3	
Non-Current Assets	£
Goodwill	
Investment in Child Ltd	
Property, Plant and Equipment	
Current Assets	
Inventories	
Receivables	
Cash & Cash Equivalents	
Total Assets	
Equity	
Ordinary Share Capital	
Retained Earnings	
Non-Current Liabilities	
Bank Loan	
Current Liabilities	
Trade and Other Payables	
Total Equity and Liabilities	

Working – Goodwill Calculation

Consideration (amount paid for the investment)	
Value of Net Assets Acquired	
Goodwill	

Working – Retained Earnings Calculation

Parent – Retained Earnings	
Subsidiary – Post-Acquisition Retained Earnings	
Consolidated Retained Earnings	

Less than 100% Ownership – Non-Controlling Interest

In each of the scenarios so far, the parent company has purchased 100% of the shares in the subsidiary. However, it is not necessary for one company to own 100% of the ordinary shares in another to create a group situation; the important aspect is that one company **controls** the other.

In IFRS 3, control is ***"the power to govern the financial and operating policies of an entity or business so as to obtain benefits from its activities".***

This simply means that the parent company is able to **control** the day to day activities, and the longer-term strategic direction, of the subsidiary, and benefit from wealth generated by it.

IAS 27 *Consolidated and Separate Financial Statements* assumes that one company will acquire control of another when it owns **more than 50%** of the voting rights in the other – these are the ordinary shares.

Although IFRS 3 and IAS 27 both identify other ways in which a company can acquire control of another, in your exam you are most likely to encounter the situation where the parent has bought more than 50% of the ordinary shares in the subsidiary.

When the **acquirer** (i.e. the parent) acquires **less than 100% (but more than 50%)** of the voting rights, there will be a proportion of the subsidiary's shares which are not owned by the parent company, these are owned by the **Non-Controlling Interest (NCI).** This Non-Controlling Interest represents an important group of shareholders; they own shares in the subsidiary, and so are entitled to a share of any profits made by the subsidiary, but are not part of the group.

Definition

The Non-Controlling Interest (NCI) is ***"the equity in a subsidiary not attributable, directly or indirectly, to a parent".***

The Non-Controlling Interest (NCI) must be shown in the Equity section of the Consolidated Statement of Financial Position, as a separate item. This will reflect the value of the subsidiary company which is owned by shareholders outside the group.

Example 7.5

J Ltd owns 80% of the share capital in K Ltd, having acquired them on 1st April 20X7 when K Ltd.'s Retained Earnings were £28,000. The summary financial statements for the two companies as at 31st March 20X8 are shown below:

STATEMENT OF FINANCIAL POSITION	J LTD	K LTD
Non-Current Assets	£	£
Investment in K Ltd	128,000	-
Property, Plant and Equipment	290,000	126,000
	418,000	**126,000**
Current Assets		
Inventories	61,000	28,000
Receivables	29,000	12,000
Cash & Cash Equivalents	30,000	2,000
	120,000	**42,000**
Total Assets	**538,000**	**168,000**
Equity		
Ordinary Share Capital	250,000	100,000
Retained Earnings	193,000	40,000
	443,000	**140,000**
Non-Current Liabilities		
Bank Loan	75,000	17,000
Current Liabilities		
Trade and Other Payables	20,000	11,000
Total Equity and Liabilities	**538,000**	**168,000**

The Consolidated Statement of Financial Position at 31st March 20X8 is shown below, along with notes to explain each of the entries.

STATEMENT OF FINANCIAL POSITION	CONSOLIDATED	NOTES
Non-Current Assets	**£**	
Goodwill	25,600	1
Investment in K Ltd		
Property, Plant and Equipment	416,000	
	441,600	
Current Assets		
Inventories	89,000	
Receivables	41,000	
Cash & Cash Equivalents	32,000	
	162,000	
Total Assets	**603,600**	
Equity		
Ordinary Share Capital	250,000	
Retained Earnings	202,600	2
Non-Controlling Interest	28,000	3
	480,600	
Non-Current Liabilities		
Bank Loan	92,000	
Current Liabilities		
Creditors	31,000	
Total Equity and Liabilities	**603,600**	

NOTES

1. There is a Non-Current Asset showing in the Statement of Financial Position of J Ltd for the value of £128,000. This refers to the purchase on 31st March 20X7 of 80% of the shares in K Ltd.

   First, we will calculate the **'net assets acquired at the date of acquisition'** as we have seen previously in this chapter. This is calculated as:

Share capital	£100,000
Plus the retained earnings <u>AT THE DATE OF ACQUISITION</u>,	£ 28,000
Plus any revaluation surplus.	-
Net assets acquired	£128,000

   To calculate the Goodwill, we will need to calculate the net assets that were acquired, consider what percentage of those assets belong to someone else and what consideration was paid for the company. To do this we would lay it out like this.

Consideration (amount we paid)	£128,000
NCI's % at acquisition (NCI owns 20% of the assets)	£ 25,600
Less - Net Assets acquired at acquisition	(£128,000)
Goodwill	£ 25,600

   All figures must be at the **date of acquisition**. There is no revaluation surplus in this example but we will look at this further on as we progress to more complex questions.

   We can now calculate what proportion of that is attributable (or belongs) to the Non-Controlling Interest (**NCI**). We know the NCI owns 20% of those assets 'at the date of acquisition' so £128,000 x 20% = £25,600.

2. When calculating the group's Retained Earnings reserve, we take the parent company's Reserves (J Ltd) plus their share of the subsidiary company's post-acquisition reserves; these are the profits made **since** the acquisition, calculated as:

Parent 100% retained earnings at 31st March 20X8	£193,000
Parents share of Sub's retained earnings post acquisition*	£ 9,600
Consolidated Retained Earnings	£ 202,600

*Note: The parents share of the subsidiary's retained earnings is calculated by finding out the profit made **since** acquisition. £40,000-£28,000= £12,000 x 80% = £9,600. Because the parent company only owns 80% of the shares in the subsidiary, the group is only 'entitled' to 80% of the post-acquisition profits (the rest belong to the NCI – see below).

3. The Non-Controlling Interest (NCI) still own 20% of the subsidiary company – and so they own 20% of the value of the subsidiary at the **<u>reporting date</u>** (31st March 20X8).

This is calculated as:

Subsidiary's Net Assets at 31st March 20X8	£140,000
x 20% =	£ 28,000

Or alternatively we can break it down separately:

Share capital attributable to NCI at end of period: *(£100,000 x 20%)*	£ 20,000
Retained Earnings attributable to NCI at end of period: *(£40,000 x 20%)*	£ 8,000
Non-Controlling Interest:	£ 28,000

Activity 7.4

Pappa Ltd owns 75% of the share capital in Kind Ltd, having acquired them on 31st December 20X2 when the retained earnings of Kind Ltd were £60,000. The summary financial statements for the two companies as at 31st December 20X3 are shown below:

STATEMENT OF FINANCIAL POSITION	Pappa Ltd	Kind Ltd
Non-Current Assets	£	£
Investment in Kind Ltd	200,000	-
Property, Plant and Equipment	600,000	240,000
	800,000	**240,000**
Current Assets		
Inventories	45,000	23,000
Receivables	38,000	9,000
Cash & Cash Equivalents	22,000	3,000
	105,000	**35,000**
Total Assets	**905,000**	**275,000**
Equity		
Ordinary Share Capital	700,000	100,000
Retained Earnings	166,000	96,000
	866,000	**196,000**
Non-Current Liabilities		
Bank Loan	22,000	50,000
Current Liabilities		
Creditors	17,000	29,000
Total Equity and Liabilities	**905,000**	**275,000**

You are required to produce the Consolidated Statement of Financial Position for the group as at 31st December 20X3.

CONSOLIDATED STATEMENT OF FINANCIAL POSITION as at 31st December 20X3	
Non-Current Assets	**£**
Goodwill	
Investment in Kind Ltd	
Property, Plant and Equipment	
Current Assets	
Inventories	
Receivables	
Cash & Cash Equivalents	
Total Assets	
Equity	
Ordinary Share Capital	
Retained Earnings	
Non-Controlling Interest	
Non-Current Liabilities	
Bank Loan	
Current Liabilities	
Creditors	
Total Equity and Liabilities	

Working – Goodwill Calculation

Consideration (amount paid)	
NCI % at acquisition	
Less – Net assets acquired at acquisition	
Goodwill	

Working – Retained Earnings Calculation

Parent – Retained Earnings	
Subsidiary – post-acquisition Retained Earnings attributable to parent	
Consolidated Retained Earnings	

Working – Non-Controlling Interest

Share Capital attributable to NCI	
Retained Earnings attributable to NCI	
Value of Non-Controlling Interest	

Fair Values in Consolidated Financial Accounts

You should already be familiar with the concept of **Fair Value**, having previously come across it whilst studying both IAS 16 *Property Plant & Equipment* and IAS 36 *Impairment Reviews.*

When one company acquires the majority of the shares (i.e. more than 50%) in another, IFRS 3 requires that the Consolidated Financial Statements (i.e. the financial statements for the group) reflect the cost of the business acquired at the fair values of all of the assets and liabilities as at the date of acquisition.

Fair Value is defined by IFRS 3 as ***"the amount for which an asset could be exchanged, or a liability settled, between knowledgeable and willing parties in an arms' length transaction"***.

This is important because whilst the subsidiary may not necessarily prepare its accounts using the fair value basis for valuing assets and liabilities, the group must. This means that there may need to be some adjustments carried out before preparation of the consolidated financial statements.

It may be necessary to adjust the given values for the subsidiary's assets – and most commonly this will affect land valuation. You may be told that the subsidiary's land was re-valued at the time of acquisition, but that this had not been reflected in the subsidiary's financial statements at that date.

In this situation, it will be necessary to adjust some of the figures in the subsidiary's Statement of Financial Position; you will need to:

Increase: Non-Current Assets

Increase: Revaluation Reserve (*with the amount of the revaluation)*

Example 7.6

T Ltd owns 60% of the share capital in W Ltd, having acquired them on 1st April 20X7 when W Ltd.'s Retained Earnings were £120,000. The summary financial statements for the two companies as at 31st March 20X8 are shown below:

STATEMENT OF FINANCIAL POSITION	T LTD	W LTD
Non-Current Assets	£	£
Investment in W Ltd	282,000	-
Property, Plant and Equipment	875,000	450,000
	1,157,000	**450,000**
Current Assets		
Inventories	81,000	49,000
Receivables	46,000	61,000
Cash & Cash Equivalents	29,000	18,000
	156,000	**128,000**
Total Assets	**1,313,000**	**578,000**
Equity		
Ordinary Share Capital	750,000	300,000
Retained Earnings	305,000	180,000
	1,055,000	**480,000**
Non-Current Liabilities		
Bank Loan	220,000	85,000
Current Liabilities		
Creditors	38,000	13,000
Total Equity and Liabilities	**1,313,000**	**578,000**

Included within the figure for Property, Plant and Equipment for W Ltd is some land which is valued at £200,000. At the acquisition date, this was professionally re-valued to £240,000. This revaluation has not been accounted for in the books of W Ltd.

It has been agreed by the directors that goodwill has been impaired by £400.

The Consolidated Statement of Financial Position at 31st March 20X8 is shown below, along with notes to explain each of the entries.

STATEMENT OF FINANCIAL POSITION	CONSOLIDATED	NOTES
Non-Current Assets	**£**	
Goodwill	5,600	1
Investment in W Ltd		
Property, Plant and Equipment	1,365,000	
	1,370,600	
Current Assets		
Inventories	130,000	
Receivables	107,000	
Cash & Cash Equivalents	47,000	
	284,000	
Total Assets	**1,654,600**	
Equity		
Ordinary Share Capital	750,000	
Retained Earnings	340,600	2
Non-Controlling Interest	208,000	3
	1,298,600	
Non-Current Liabilities		
Bank Loan	305,000	
Current Liabilities		
Creditors	51,000	
Total Equity and Liabilities	**1,654,600**	

NOTES

1. There is a Non-Current Asset showing in the Statement of Financial Position of T Ltd for the value of £282,000. This refers to the purchase on 31st March 20X7 of 60% of the shares in W Ltd.

   Calculation of the net assets acquired at the date of acquisition is as follows:

Ordinary Shares (at nominal value)	£300,000	
Retained Profit	£120,000	*PRE-acquisition reserves*
Revaluation of land	£ 40,000	
	£460,000	

Therefore the goodwill is calculated:

Consideration (amount paid)	£282,000
NCI % at acquisition *(£460,000 x 40%)*	£184,000
Less - Net assets acquired	(£460,000)
Goodwill	£6,000
Impairment of goodwill	(£400)
Goodwill in SFP	£5,600

2. When calculating the group's Retained Earnings reserve, we take the parent company's Reserves (W Ltd) plus their share of the subsidiary company's post-acquisition reserves; these are the profits made **since** the acquisition, calculated as:

Parent 100% retained earnings at 31st March 20X8	£305,000
Parents share of Sub's retained earnings post acquisition *	£36,000
Goodwill impairment	(£400)
Consolidated Retained Earnings	£340,600

*Note: The parents share of the subsidiary's retained earnings is calculated by finding out the profit made since acquisition. £180,000 - £120,000= £60,000 x 60% = £36,000. Because the parent company only owns 60% of the shares in the subsidiary, the group is only 'entitled' to 60% of the post-acquisition profits (the rest belong to the NCI – see below).

3. The Non-Controlling Interest (NCI) still owns 40% of the subsidiary company – and so they own 40% of the value of the subsidiary at the **reporting date** (31st March 20X8).

This is calculated as:

Share Capital attributable to NCI	£120,000	*(£300,000 x 40%)*
Retained Earnings attributable to NCI	£ 72,000	*(£180,000 x 40%)*
Revaluation attributable to NCI	£ 16,000	*(£40,000 x 40%)*
Non-controlling Interest total	£208,000	

Activity 7.5

Monpere Ltd owns 90% of the share capital in Monfils Ltd, having acquired them on 31st December 20X6 when the retained earnings of Monfils Ltd were £240,000. The summary financial statements for the two companies as at 31st December 20X7 are shown below:

STATEMENT OF FINANCIAL POSITION	Monpere Ltd	Monfils Ltd
Non-Current Assets	£	£
Investment in Monfils Ltd	1,200,000	-
Property, Plant and Equipment	2,600,000	950,000
	3,800,000	**950,000**
Current Assets		
Inventories	355,000	84,000
Receivables	418,000	38,000
Cash & Cash Equivalents	98,000	16,000
	871,000	**138,000**
Total Assets	**4,671,000**	**1,088,000**
Equity		
Ordinary Share Capital	3,000,000	500,000
Retained Earnings	1,050,000	490,000
	4,050,000	**990,000**
Non-Current Liabilities		
Bank Loan	300,000	74,000
Current Liabilities		
Creditors	321,000	24,000
Total Equity and Liabilities	**4,671,000**	**1,088,000**

Included within the figure for Property, Plant and Equipment for Monfils Ltd is some land which is valued at £180,000. At the acquisition date, this was professionally re-valued to £480,000. This revaluation has not been accounted for in the books of Monfils Ltd.

You are required to produce the Consolidated Statement of Financial Position for the group as at 31st December 20X7. Use the working boxes to help you.

CONSOLIDATED STATEMENT OF FINANCIAL POSITION as at 31st December 20X7	
Non-Current Assets	**£**
Goodwill	
Investment in Monfils Ltd	
Property, Plant and Equipment	
Current Assets	
Inventories	
Receivables	
Cash & Cash Equivalents	
Total Assets	
Equity	
Ordinary Share Capital	
Retained Earnings	
Non-Controlling Interest	
Non-Current Liabilities	
Bank Loan	
Current Liabilities	
Creditors	
Total Equity and Liabilities	

Working – Goodwill Calculation

Consideration (amount paid)	
NCI % at acquisition	
Less - Value of Net Assets Acquired	
Goodwill	

Working – Retained Earnings Calculation

Parent – Retained Earnings	
Subsidiary – Post-Acquisition Retained Earnings	
Consolidated Retained Earnings	

Working – Non-Controlling Interest

Share Capital attributable to NCI	
Retained Earnings attributable to NCI	
Revaluation attributable to NCI	
Value of Non-Controlling Interest	

Intra-Group Transactions

It is likely that the separate companies, which together make a group, will have **intra-group transactions** – that is, transactions with another member of the same group.

These transactions could involve:

- **Loans** from one company to another.
- **Sales of goods or services** from one company to another.
- **Payment of dividends** paid by one company to another.

Each company involved must account for any of these transactions as normal in their own financial statements.

The consolidated statements sole purpose is to present the parent and its subsidiaries as one trading entity. Therefore IFRS 10 states that all of the above must be **eliminated in full** from the group accounts.

Loans

When one company makes a loan to another within the group, each company will record this in their financial statements. However, from the group's perspective these two items will cancel each other out. There is no obligation (liability) between the group and the outside world, and so there is no need to record the loan in the consolidated accounts and we must remove it.

Example 7.7

Harvey Ltd is a subsidiary of Eric Ltd. On 1st April 20X7 Harvey Ltd lends £800,000 over 12 months to Eric Ltd.

Required

How would this loan would be shown in the financial statements of both Harvey Ltd and Eric Ltd at 31st December 20X7?

Answer

Eric Ltd would show the loan as a current liability, whilst Harvey Ltd would show the loan as a current asset. If the loan had been over a period of more than 12 months, it would be shown as a non-current liability and non-current asset respectively.

However, when the **consolidated financial statements** are prepared, the aim is to show the position of the **group** as one single entity. It can be helpful to think of three 'parties' in consolidated accounts – the **group**, the **non-controlling interest** and the **outside world**.

The **group** is made up of the parent company plus its share of the subsidiary, the **non-controlling interest** is made up of the other shareholders of the subsidiary, and the **outside world** is anybody else who is not part of the group.

As the consolidated financial statements seek to show the position of the group, we must be careful to consider the effect of any intra-group transactions. This is because there is a danger of overstating assets and liabilities, and profits.

Example 7.8

Vateri Ltd owns 80% of the shares in Muttery Ltd.

Extracts from the statement of financial position of both companies (at 31st December 20X3) are shown below.

		Vateri Ltd		Muttery Ltd
Non-Current Assets		£		£
PPE		3,400,000		1,450,000
Investment in Muttery Ltd		750,000		-
Loan to Vateri Ltd		-		300,000
		4,150,000		**1,750,000**
Non-Current Liabilities				
Bank Loans		940,000		188,000
Loan from Muttery Ltd		300,000		-
		1,240,000		**188,000**

Required

Calculate the value of loans to be included in the consolidated statement of financial position for the group as at 31st December 20X3.

Answer

The value of loans should represent the total obligation of the group to the **outside world** – and therefore should not include any intra-group indebtedness. There is a loan of £300,000 from Muttery Ltd to Vateri Ltd – this must be removed for the consolidated accounts.

Therefore, the total value of non-current liabilities in the consolidated SFP will be £940,000 + £188,000 = **£1,128,000.**

Intra-Group Sales

Similarly, when one company in the group sells to another, this will create 'mirror image' accounting in the individual statements of the two companies. The selling company will record a sale whilst the buying company will record a purchase.

Where sales are made on credit, the selling company will record the sale made on credit and this will increase **trade and other receivables**, whilst the buying company will record the purchase made on credit which leads to an increase in their **trade and other payables**.

Again, the entries in these should cancel each other out when preparing the consolidated SFP. From the **group's** perspective, intra-group transactions do not affect the level of obligation to the outside world, and therefore must be removed in the consolidated statements.

It may be necessary to make adjustments to the individual company balances at the year end to reflect items **'in transit'** – this could be cash or goods which have been accounted for in one entity's accounts, but not the other.

Example 7.9

Pops Ltd owns 75% of Kidder Ltd. At the year end, Pops Ltd has trade receivables of £180,000 and trade payables of £105,000. Kidder Ltd has trade receivables of £72,000 and trade payables of £45,000. These figures include an outstanding invoice from Pops Ltd to Kidder Ltd for goods of £12,000.

Required

Calculate the amount for trade receivables and trade payables to be included in the consolidated SFP.

Answer

Trade Receivables = £180,000 + £72,000 - £12,000 = **£240,000**

Trade Payables = £105,000 + £45,000 - £12,000 = **£138,000**

The outstanding receivables in the accounts of Pops Ltd of £12,000 and the £12,000 outstanding payables in the accounts of Kidder Ltd have now been removed.

Intra-Group Sales with Unrealised Profits

If the parent and subsidiary trade with each other, goods that are sold may include a profit element.

When one company in a group sells goods to another, it will usually do so on a commercial basis – in other words, the selling company will make a profit on the goods sold, and this is recorded in that company's financial statements. When the other company subsequently sells these goods to the outside world, it too will do so at a profit which will be recorded in its own financial statements.

So long as all the goods have been sold to the outside world then there is no problem. The profit element of an intra-group sale is recorded in the selling company's SPL and retained earnings in the SFP, but this is effectively cancelled out by the purchasing company recording the cost of these goods in its Cost of Sales computation. All profits made by the purchasing company selling the goods to the outside world are then captured in its own SPL and retained earnings in the SFP, and as these profits belong to the group, these are included in the consolidated accounts.

Example 7.10

Pappy Ltd owns 100% of the shares in Laddo Ltd. In the year ended 31st December 20X1, Pappy Ltd sold goods which had cost £30,000 to Laddo Ltd for £45,000. Laddo Ltd had subsequently sold all of these goods to external customers for £70,000.

Required

Calculate the profit to be shown in the individual company accounts, and also in the consolidated accounts, in relation to these goods.

Answer

Pappy Ltd

Profit = £45,000 - £30,000 = **£15,000**

Laddo Ltd

Profit = £70,000 - £45,000 = **£25,000**

The consolidated profit reflects the original cost of the goods (bought by Pappy Ltd from the outside world) and the final sales revenue (when sold by Laddo Ltd to the outside world).

Group Profit = £70,000 - £30,000 = **£40,000**

We can see that the consolidated profit can also be calculated by adding together the two individual profits from the two companies (£15,000 + £25,000 = £40,000).

However, if Laddo Ltd has **not sold all the goods** to the outside world at the year end, a problem arises.

Provisions for Unrealised Profits (PUPs)

In this situation, if we simply add together the profits of the two companies, there will be **unrealised profits**. Where goods have not yet been sold to outside of the group, the profit in question is seen as **unrealised**. This can cause a problem with the profit and closing inventory of the group because they will be overstated.

This is because the selling company will have recorded profit which was earned within the group, rather than from the outside world. Secondly, the remaining (unsold) inventory will be included in the current assets of the subsidiary company's SFP at the cost to the company rather than the cost to the group.

Unrealised profit must be removed from the consolidated statements. Therefore, a **provision for unrealised profit** (PUP) must be made. This provision reduces the profit and the value of the closing inventory.

The adjustments required to resolve these problems will be determined by whether it is the parent company or the subsidiary company which made the sale in the intra-group transaction.

If the parent company sold the goods to the subsidiary:

Reduce	Parent's Closing Retained Earnings
Reduce	Value of inventory (SFP)

If the subsidiary company sold the goods to the parent:

Reduce	Subsidiary's Closing Retained Earnings
Reduce	Profit attributable to the NCI (SFP)
Reduce	Value of Inventory (SFP)

Note: The PUP is subtracted from the profits (the retained earnings) of the company which originally sold the goods to the other and reduces the value of the inventory for the group.

Therefore, if the parent sold to the subsidiary, no adjustment is needed to the NCI. However, if the subsidiary is the seller, the subsidiary will have recorded the sale to the parent at the full price and therefore the full cost will have been included in the subsidiary's accounts. Since the subsidiaries profit will need to be reduced on consolidation, then equally the **share of the profit belonging to the NCI** must also be reduced.

Example 7.11a

Materic Ltd owns 80% of the shares in Dorter Ltd. At the year end, Materic Ltd's SFP showed inventories of £220,000 and Dorter Ltd's SFP showed inventories of £146,000. During the year, Materic Ltd sold goods to Dorter Ltd for £40,000 – these goods had originally cost Materic Ltd £18,000. At the end of the year, 75% of these goods had been sold, but 25% remained in Dorter Ltd's inventories.

Required

Calculate the adjustment required in relation to this information, and calculate the value of closing inventory for inclusion in the consolidated SFP.

Answer

The parent company (Materic Ltd) sold the goods to the subsidiary (Dorter Ltd). However, as not all of these goods have been sold, there are unrealised profits which must be deducted from the group's profits and also from the value of the group's inventory. Therefore, a provision for unrealised profit must be made.

Calculation of unrealised profit is:

(£40,000 - £18,000) x 25% = £5,500

The following adjustments will need to be made:

Reduce	Retained Earnings	£5,500 (*reduces the group's profit)*
Reduce	Inventory	£5,500 *(reduces the value of inventory)*

The value of inventory in the current assets of the consolidated SFP is therefore:

£220,000 + £146,000 - £5,500 = **£360,500**

Example 7.11b

Now let us consider the adjustments if the sale had been from the subsidiary (Dorter Ltd) to the parent (Materic Ltd).

Materic Ltd owns 80% of the shares in Dorter Ltd. At the year end, Materic Ltd's SFP showed inventories of £220,000 and Dorter Ltd's SFP showed inventories of £146,000. During the year, Dorter Ltd sold goods to Materic Ltd for £4

0,000 – these goods had originally cost Dorter Ltd £18,000. At the end of the year, 75% of these goods had been sold, but 25% remained in Materic Ltd's inventories.

Required

Calculate the adjustment required in relation to this information, and calculate the value of closing inventory for inclusion in the consolidated SFP.

Answer

The subsidiary company (Dorter Ltd) sold the goods to the parent (Materic Ltd). However, as not all of these goods have been sold, there are unrealised profits which must be deducted from the group's profits, and also from the value of the group's inventory. Therefore, a provision for unrealised profit must be made.

Again, the calculation of unrealised profit is:

(£40,000 - £18,000) x 25% = £5,500

The following adjustments will need to be made:

Reduce	Retained Earnings of Dorter Ltd	£4,400 *(£5,500 x 80%)*
Reduce	Profit attributable to the NCI	£1,100 *(£5,500 x 20%)*
		£5,500
Reduce	Inventory	£5,500

We can see that the subsidiary's profits have been reduced by the amount attributable to the group, then the **share of profit belonging to the NCI** has also been reduced.

The value of inventory in the current assets of the consolidated SFP remains:

£220,000 + £146,000 - £5,500 = **£360,500**

Activity 7.6

Oldman Ltd owns 75% of Yung Gi Ltd. During the year Yung Gi Ltd sold goods to Oldman Ltd which had originally cost them £140,000. The goods were sold with a mark-up of 30%.

At the year end, Oldman Ltd still had one quarter of the goods in inventory.

Required

Calculate the value of inventory for the group which should be included in the Consolidated SFP, and the adjustments that will be needed to the group's consolidated reserves and the non-controlling interest.

Answer

Adjustment to Inventory	
Adjustment to Retained Earnings	
Adjustment to NCI	

Example 7.12

In 20X3 Profen Ltd acquired 70% of the ordinary share capital of Cupra Ltd, when Cupra Ltd.'s retained earnings were £890,000. At 31 March 20X4, the statements of financial position of both companies were:

Statement of Financial Position	Profen	Cupra
	£000	£000
Assets		
Investment	11,200	
Non-currents Assets	18,800	3,200
Current Assets:		
Inventories	4,680	2,500
Trade and other receivables	7,230	4,152
Cash and cash equivalents	2,990	1,100
	14,900	7,752
Total Assets	**44,900**	**10,952**
Equity and Liabilities		
Equity		
Share Capital	13,000	4,500
Share Premium	2,500	1,000
Retained Earnings	15,500	1,200
Total Equity	**31,000**	**6,700**
Non-current liabilities	5,800	1,200
Current liabilities:		
Trade payables	6,850	2,240
Tax liability	1,250	812
Total Liabilities	13,900	4,252
Total equity and liabilities	**44,900**	**10,952**

Additional information:

During the year Cupra sells £200,000 of goods to Profen at a profit margin of 40%. One quarter of the goods remain in Profen's inventory at the end of the year.

Required

Calculate the unrealised profit and complete the working boxes to enter into the consolidated accounts.

Answer

Profit margin on goods £200,000 x 40% = £80,000

Unrealised profit £80,000 / 4 = £20,000 *(one quarter remains in inventory)*

One quarter of the goods remain in the inventory. This means that the profits made by Cupra Ltd on these goods are unrealised, so we must remove them from the consolidated accounts.

Therefore, because the seller is the subsidiary, we must make the following adjustments as we saw before.

Net Assets	**£000**
Subsidiary's Share capital	5,500
Subsidiary's Retained earnings *(pre-acquisition)*	890
Net Assets	6,390

Goodwill	**£000**
Consideration (amount paid for the company)	11,200
NCI's share of net assets at acquisition *(net assets x NCI%)*	1,917
Less – Value of net assets *(working box above)*	6,390
Goodwill	6,727

Retained Earnings	**£000**
100% Parents Retained Earnings	15,500
% of Retained earnings attributable to the parent – post acquisition profit *(Subsidiary profit - pre acquisition profit - PUP) x P%*	203
Retained Earnings	15,703

Non-controlling Interest	**£000**
% of Share Capital attributable to NCI *(x 30%)*	1,650
% of Retained Earnings attributable to NCI *(less PUP) x 30%*	354
NCI	2,004

Activity 7.7

In 20X4 Poppop Ltd acquired 80% of the ordinary share capital of Tiny Ltd, when Tiny Ltd.'s reserves were £90,000. At 31 March 20X5, the statements of financial position of both companies were:

	Poppop Ltd £	Tiny Ltd £
Non-Current Assets		
PPE	1,000,000	625,000
Investment in Tiny Ltd	300,000	-
	1,300,000	625,000
Current Assets		
Inventory	70,000	58,000
Receivables	50,000	30,000
Cash	25,000	12,000
	145,000	100,000
Total Assets	**1,445,000**	**725,000**
Equity		
Share Capital	500,000	200,000
Retained Earnings	610,000	314,000
Total Equity	**1,110,000**	**514,000**
Non-Current Liabilities		
Loans	230,000	115,000
Current Liabilities		
Trade Payables	82,000	74,000
Tax	23,000	22,000
Total Equity & Liabilities	**1,445,000**	**725,000**

The following information is also relevant:

a. Included in Poppop Ltd.'s receivables, is £11,000 due from Tiny Ltd. This amount is also included as a payable in Tiny Ltd.'s Statement of Financial Position.

b. During the year Poppup Ltd sold goods to Tiny Ltd for £27,000 and which were sold with a mark-up of 50%. As at 31st March 20X5 80% of these goods had been sold by Tiny Ltd, with the other 20% still in inventory.

Prepare the consolidated statement of financial position as at 31 March 20X5. Use the workings boxes on the following page to help you.

CONSOLIDATED STATEMENT OF FINANCIAL POSITION as at 31st March 20X5	
Non-Current Assets	**£**
Goodwill	
Investment in Tiny Ltd	
Property, Plant and Equipment	
Current Assets	
Inventories	
Receivables	
Cash & Cash Equivalents	
Total Assets	
Equity	
Ordinary Share Capital	
Retained Earnings	
Non-Controlling Interest	
Non-Current Liabilities	
Bank Loan	
Current Liabilities	
Creditors	
Taxation	
Total Equity and Liabilities	

Working – Adjustment for Non-Realised Profit

Working – Goodwill Calculation

Consideration (amount paid)	
NCI% at acquisition	
Less - Value of Net Assets Acquired	
Goodwill	

Working – Adjustment to Inventories

Inventories of Poppop Ltd	
Inventories of Tiny Ltd	
Less adjustment for unrealised profit	

Working – Adjustment to Receivables

Receivables of Poppop Ltd	
Receivables of Tiny Ltd	
Less adjustment for intra-group trading	

Working – Adjustment to Payables

Payables of Poppop Ltd	
Payables of Tiny Ltd	
Less adjustment for intra-group trading	

Working – Retained Earnings Calculation

Parent – Retained Earnings	
Subsidiary's post-acquisition Retained Earnings attributable to parent	
Less adjustment for unrealised profit	
Consolidated Retained Earnings	

Working – Non-Controlling Interest

Share Capital attributable to NCI	
Retained Earnings attributable to NCI	
Value of Non-Controlling Interest	

Assessment 7.1

You are now required to log-in to your ROGO account to complete your online assessment before progressing on to the next part of this chapter.

The Consolidated Statement of Profit or Loss

So far, we have focussed on the preparation of the Consolidated Statement of Financial Position (SFP). It is now time to consider the second half of the consolidated statements – the Consolidated Statement of Profit or Loss.

As with the Consolidated SFP, the basic approach is to add together to individual line items in each of the individual companies' statements to create the 'group' picture. However, there are a number of adjustments which then need to be made to show the consolidated position correctly.

Again, the Consolidated Statement of Profit or Loss considers how profitable the group as a whole has been through its transactions with the outside world. If a subsidiary buys goods from the parent company (or vice versa), any profit on this transaction is recorded in the selling company's individual SPL, but this profit is unrealised from the group's perspective until the goods are subsequently sold on to the outside world.

The (adjusted) profit of the group belongs primarily to the shareholders of the parent company. However, where there is a non-controlling interest (NCI) in the subsidiary, the NCI is entitled to receive a percentage share of the **subsidiary's profits only**. This proportion of the group's profits which 'belongs' to the NCI should be calculated first, with the proportion 'belonging' to the parent company then being calculated as a balancing figure.

Example 7.13

Momma Ltd own 75% of the shares in Bubba Ltd. Here are extracts of Momma Ltd and Bubba Ltd Statements of Profit or Loss for the end ended the 31 December 20X2.

Statement of Profit or Loss Extract	Momma	Bubba
	£000	**£000**
Revenue	9,200	4,420
Cost of Sales	-5,400	-2,640
Gross Profit	3,800	1,780
Other income	0	0
Operating Expenses	-1,740	-860
Profit before tax	2,060	920
Tax	-600	-240
Profit for the period from continuing operations	1,460	680

Firstly, we should add together each line.

Consolidated Statement of Profit or loss	£000	Workings
Revenue	13,620	*9,200+4,420*
Cost of Sales	-8,040	*5,400 + 2,640*
Gross Profit	5,580	
Other income	-	
Operating expenses	-2,600	*1,740 + 860*
Profit before tax	2,980	
Tax	-840	*600 + 240*
Profit from continuing operations	**2,140**	
Attributable to:		
Equity holders		
Non-Controlling Interests		

Now we need to calculate the profit attributable to the equity holders (the parent) and the profit attributable to any non-controlling interest.

Consolidated Statement of Profit or loss	£000	Workings
Revenue	13,620	*9,200+4,420*
Cost of Sales	-8,040	*5,400 + 2,640*
Gross Profit	5,580	
Other income	-	
Operating expenses	-2,600	*1,740 + 860*
Profit before tax	2,980	
Tax	-840	*600 + 240*
Profit from continuing operations	**2,140**	
Attributable to:		
Equity holders	**1,970**	***2,140 - 170***
Non-Controlling Interests	**170**	****680 x 25%***

*The Non-Controlling Interest is only entitled to a percentage of the **Subsidiary's profit only**. The Non-Controlling Interest of the Subsidiary has no right to any of the Parent's profit.

Profit attributable to NCI – £680,000 x 25% = **£170,000**

Group profit – Balancing Figure (£2,140,000 - £170,000) = **£1,970,000**

Example 7.14

Dada Ltd owns 80% of the issued share capital of Kidder Ltd. As at 30th April 20X3, the following information has been extracted from the financial statements of each company.

	Dada Ltd £000	Kidder Ltd £000
Profit from Operations	920	135
Other income *(dividend from Kidder Ltd)*	25	-
Profit Before Tax	945	135
Tax	208	30
Profit for the Year	737	105

Required

Complete the extract of the consolidated Statement of Profit or Loss shown below.

Consolidated Statement of Profit or Loss for the year ended 30th April 20X3	£000
Profit from Operations	
Other Income	
Profit Before Tax	
Taxation	
Profit for the Year from Continuing Operations	
Attributable to:	
Equity Holders of the Parent	
Non-Controlling Interest	

Answer

Consolidated Statement of Profit or Loss for the year ended 30th April 20X3	£000
Profit from Operations	1,055
Other Income	-
Profit Before Tax	1,055
Taxation	238
Profit for the Year from Continuing Operations	817
Attributable to:	
Equity Holders of the Parent *(Balancing Figure)*	796
Non-Controlling Interest *(£105,000 x 20%)*	21

You should note that the dividends paid by Kidder Ltd to Dada Ltd (£25,000) are excluded from the consolidated SPL. This is because these represent intra-group receipts – again, they are not paid from 'outside' the group and should be excluded.

Activity 7.8

Vater Ltd owns 90% of the issued share capital of Kind Ltd. As at 30th September 20X7, the following information has been extracted from the financial statements of each company.

	Vater Ltd £000	Kind Ltd £000
Sales	1,580	948
Cost of Sales	745	311
Gross Profit	835	637
Distribution Costs	201	153
Administrative Expenses	225	174
Profit from Operations	409	310
Finance Costs	91	45
Profit Before Tax	318	265
Tax	74	55
Profit for the Year	244	210

During the year Kind Ltd paid £85,000 dividends to its parent company. There were no other intra-group transactions during the year.

Required

Complete the extract of the consolidated Statement of Profit or Loss shown below.

Consolidated Statement of Profit or Loss for the year ended 30th April 20X7	£000
Sales	
Cost of Sales	
Gross Profit	
Distribution Costs	
Administrative Expenses	
Profit from Operations	
Finance Costs	
Profit Before Tax	
Taxation	
Profit for the Year from continuing operations	
Attributable to:	
Equity Holders of the Parent	
Non-Controlling Interest	

Intra-Group Transactions in the Consolidated SPL

As with the consolidated Statement of Financial Position, some adjustments are required when the two companies in the group trade with each other. This is for the same reason as before – namely that the consolidated financial statements must show the financial position and performance of the group as a whole. Therefore, although each company must show these transactions as normal in their own individual financial statements, when these are consolidated they must be eliminated.

There are two adjustments which must be made in such circumstances:

- Eliminate intra-group transactions from the revenue and cost of sales figures.
- Eliminate unrealised profits on goods still in inventory at the year end.

Let's look at each of these in turn:

Eliminating intra-group transactions from the revenue and cost of sales figures.

When one company sells goods to the other, they will record these in their revenue figure. Similarly, the buying company will record these purchases as part of their cost of sales figure.

From the group perspective, these must be eliminated when preparing the consolidated statements, otherwise revenue and cost of sales will be overstated (although the gross profit would remain unaffected).

Example 7.15

Dude Ltd owns 80% of Geek Ltd. During the year ended 31st May 20X3 Dude Ltd sold goods to Geek Ltd for £400,000 which had originally cost £230,000. The extract from the two companies' statements of profit or loss are shown below.

	Dude Ltd £000	Geek Ltd £000
Sales	2,455	1,052
Cost of Sales	1,086	652
Gross Profit	1,369	400
Distribution Costs	341	104
Administrative Expenses	188	116
Profit from Operations	840	180

Required

Calculate the consolidated sales, cost of sales and gross profit for the group for the year ended 31st May 20X3.

Answer

All figures are shown in £000.

Consolidated Sales	£2,455 + £1,052 = £3,507 - £400 = **£3,107**
Consolidated Cost of Sales	£1,086 + £652 = £1,738 - £400 = **£1,338**
Consolidated Gross Profit	£3,107 - £1,338 = **£1,769**

You should note that it is the **full sales value** which is deducted from both the sales and the cost of sales figures to remove the intra-group transaction. Even after removing the intra-group transaction, the gross profit figure remains the same as it would if the intra-group transaction had not been removed, however the sales and cost of sales of the group are no longer overstated.

<u>Eliminating unrealised profits on goods still in inventory at the year end.</u>

When there are intra-group transactions during the year, the only adjustment needed is to the sales and cost of sales figures (as illustrated above) **so long as all the goods have been sold to the outside world by the end of the financial year.**

Where some of the goods are unsold at the year end, a further adjustment is needed. This is because the company which sold the goods (within the group) will have recorded a profit on the sale in their individual SPL, but this profit will not have been realised from the group's perspective if the goods have not been sold to the outside world.

This unrealised profit must be eliminated by increasing the consolidated cost of sales, and reducing the consolidated inventories in the consolidated SFP. We will increase the cost of sales because if we reduce the closing inventories in the SFP, we also need to reduce the closing inventories recorded in the SPL. By increasing the cost of sales we are effectively adjusting (reducing) the closing inventory and by increasing the cost of sales we reduce the gross profit.

Furthermore, if the subsidiary makes a sale to the parent, the amount of profit attributable to the non-controlling interest must also be reduced by their share of the unrealised profit.

Example 7.16

Womble Ltd owns 75% of the issued share capital of Wimble Ltd. During the year, Wimble Ltd made sales of goods for £500,000 to Womble Ltd, which had originally cost £200,000. At the end of the financial year, 50% of these goods remained in the inventory of Womble Ltd.

Womble Ltd.'s sales for the year were £3,400,000 and it's cost of sales were £1,800,000. Wimble Ltd.'s sales were £1,700,000 and it's cost of sales were £950,000. The combined inventories of both companies were valued at £780,000 at the year end.

Required

Identify the adjustments required to reflect this intra-company trading.

Answer

Firstly, eliminate the sale:

Consolidated sales = £3,400,000 + £1,700,000 - £500,000 = **£4,600,000**

Consolidated cost of sales = £1,800,000 + £950,000 - £500,000 = **£2,250,000**

Secondly, eliminate the unrealised profit on the transaction. The unrealised profit is calculated as £500,000 - £200,000 = £300,000 x 50% *(as 50% of the goods remain in inventory at the year end)* = **£150,000**.

The adjustments are:

Consolidated Cost of Sales = £2,250,000 + £150,000 = **£2,400,000**

Consolidated Inventories (SFP) = £780,000 - £150,000 = **£630,000**

If we did not make an adjustment for the unrealised profit, the group would be recording a profit of £150,000 from selling inventory to itself. This will inflate the value of the group inventory in the statement of financial position and the profit in the statement of profit or loss. Remember, closing inventory is a part of the cost of sales so the adjustment for unrealised profits affects both the statement of profit or loss and the statement of financial position.

The sale was from the subsidiary (Wimble Ltd) to the parent (Womble Ltd) and therefore the profit attributable to the NCI must also be adjusted. This adjustment will be a reduction of 25% x £150,000 = **£37,500**.

Activity 7.9

Terry Ltd owns 80% of the issued share capital in Colin Ltd. The statements of profit or loss for each company for the year ended 31st October 20X9 are shown below.

	Terry Ltd £000	Colin Ltd £000
Sales	2,148	1,580
Cost of Sales	985	496
Gross Profit	**1,163**	**1,084**
Distribution Costs	184	205
Administrative Expenses	209	221
Profit from Operations	**770**	**658**
Finance Costs	67	71
Profit Before Tax	**703**	**587**
Tax	148	139
Profit for the Year	**555**	**448**

During the year Terry Ltd sold some goods to Colin Ltd which had originally cost £480,000 and which were sold for £850,000. At the end of the year Colin Ltd had only sold 60% of these goods with the remaining 40% in inventory.

Required

Prepare the consolidated statement of profit or loss for the group for the year ended 31st October 20X9.

Consolidated Statement of Profit or Loss for the year ended 31st October 20X9	£000	Notes
Sales		
Cost of Sales		
Gross Profit		
Distribution Costs		
Administrative Expenses		
Profit from Operations		
Finance Costs		
Profit Before Tax		
Taxation		
Profit for the Year from cont. Operations		
Attributable to:		
Equity Holders of the Parent		
Non-Controlling Interest		

Activity 7.10

Margo Ltd owns 60% of the issued share capital in Norma Ltd. The statements of profit or loss for each company for the year ended 31st May 20X1 are shown below.

	Margo Ltd £000	Norma Ltd £000
Sales	5,580	3,140
Cost of Sales	2,962	1,960
Gross Profit	**2,618**	**1,180**
Distribution Costs	852	301
Administrative Expenses	617	295
Profit from Operations	**1,149**	**584**
Finance Costs	201	92
Profit Before Tax	**948**	**492**
Tax	158	81
Profit for the Year	**790**	**411**

During the year Norma Ltd sold some goods to Margo Ltd which had originally cost £200,000 and which were sold for £380,000. At the end of the year Margo Ltd had only sold 25% of these goods with the remaining 75% in inventory.

Required

Prepare the consolidated statement of profit or loss for the year ended 31st May 20X1.

Consolidated Statement of Profit or Loss for the year ended 31st May 20X1	£000	Notes
Sales		
Cost of Sales		
Gross Profit		
Distribution Costs		
Administrative Expenses		
Profit from Operations		
Finance Costs		
Profit Before Tax		
Taxation		
Profit for the Year from continuing operations		
Attributable to:		
Equity Holders of the Parent		
Non-Controlling Interest		

Assessment 7.2

You are now required to log-in to your ROGO account to complete your online assessment before progressing on to the next chapter.

Chapter 8: Financial Ratios

By the end of this chapter you should:

- Be able to calculate the ratios on profitability, efficiency, liquidity and financial position.
- Understand the meaning of each ratio
- Be able to recognise whether a ratio is better or worse as compared to a comparative ratio
- Understand the limitations of ratio analysis

Introduction

In this chapter, we will look at a range of **performance indicators**; these are financial and non-financial measures which an organisation uses to judge its performance. Inevitably, many of the performance indicators we use will be **financial** in nature, but there are also many **non-financial** indicators which can be developed.

It is unlikely that a single performance indicator will ever be able to tell the whole story about an organisation's performance; indeed, we should be wary of attaching too much significance to a single (or small number of) indicators. Indicators should be used to build a broad picture of the organisation's performance in a given time period, which usually means using a wide range of indicators.

Who was the Best?

Let's start with a non-accounting related question…

Who was the better tennis player – Bjorn Borg or Pete Sampras?

This kind of question could keep you thinking for days… you might already have a favourite, or it might be something you've never really thought about before.

If you were to try to answer this question, you would probably want to know a bit more about each of the players, so that you could analyse their respective careers in order to make a judgement. To do this you would need a variety of data, considering a number of different aspects.

Let's look at the data:

	Bjorn Borg	***Pete Sampras***
Duration of career	1973-1983	1988-2002
Number of weeks ranked as Number 1 in the world	109	286
Number of Grand Slam titles	11	14
Number of career titles	64	64
Win ratio	82.74%	77.44%
Career winnings	$3,633,751	$43,280,489
Other Information	Retired aged 26 Only played Australian Open once	

Both Borg and Sampras were great players, and there are good reasons to favour either one over the other. Sampras's career was longer; he won more Grand Slams and a greater range, and spent a significantly greater number of weeks ranked as the world's best player.

Borg, on the other hand, achieved his success in a much shorter career, retiring at the age of 26. He had a significantly higher win ratio (how many of the matches he played that he won) – winning 82.74% of his matches compared to Sampras' 77.44%. Sampras, of course, had far higher career earnings, which can be explained by a number of factors, including that his career was longer, and there was far more money in the sport during Sampras' career (in 1990 he won $2 million just for winning the inaugural Grand Slam Cup in Munich – when Borg won Wimbledon in 1980 – only ten years earlier - the prize money was just £20,000!).

Borg and Sampras never played each other, so the discussion as to who was the greatest is almost unsolvable. Yet the processes that we have just gone through here are used all the time in business, in analysing the financial statements of companies.

Financial Analysis

Just as we looked at a number of factors in our analysis of Borg and Sampras – weeks ranked as Number one in the world, career titles, Grand Slam titles etc – so we must look at different factors when analysing corporate financial statements. What we look at, and how we look at it, will be determined by WHY we are carrying out the analysis. Financial statements are analysed for a wide variety of users, but in this unit, we are particularly concerned with the way in which **management** can develop and interpret ratios to better understand how the organisation is performing.

DIFFERENT MEASURES

It can be useful to think of the many different ways of measuring financial performance and financial position as being 'grouped' together according to what they look at. Common groupings include:

PROFITABILITY

Profitability measures look at how successfully the business has made money during the period. All businesses need to make profits in the long term, to enable them to:

- Re-invest in assets to enable the business to grow. These assets could include:
    - non-current assets
    - property, plant and equipment
    - expansion of the business
    - investments in other businesses
    - current assets
    - inventories – new product lines
    - cash reserves

- Make payments to owners to reward them for their investment (in limited companies these are dividends).

LIQUIDITY

Liquidity means the ability of the business to meet its financial obligations – including paying trade and other suppliers, VAT and other tax liabilities and interest charges on debts.

EFFICIENCY

Efficiency covers a range of measures which analyse how well the business is managed, and how successfully it uses the resources (inventories, receivables and cash) in its day to day operations.

FINANCIAL POSITION

The financial position of the business looks at how well the business is structured to ensure its long-term security. In particular it looks at how the business is financed – the proportion which is financed by debt as opposed to that financed by the equity holders.

Ways of Calculating Financial Measures

There are a number of different ways to calculate relevant financial ratios. The most common of these are:

- As a ratio
- As a percentage

WHAT IS A RATIO?

A ratio is simply a way of expressing how two figures relate to each other.

A ratio is expressed in the following way:

A : B

Let's take a simple example:

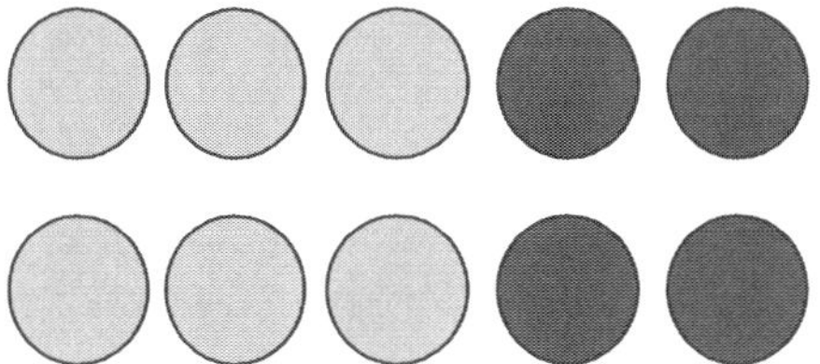

Here the ratio of light coloured counters to dark coloured counters is 6:4 – although this would be better written as 3:2 (this is known as expressing the ratio in its simplest form).

WHAT IS A PERCENTAGE?

A percentage is used when one number is expressed as a proportion of another.

The percentage of all counters that are light is 6 / 10 x 100 = 60%

Similarly, the percentage of dark counters is 4 / 10 x 100 = 40%

THE FINANCIAL STATEMENTS

The two main financial statements prepared by limited companies are:

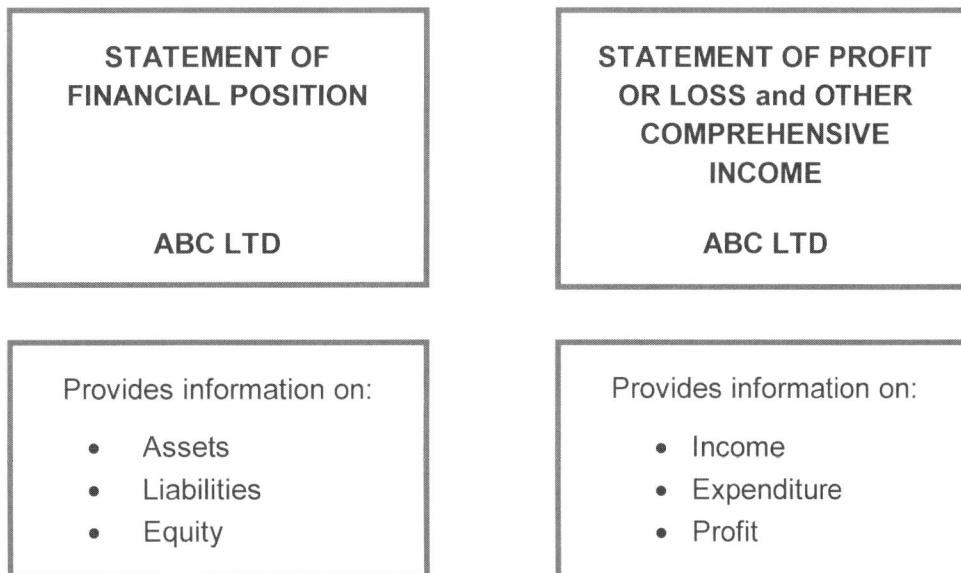

STATEMENT OF FINANCIAL POSITION **ABC LTD**	**STATEMENT OF PROFIT OR LOSS and OTHER COMPREHENSIVE INCOME** **ABC LTD**
Provides information on: • Assets • Liabilities • Equity	Provides information on: • Income • Expenditure • Profit

The data we need to analyse a company's financial performance and financial position can all be found in these two financial statements. However, the financial statements of limited companies contain a huge amount of other information, and it is not always easy to instantly identify the key figures. Also, as we have seen, we are often interested in the **relationship** between two figures, which means digging a little deeper.

Fortunately, we have a set of analytical tools (called the financial ratios) which we can use to help to analyse a company.

THE FINANCIAL RATIOS

Accountants have identified many different financial ratios; the ones that you need to know and understand in this unit are shown below:

PROFITABILITY RATIOS	LIQUIDITY RATIOS	EFFICIENCY RATIOS	FINANCIAL POSITION RATIOS
Gross Profit Percentage (GP%)	Current Ratio	Working Capital Cycle	Interest Cover
Operating Profit Percentage (OP%)	Acid Test (Quick) Ratio	Trade Receivables Collection Period (Days)	Gearing
Return on Capital Employed (ROCE)		Trade Payables Payment Period (Days)	
Return on Shareholder Funds		Asset Turnover (Non-current and net assets)	
Capital Employed		Inventory Holding Period (Days)	
Expense / revenue %		Inventory Turnover	

As you can see there are **sixteen** ratios to learn; you will need to know all of these, meaning that you will need to be able to:

- Remember the correct formula
- Calculate the ratio from given figures
- Explain what the ratio means

Whilst this might seem a lot at the moment to remember, the key thing is not to try to just remember the formulas by heart, but to **understand** what each one shows us in the context of a set of financial statements.

Ratios – A Toolbox

Most people have a toolbox at home – and in that toolbox, will be (at the very least) some basic tools:

- Hammer
- Screwdrivers
- Pliers
- Spirit Level
- Saw and so on.

The point is that to complete any job around the house you wouldn't always use the same tool – you wouldn't (hopefully) try to change a plug with a hammer! Similarly, you will use different financial ratios for different purposes – they are a set of tools in a tool box for you to use as appropriate.

Making Comparisons

Imagine you run your own business, and you calculate that your Operating Profit Percentage is 9.3%

Is this good?

The simple answer is that it is impossible to say whether 9.3% is good or not, without something to **compare** it with. If our OP% was 15% last year, this would suggest we have not performed as well as we did twelve months ago. If our target (that we set at the start of this financial year) was only 6% we would seem to have performed better than expected. And if our competitors (similar businesses in the same industry sector as ourselves) achieved an Operating Profit Percentage of 12.8% we would probably be pretty disappointed.

The same is true of all the ratios – on their own, without something to compare them with, they are fairly meaningless.

So, there are three main comparators – things with which to compare our performance:

- Our own performance in previous years
- Our performance this year against our own targets or benchmarks
- Our performance this year against the performance of our competitors

Although, as we shall see, there are some guidelines as to what is considered to be a 'generally acceptable' ratio, you must exercise great care with these, as they are only guidelines, and can vary wildly between different industries.

Profitability Ratios

All companies need to make profits in the long run to ensure their economic sustainability. Whilst companies may be able to sustain occasional losses, any company which consistently makes losses will eventually cease trading.

Profits (representing the excess of income over expenses) are required in limited companies for two major reasons:

- Shareholders (the owners of the company) expect to receive a reward for the risk they have taken in investing their money in the business – this reward is the **dividends** paid out of the profits made by the company.
- The business will not, however, necessarily pay out all of its profits to shareholders – it is likely to retain some of the profits made so that it can either re-invest this in new assets, or perhaps to ensure it can also pay out a dividend in the following year if, for example, it didn't perform as well.

Measuring profitability (how successful a business is at making profits) is obviously therefore a really important issue for the users of financial statements – particularly investors and potential investors.

The starting point is clearly going to the Statement of Profit or Loss – after all, the whole purpose of this statement is to show how much profit the business made. However, we must also take into account other factors when analysing the company's performance.

Example 8.1

A Ltd and B Ltd both made an Operating Profit of £100,000 in the year ended 31st December 20X7. You might conclude that both companies have performed equally as well.

However, if you are given the following additional information it should be quite clear that A Ltd has performed better than B Ltd.

	A Ltd	B Ltd
Operating Profit	£100,000	£100,000
Capital Employed	£50,000	£500,000
Number of employees	4	50
Value of assets	£20,000	£300,000
Turnover	£160,000	£500,000

Why has A Ltd done better? It is apparent from the additional information that A Ltd is a much smaller company – it has less capital employed, fewer assets, fewer employees and much lower sales turnover – yet it still made £100,000 profit.

Imagine A Ltd is a small independent high street store, and B Ltd is a bigger chain. A Ltd.'s profit of £100,000 is much more impressive than B Ltd.'s – for every £1 of sales they make, for every £1 of assets they own, and for every employee, they make more profit than B Ltd.

The Profitability Ratios

GROSS PROFIT PERCENTAGE (GP%) (Also called Gross Profit Margin)	
Formula	**Notes**
Gross Profit x 100 **Revenue**	This percentage shows how much gross profit a business makes for every £1 of sales revenue it earns. There is no such thing as a 'typical' GP% - it depends very much on the type of business. For example, a designer handbag shop would expect to make a much higher GP% than a discount clothing store. The GP% will typically remain fairly constant from year to year – businesses will try to avoid having large fluctuations over time. A rising GP% is a good thing – it indicates that the business has either been able to increase prices without increasing its cost of sales, or has been able to reduce the cost of sales relative to the selling price. A falling GP% could be an indicator of falling sales price (caused, perhaps, because of competitive pressures or the product being towards the end of its **product life cycle**), or increasing costs of sales (e.g. increasing prices from suppliers of raw materials or increasing wage costs).

OPERATING PROFIT PERCENTAGE (OP%) (also called Net Profit Margin)	
Formula	**Notes**
Operating Profit x 100 **Revenue**	The GP% doesn't take into account a business's overheads – the other expenses which it incurs throughout the year. The Operating Profit Percentage (OP%) is measured using the profit figure **before** finance costs (interest) and taxation charges. A decrease in the OP% could be caused by a decrease in the GP%, or because of rising costs in other expenses, such as administration or distribution costs. Increasing OP% could be caused by a corresponding increase in the GP%. It is often also an indicator that the business has been able to better control its expenses this year, perhaps by planned cost control measures such as restructuring, redundancies, reduced expenditure on advertising etc.

EXPENSE / REVENUE PERCENTAGE	
Formula	**Notes**
Expense x 100 **Revenue**	This ratio can be applied to **any** chosen expense item contained within the Statement of Profit or Loss. A user of the financial statements may wish to compare how well two entities control their expenses – and in particular if one entity spends a higher proportion of its revenue on a particular expense. For example, calculating the **advertising expense: revenue** ratio gives an indication of how effective the company's advertising is in generating sales.

RETURN ON CAPITAL EMPLOYED (ROCE) %	
Formula	**Notes**
Operating Profit x 100 **Capital Employed** **Capital Employed** **= Total Equity + Non-Current Liabilities**	This is sometimes known as the **Primary Ratio** and is one of the most commonly used ratios in measuring company performance. In essence, ROCE looks at two aspects; the business's performance (its operating profit) compared to its size (capital employed). We would all expect a company such as Tesco to have a higher profit figure than a corner shop – but is this simply because it is so much bigger or has it actually performed better? By dividing the operating profit by the capital employed we devise a ratio which is comparable across all businesses. The higher ROCE is, the better it has performed. **Capital Employed** includes all equity (i.e. shareholder funds – share capital and reserves) and also non-current liabilities (usually debt such as loans and debentures). This is because the funds included in non-current liabilities can be considered as being available to the company for a reasonably long period of time. ROCE is particularly useful to potential investors, who can compare the different ROCE %s of different companies to provide an indicator as to which to possibly invest in – as well as other alternative investments such as bank accounts. Because investing in shares is inherently risky (their value can go down as well as up) potential investors would look for a higher rate of return (as measured by ROCE) to compensate for this increased risk. Increases in ROCE could be caused by an increase in profits whilst the business has stayed the same size, or a decrease in value of the business (e.g. by repayment of long term loans) without significantly affecting the profits made.

<table>
<tr><th colspan="2">RETURN ON SHAREHOLDER FUNDS %</th></tr>
<tr><th>Formula</th><th>Notes</th></tr>
<tr><td><u>Profit after Tax *</u> x 100
Total Equity

* If there are any preference share dividends or non-controlling interest dividends, these should be deducted from the Profit after Tax. This is to leave the figure that (in theory) could all be distributed to ordinary shareholders</td><td>This ratio is specifically focussed on providing information to ordinary shareholders.

Ordinary shareholders expect a return on their investment. The amount of profit available to ordinary shareholders is the profit after tax; in theory, the company could pay all of this to its ordinary shareholders. The shareholders' investment in the company is measured as total equity; this can be found from the Equity section of the Statement of Financial Position.

This ratio is therefore similar to ROCE, but ignores the non-equity elements of the company's long-term financing, and uses a different measure of profit. Ordinary shareholders will use this measure when comparing existing or potential investments in different companies.</td></tr>
</table>

Activity 8.1

Flamingo Ltd had the following results in 20X7, 20X8 and 20X9.

	20X7	20X8	20X9
Revenue	£950,000	£820,000	£865,000
Cost of Sales	£320,000	£295,000	£315,000
Gross Profit	£630,000	£525,000	£550,000
Expenses	£260,000	£210,000	£235,000
Operating Profit	£370,000	£315,000	£315,000
Equity	£1,250,000	£1,400,000	£1,400,000
Non-Current Liabilities	£72,000	£76,000	£66,000

Required

(a) Calculate the following ratios to 2 decimal places.

	20X7	20X8	20X9
Gross Profit Percentage			
Operating Profit Percentage			
Return on Capital Employed			

(b) Write a short note to your manager explaining the changes in the ratios over the three years.

Liquidity Ratios

Liquidity is vital for a business – it means the ability to meet its liabilities in the short term. All companies will have current liabilities – to trade suppliers, suppliers of other services such as utilities, insurance and advertising, to staff (payroll) and to the HMRC (VAT and other tax authorities). Failure to pay these liabilities can have serious consequences for the business – ultimately leading to possible legal action and eventually the closure of the business.

Maintaining liquidity is a key financial performance indicator for all businesses. Two key ratios are used.

Current Ratio	
Formula	**Notes**
$\frac{\text{Current Assets}}{\text{Current Liabilities}}$	This ratio shows how many times the company will be able to pay its current liabilities using its current level of short-term assets – inventories, trade receivables and bank and cash balances. The figure is expressed as a ratio in the form X:1. Whilst some sources suggest businesses should ideally have a current ratio of 1.5:1 or even 2:1, the reality is that this will vary significantly according to the type of business. Cash rich businesses such as supermarkets can easily operate on much lower ratios, whilst businesses which often have delayed receipts from customers (e.g. builders) may need much higher ratios to remain comfortably liquid.

Quick Ratio (also called Acid Test Ratio)	
Formula	**Notes**
$\frac{\text{Current Assets-Inventory}}{\text{Current Liabilities}}$	The calculation for the quick ratio is exactly the same as the calculation for the current ratio, except the value of inventories is excluded from the current assets figure. This is because in many businesses there can be a significant delay before inventories can be converted into cash with which liabilities can be paid. Inventory must firstly be sold (which can of course take time) and if the sale is on credit, there will then be a further delay until the cash is received. Therefore, this ratio provides an even more robust measure of a company's liquidity. It will always be lower than the current ratio, and again there is no 'ideal' value which will apply to all businesses. A quick ratio of less than 1:1 is often seen as a sign of a risky level of liquidity – but this will not be the case in all businesses.

Activity 8.2

Generation Ltd has produced its financial statements for 20X5, and an extract (including comparatives from 20X4) is shown below.

	20X4 £	20X5 £
Current Assets		
Inventories	61,150	64,970
Trade Receivables	44,280	48,630
Cash & Cash Equivalents	8,650	1,850
	114,080	**115,450**
Current Liabilities		
Trade Payables	65,530	73,380
Taxation	13,690	16,570
	79,220	**89,950**

Required

(a) Calculate the following ratios for 20X4 and 20X5 (to 2dp).

	20X4 £	20X5 £
Current Ratio		
Quick (Acid Test) Ratio		

(b) Write a short note explaining why both the quick ratio and the current ratio have fallen in 20X5.

Efficiency Ratios

The following ratios can be used to identify how efficiently a business uses its resources on a day to day basis. They are concerned with the company's management of its **working capital** – the balance between the company's current assets and current liabilities. They therefore 'feed' into the liquidity ratios, but help to explain any changes in the liquidity ratios.

Inventory	
Formula	**Notes**
Inventory Holding Days = $\frac{\text{Inventory}}{\text{Cost of Sales}} \times 365$ **Inventory Turnover (Times) =** $\frac{\text{Cost of Sales}}{\text{Inventory}}$	This shows how efficiently the company sells its products. It is expensive to hold high volumes of inventories – they have to be paid for (which affects liquidity), but also must be stored, insured and may suffer deterioration. This ratio calculates how long it takes the company (on average) to sell its goods – in other words, how long an item is held in inventory before it is sold. Ideally it will be as low as possible – but the ratio will very much depend on the type of business. A bakery should have a much shorter inventory holding period than a jewellery shop. Inventory turnover represents exactly as it states, the turnover of inventory. It shows us on average how many **times** the company has sold its total inventory during the period. So, to run effectively there needs to be balance between of being able to send out goods to customers in a timely manner but also not having too much money tied up in stock. A company should try to keep inventory holding days low and inventory turnover high.

Receivables Collection Period (in days)	
Formula	**Notes**
$\frac{\text{Receivables}}{\text{Turnover}} \times 365$	Another aspect of working capital management is the way in which the organisation manages its trade receivables – customers who owe it money. If the business offers credit terms to customers (e.g. 30 days) it must ensure it has appropriate systems in place to chase payments up. The higher the receivables collection period, the longer it takes the company to collect its debts. This has a negative impact on the company's cash flow and liquidity. Ideally the calculation should be in line with the credit period offered to customers, and if it significantly exceeds this the company should take steps to reduce it.

Payables Collection Period (in days)	
Formula	**Notes**
Trade Payables x 365 **Cost of Sales**	This measures how long (on average) it takes the company to pay its debts. This will depend largely on the credit terms which it is able to secure from its suppliers. The longer the company takes to pay its bills, the better for its cash-flow and liquidity. However, taking too long to pay bills risks suppliers becoming disgruntled, perhaps removing credit facilities or taking legal action. Furthermore, possible discounts may be lost.

WORKING CAPITAL CYCLE (Days)	
Formula	**Notes**
Inventory Days + **Receivable Days** - **Payable Days**	The working capital cycle is not strictly a ratio, but it uses the results of the three efficiency ratios to provide a measure of how well an organisation manages its working capital. The working capital cycle reflects that most organisations must finance the period of time from when they first pay for goods or materials to the time when they receive payment from customers for sales made to them. The shorter the working capital cycle is, the less likely it is that the company will suffer cash shortages. Improvements in the working capital cycle can be made by making improvements in one or more of the three ratios. For example, reducing inventory days or receivable days, or increasing payable days, will all lead to an improvement in the working capital cycle.

ASSET TURNOVER (times)	
Formula	**Notes**
Asset turnover (net assets) $\frac{\textbf{Revenue}}{\textbf{Total Assets – Current Liabilities}}$ **Or** **Asset turnover (non-current assets)** $\frac{\textbf{Revenue}}{\textbf{Non-current assets}}$	Whereas the profit percentage ratios measure profit, the **asset turnover** ratio considers how well the company generates revenue (i.e. sales) from its assets. Revenue is not the same as profit – some organisations may be very good at generating high volumes of sales but will make relatively low profits because their costs are relatively high and so their profit margins are low. As ever, be wary of making assumptions based on one ratio alone. This ratio, for example, could appear to have worsened from one year to the next, but this may have been caused by investment in high-value assets which have not yet started to generate the expected level of income.

We can see that there is a relationship between the ROCE, Operating Profit Percentage and Asset Turnover ratios.

ASSET TURNOVER x OPERATING PROFIT PERCENTAGE = ROCE

This is because when the two equations are multiplied together, the top line of Asset Turnover cancels out the bottom line of the Operating Profit Percentage:

$$\frac{\text{Rev}\cancel{\text{enue}}}{\text{C}\cancel{\text{apit}}\text{al Employed}} \times \frac{\text{Operatin}\cancel{\text{g Profit}}}{\cancel{\text{R}}\text{evenue}} = \frac{\text{Operating Profit}}{\text{Capital Employed}}$$

The significance of this relationship is that any change in the Return on Capital Employed can be explained by a change in either or both of the company's operating profit or capital employed.

Activity 8.3

Sheeran Ltd has produced its financial statements for 20X8, and an extract (including comparatives from 20X7) is shown below.

	20X7 £	20X8 £
Current Assets		
Inventories	442,500	486,650
Trade Receivables	196,600	210,480
Cash & Cash Equivalents	18,850	2,680
	657,950	**699,810**
Current Liabilities		
Trade Payables	204,860	229,640
Taxation	34,750	41,800
	239,610	**271,440**
Turnover	4,840,360	4,610,070
Cost of Sales	1,986,070	1,940,300

Required

(a) Calculate the following ratios (to the nearest day) for 20X7 and 20X8.

	20X7	20X8
Inventory Holding Period (days)		
Receivables Collection Period (days)		
Payables Payment Period (days)		
Working Capital Cycle (days)		

(b) Comment on whether the ratios have improved or worsened from 20X7 to 20X8, and what impact these changes will have on the company's working capital.

Financial Position Ratios

The final two ratios included in this unit are concerned with the long-term financial security of the company. All companies are financed through a combination of owners' investment and retained profits (**equity**) and **total debt** (such as mortgages and bank loans). In general, the higher the proportion of debt the riskier the business is – this is because the company must pay **finance charges** (interest) on debt, and is often susceptible to upward changes in the interest rate. However, having little or no debt may also indicate a business which is 'missing' opportunities to expand; by borrowing money, the company could finance growth or new assets.

The balance between equity and debt is known as **gearing** – a highly geared company has a higher proportion of debt. When using the gearing ratio for financial analysis (as in this unit) it is usual to **exclude current liabilities** in the total debt – this may not be the case for other interpretations of the gearing ratio, where both long-term debt and current liabilities are included.

There are two ratios.

Gearing (%)	
Formula	**Notes**
$\frac{\text{Non-Current Liabilities}}{\text{Total Equity + Non-Current Liabilities}} \times 100$ **Or** $\frac{\text{Total Debt}}{\text{Total Debt + Total Equity}} \times 100$ **(where total debt is all non-current liabilities only)***	This ratio calculates how much of the **total** value of the business is financed through debt. Generally speaking the higher the gearing ratio, the riskier the business's long-term future. A gearing ratio of between 20% and 45% is generally considered typical; a ratio above 50% is usually considered to be high. For the purposes of this exam 'total debt' will **only** include 'non-current liabilities'.

Interest Cover (number of times)	
Formula	**Notes**
<u>**Profit from Operations**</u> **Interest**	This calculation shows how many times a company is able to 'cover' (i.e. pay) its interest charges out of its profits. The more times a company can cover its interest charges the better – this means it is less likely to have problems should interest rates rise in the future.

Activity 8.4

Tipping Ltd is a large manufacturing company in the clothing industry. The following information is available for the years ended 30 September 20X8 and 20X9.

SPL for y/e 30/09	20X8		20X9	
	£000	**£000**	**£000**	**£000**
Revenue		7,265		7,890
Opening Inventory	488		399	
Purchases	3,924		4,642	
Less Closing Inventory	399		445	
Cost of Sales		4,013		4,596
Gross Profit		**3,252**		**3,294**
Selling and Distribution	818		948	
Administration	1,567	2,385	1,775	2,723
Operating Profit		867		571
Interest Charges		40		48
Profit Before Taxation		827		523
Taxation		155		119
Profit After Taxation		**672**		**404**

SFP at 30/9	20X8		20X9	
	£000	£000	£000	£000
Non-current Assets		6,125		6,432
Current Assets:				
Inventory	399		445	
Receivables	715		699	
Cash at Bank	756		844	
		1,870		1,988
TOTAL ASSETS		**7,995**		**8,420**
Equity:				
Ordinary Shares		2,000		2,000
Retained Profits (Reserves)		3,767		4,171
		5,767		**6,171**
Non-current Liabilities:				
Bank Loan		1,750		2,080
Current Liabilities:				
Trade Payables	397		101	
Taxation	81		68	
		478		169
Total Liabilities		**2,228**		**2,249**
TOTAL EQUITY & LIABILITIES		**7,995**		**8,420**

Required

Carry out an analysis of the ratios listed below for Tipping Ltd and comment on the results:

Ratio	20X8	20X9
Gross Profit %		
Comments		

Ratio	20X8	20X9
Operating Profit %		
Comments		

Ratio	20X8	20X9
ROCE		
Comments		

Ratio	20X8	20X9
Asset Turnover (net)		
Comments		

Ratio	20X8	20X9
Current Ratio		
Comments		

Ratio	20X8	20X9
Acid Test Ratio		
Comments		

Ratio	20X8	20X9
Inventory Holding Period (days)		
Comments		

Ratio	20X8	20X9
Receivables Collection Period (days)		
Comments		

Ratio	20X8	20X9
Payables Collection Period (days)		
Comments		

Ratio	20X8	20X9
Gearing Ratio		
Comments		

Ratio	20X8	20X9
Interest Cover		
Comments		

Limitations of Ratio Analysis

As we have seen, ratio analysis can be used to help us interpret the information provided in the financial statements. This helps us to build a picture of on an organisation and make comparative judgements on performance and profitability etc. However, there a number of limitations you should consider when carrying out ratio analysis and making interpretations.

Ratio analysis uses historical information. This means that the financial information provided is up to that point time, but is not current. This means the ratios are looking at the past and not the present.

Ratio analysis does not consider external factors, such as economical factors and the business environment for that industry, recession and inflation.

Ratio analysis does not measure the human element of an organisation. For example, product quality, customer service and employee morale can all play a part and be an important factor in terms of financial performance.

Ratio analysis can be only truly be useful when comparing with other businesses of the same size and type.

Financial information can be manipulated to give a misleading presentation of an organisation. This can make the financial information look favourable or 'more attractive', for example, including or delaying transactions to make turnover or cash balances more desirable.

Therefore, it is important to consider these limitations when in using ratio analysis. Ratios can build a picture of an organisation and allow us to make assumptions we can base our findings upon, but might not show a true picture. The ratios might not answer all questions, however they can highlight areas where questions need to be asked and more information may be required.

Assessment 8

You are now required to log-in to your ROGO account to complete your online assessment and final assessment before progressing on to the mock exam.

This page is left intentionally blank.

Mock Exam

You have **2 hours and 30 minutes** to complete this practice assessment.

- This assessment contains 7 tasks and you should attempt to complete all elements of each task.
- There are a total of **120 marks available** in the assessment.
- You must use a full stop to indicate a decimal place where required. For example, write 500.75 not 500,75, 50075, or 500 75.
- You may use a comma as a thousand separator but both 100,000 or 100000 are acceptable.
- Read every task carefully to ensure you understand what is required.

Task 1 (23 marks)

You have been asked to help prepare the financial statements of Gerbil Ltd for the year ended 31st December 20X6. The company's trial balance as at 31st December 20X6 and additional information can be seen below.

Trial Balance for Gerbil Ltd as at 31st December 20X6.

	£000	£000
Sales		515,840
Purchases	301,568	
Distribution Costs	29,953	
Administration Expenses	51,465	
Inventories at 01/01/20X6	31,958	
Dividends Paid	7,900	
Interest Paid	1,000	
Share Capital		120,000
Retained Earnings at 01/01/20X6		64,520
8% Bank Loan repayable 20Y4		25,000
Trade and Other Payables		27,341
Property, Plant & Equipment at cost	324,980	
Property, Plant & Equipment Acc. Depreciation at 31/12/20X6		41,185
Trade Receivables	31,160	
Allowance for doubtful debts 01/01/20X6		1,242
Cash at Bank	15,144	
	795,128	**795,128**

Additional Information:

- Share capital of the company consists of Ordinary Shares with a nominal value of £1 each.
- The inventories at the close of business on 31/12/20X6 cost £33,108,000.
- Rent expenditure of £216,000 relating to the period 1st October 20X6 to 30th September 20X7 was paid on 7th October 20X6. This payment has been included in the Administrative Expenses in the trial balance.
- Costs of £18,000 relating to the repair of the company's delivery vehicles have been included in the cost of Property, Plant and Equipment in the trial balance.
- The Allowance for Doubtful Debts is to be increased to 5% of the Trade Receivables figure. Doubtful Debts are treated as a distribution cost by Gerbil Ltd.
- The Corporation Tax charge for the year has been estimated at £8,245,000.
- Land included in Property, Plant and Equipment at a carrying amount of £30,000,000 is to be revalued at the end of the year to £35,000,000.
- Interest on the bank loan for the final six months of the year has not been paid yet, nor has it been included in the accounts.
- All of the operations are continuing operations.

1a. Complete the following workings boxes to calculate the correct figures for Cost of Sales, Distribution Costs and Administration Expenses.

Cost of Sales	
	£000
Opening Inventories	
Purchases	
Closing Inventories	

Distribution Costs	
	£000
Distribution Costs	
Doubtful Debts Adjustment	
Servicing Costs	

Administrative Expenses	
	£000
Administrative Expenses	
Prepayment	

1b. Draft the statement of profit or loss and other comprehensive income for Gerbil Ltd for the year ended 31st December 20X6.

Gerbil Ltd Statement of Profit or Loss and Other Comprehensive Income for the year ended 31/12/20X6	
	£000
Revenue	
Cost of Sales	
Gross Profit	
Distribution Costs	
Administration Expenses	
Profit from Operations	
Finance Costs	
Profit Before Tax	
Taxation	
Profit for the Year from Continuing Operations	
Other Comprehensive Income for the Year	
Total Comprehensive Income for the Year	

1c. Draft the Statement of Changes in Equity for Gerbil Ltd for the year ended 31st December 20X6.

	Share Capital £000	Revaluation £000	Retained Earnings £000	Total Equity £000
Balance at 1st January 20X6				
Changes in Equity				
Total Comprehensive Income				
Dividends				
Balance at 31st December 20X6				

1d. Complete the following workings boxes to calculate the correct figures for Property, Plant & Equipment, Trade & Other Receivables, Trade & Other Payables and Retained Earnings.

Property, Plant and Equipment	
	£000
PPE at cost	
Accumulated Depreciation	
Revaluation	
Servicing Costs	

Trade and Other Receivables	
	£000
Trade Receivables	
Allowance for Doubtful Debts	
Prepayments	

Trade and Other Payables	
	£000
Trade and other Payables	
Accrual – Finance Costs	

Retained Earnings	
	£000
Retained Earnings @ 01/01/20X8	
Dividends Paid	
Profit for the Year	

1e. Draft the Statement of Financial Position for Gerbil Ltd as at 31st December 20X6.

ASSETS	£000
Non-Current Assets	
Property Plant and Equipment	
Current Assets	
Inventories	
Trade and Other Receivables	
Cash and Cash Equivalents	
Total Assets	
EQUITY AND LIABILITIES	
Equity	
Share Capital	
Retained Earnings	
Revaluation Reserve	
Total Equity	
Non-Current Liabilities	
Bank Loans	
Current Liabilities	
Trade and Other Payables	
Tax Liability	
Total Liabilities	
Total Equity and Liabilities	

Task 2 (17 marks)

You have been asked to prepare the Statement of Cash Flows for Hamster Ltd for the year ended 31st October 20X8.

The most recent Statement of Profit or Loss and Statement of Financial Position (with comparatives for the previous year) of Hamster Ltd can be seen below.

Hamster Ltd – Statement of Profit or Loss for the year ended 31/10/20X8	
	£000
Revenue	82,105
Cost of Sales	(43,658)
Gross Profit	**38,477**
Gain on Disposal of PPE	16
Dividends Received	101
	38,594
Distribution Costs	(12,202)
Administrative Expenses	(7,985)
Profit from Operations	**18,407**
Finance Costs	(66)
Profit Before Taxation	**18,341**
Taxation	(2,926)
Profit from Continuing Operations	**15,415**

Additional Information:

- The total depreciation charge for the year was £2,275,000.
- PPE with a carrying value of £360,000 was sold during the year.
- All sales and purchases were made on credit. All expenses were paid for in cash.
- A dividend of £1,200,000 was paid during the year, and a further dividend of £950,000 was declared on 23rd December 20X8, before the financial statements were authorised for issue.

Hamster Ltd – Statement of Financial Position as at…		
	31/10/20X8 £000	**31/10/20X7 £000**
ASSETS		
Non-Current Assets		
Property Plant and Equipment	44,256	33,108
Investments at cost	6,000	6,000
	50,256	**39,108**
Current Assets		
Inventories	2,558	1,896
Trade Receivables	12,131	8,516
Cash and Cash Equivalents	3,797	-
	18,486	**10,412**
TOTAL ASSETS	**68,742**	**49,520**
EQUITY AND LIABILITIES		
Equity		
Share Capital	10,900	9,600
Share Premium	3,500	2,100
Retained Earnings	35,493	21,278
Total Equity	**49,893**	**32,978**
Non-Current Liabilities		
Bank Loans	8,900	5,800
	8,900	**5,800**
Current Liabilities		
Trade Payables	7,023	6,185
Tax Liabilities	2,926	3,105
Bank Overdraft	-	1,452
	9,949	10,742
Total Liabilities	**18,849**	**16,542**
TOTAL EQUITY AND LIABILITIES	**68,742**	**49,520**

2a. Complete the following workings boxes to calculate the correct figures for Proceeds on Disposal of PPE and Purchases of PPE.

Proceeds on Disposal of PPE	
	£000
Carrying amount of PPE sold	
Gain / Loss on disposal of PPE	

Purchases of PPE	
	£000
PPE at start of year	
Depreciation Charge	
Carrying amount of PPE sold	
PPE at end of year	
Total PPE additions	

2b. Prepare a reconciliation of profit from operations to net cash from operating activities for Hamster Ltd for the year ended 31st October 20X8.

	£000
Profit from Operations	
Adjustments For:	
Depreciation	
Gain / Loss on disposal of PPE	
Dividends received	
Adjustment in respect of inventories	
Adjustment in respect of trade receivables	
Adjustment in respect of trade payables	
Cash Generated by Operations	
Interest Paid	
Taxation Paid	
Net Cash from Operating Activities	

2c. Prepare the Statement of Cash Flows for Hamster Ltd for the year ended 31st October 20X8.

	£000
Net Cash from Operating Activities	
Investing Activities	
Purchases of PPE	
Proceeds on Disposal of PPE	
Dividends Received	
Net Cash Used in Investing Activities	
Financing Activities	
Increase in share capital & premium	
Increase in loan	
Dividends paid	
Net Cash From Financing Activities	
Net increase / (decrease) in cash and cash equivalents	
Cash and cash equivalents at beginning of year	
Cash and cash equivalents at end of year	

Task 3 (8 marks)

a) What is the objective of Financial Statements, according to the IASB Conceptual Framework?

b) Define the three elements of financial statements which would appear in the Statement of Financial Position.

Task 4 (12 marks)

a) Chinchilla Ltd is preparing its financial statements following its year end of 31st December 20X5. A number of issues have been brought to your attention regarding events which have happened to the company. You should write a report to the Directors of Chinchilla Ltd **explaining** how each of the following should be reported in the financial statements for the year to 31st December 20X5.

Event A – On 6th January there was a fire at one of Chinchilla Ltd.'s offices. Although most of the damage was superficial the fire significantly damaged a manufacturing machine valued in the accounts of Chinchilla Ltd on 31st December 20X5 at £68,000. The machine was damaged beyond repair and is now considered to be worthless. The machine was unfortunately not covered under the company's insurance policy.

Event B – On 10th January a former employee sued the company for wrongful dismissal. Chinchilla Ltd have now received notification from the former employee's solicitor that he will be suing them for £210,000 compensation.

Event C – Ratty Ltd is a major customer of Chinchilla Ltd. On 29th January 20X6, Ratty Ltd issued a statement announcing that they were going into liquidation with immediate effect. The balance on Ratty Ltd.'s account for Chinchilla Ltd as at 31st December 20X5 was £45,000.

Event D – On 8th February the directors of Chinchilla Ltd proposed a final dividend totalling £40,000.

b) Mouse Ltd carries out an impairment review on three of its assets. Details of the assets are as shown below:

	Carrying Amount	Fair Value less Costs to Sell	Value in Use
	£000	**£000**	**£000**
Asset A	55	48	57
Asset B	41	33	36
Asset C	24	25	28

i. Which asset is impaired?

ii. How much is the impairment loss?

c) Which of these is not a criterion for determining whether expenditure on development can be capitalised?

	✓
It is technically feasible to be able to complete the development so that the asset will be available for use or sale.	
The business has the intention to complete, and then use or sell, the asset.	
It is probable that the asset will generate future economic benefits.	
The business has available resources to complete the development.	
It is possible to measure all future income reliably.	

d) Mole Ltd has three lines of inventory. At the year end the following information is extracted:

	Cost	Net Realisable Value	Replacement Cost
	£	**£**	**£**
Product Line A	16,780	22,105	18,960
Product Line B	31,140	29,975	32,025
Product Line C	21,180	29,960	24,450

According to IAS 2 *Inventories* what is the total valuation of Mole Ltd.'s inventory at the year end?

e) An intangible asset is defined as:

"An ______1______, _________2________ asset without ________3___________"

Complete the missing words.

	✓
1. Identifiable, 2. monetary, 3. real form	
1. Invisible, 2. non-real, 3. identifiable value	
1. Identifiable, 2. non-monetary, 3. physical substance	
1. Identifiable, 2. non-physical, 3. ascertainable value	

f) Vole Ltd is currently suing a rival company, Guinea Ltd, for breach of contract. At 31st December 20X8, Guinea Ltd.'s year end, the court case is still ongoing, with an outcome not expected for at least another six months. Guinea Ltd.'s solicitor has indicated that he is not particularly confident that Guinea Ltd will win the case – in fact, he thinks it is around 40% likely that the case will be lost. He has advised that if this happens, the company would have to pay damages of £1.8 million.

How should Guinea Ltd show this in the accounts for the year ended 31st December 20X8?

	✓
Record an expense of £1.8 million in the SPLOCI, and show a payable of £1.8 million in the SFP.	
Record a provision in the SFP for £1.8 million, with an expense for the same amount in the SPLOCI.	
Disclose the possible liability in a note to the accounts, describing the situation.	
No disclosure at all.	

Task 5 (30 marks)

Rabbit Ltd acquired 90% of the issued share capital and voting rights of Hare Ltd on 1st September 20X7 for £2,000,000. At that date Hare Ltd had issued share capital of £800,000 and retained earnings of £600,000.

Extracts of the Statement of Financial Position for the two companies one year later at 31st August 20X8, as well as further information, are shown below:

Statement of Financial Position as at 31st August 20X8		
	Rabbit Ltd £000	**Hare Ltd £000**
ASSETS		
Non-Current Assets		
Property Plant and Equipment	4,258	2,350
Investments in Hare Ltd	2,000	-
	6,258	**2,350**
Current Assets		
Inventories	985	186
Trade Receivables	765	305
Cash and Cash Equivalents	402	104
	2,152	**595**
TOTAL ASSETS	**8,410**	**2,945**
EQUITY AND LIABILITIES		
Equity		
Share Capital	3,800	800
Retained Earnings	2,950	1,360
Total Equity	**6,750**	**2,160**
Non-Current Liabilities		
Bank Loans	680	240
	680	**240**
Current Liabilities		
Trade Payables	658	440
Tax Liabilities	322	105
	980	**545**
Total Liabilities	**1,660**	**785**
TOTAL EQUITY AND LIABILITIES	**8,410**	**2,945**

Further information:

- The fair value of the non-current assets of Hare Ltd at 1 September 20X7 was £2,000,000. The book value of the non-current assets at 1 September 20X7 was £1,600,000. The revaluation has not been recorded in the books of Hare Ltd (ignore any effect on the depreciation for the year).
- During the year Rabbit Ltd sold some of its inventory to Hare Ltd for £36,000. The goods had cost Rabbit Ltd £20,000. One half of these goods were still in Hare Ltd.'s inventory at 31st August 20X8. There were no inter-company balances outstanding at

the end of the year in respect of this transaction in Trade Receivables or in Trade Payables.

- Hare Ltd has decided that the non-controlling interest will be valued at their proportionate share of net assets.

5a. Complete the following workings boxes to calculate the correct figures for Goodwill, Inventories, Retained Earnings and Non-Controlling Interest.

Goodwill	
	£000
Consideration	
Non-controlling interest at acquisition	
Less: Net assets acquired	
Goodwill	

Inventories	
	£000
Consolidated Inventories (before any inter-company adjustment)	
Inter-company adjustment	

Retained Earnings	
	£000
Rabbit Ltd	
Hare Ltd attributable to Rabbit Ltd (excluding any inter-company adjustment)	
Inter-company adjustment	

Non-Controlling Interest (NCI)	
	£000
Share Capital Attributable to NCI	
Retained Earnings Attributable to NCI	
Revaluation Reserve Attributable to NCI	

5b. Draft the Consolidated Statement of Financial Position for Rabbit Ltd as at 31st August 20X8.

ASSETS	£000
Non-Current Assets	
Goodwill	
Property, Plant and Equipment	
Current Assets	
Inventories	
Trade Receivables	
Cash and Cash Equivalents	
Total Assets	
EQUITY AND LIABILITIES	
Equity	
Share Capital	
Retained Earnings	
Non-Controlling Interest	
Total Equity	
Non-Current Liabilities	
Bank Loans	
Current Liabilities	
Trade Payables	
Taxation	
Total Liabilities	
Total Equity and Liabilities	

Task 6 (8 marks)

You have been given the financial statements for Capybara Ltd for the year ending 31st May 20X3. You are now required to prepare financial ratios to assist your manager in his analysis of the company.

Capybara Ltd.'s Statement of Profit or Loss and other Comprehensive Income and Statement of Financial Position can be viewed by clicking on the buttons below.

Capybara Ltd – Statement of Profit or Loss and Other Comprehensive Income for the year ended 31/05/20X3	
	£000
Revenue	334,630
Cost of Sales	131,980
Gross Profit	**202,650**
Distribution Costs	29,892
Administrative Expenses	18,645
Profit from Operations	**154,113**
Finance Costs	25,885
Profit Before Taxation	**128,228**
Taxation	22,748
Profit from Continuing Operations	**105,480**

Capybara Ltd – Statement of Financial Position	
	£000
ASSETS	
Non-Current Assets	
Property Plant and Equipment	634,580
	634,580
Current Assets	
Inventories	55,940
Trade Receivables	21,158
Cash and Cash Equivalents	14,396
	91,494
TOTAL ASSETS	**726,074**
EQUITY AND LIABILITIES	
Equity	
Share Capital	300,000
Retained Earnings	149,935
Total Equity	**449,935**
Non-Current Liabilities	
Bank Loans	200,000
	200,000
Current Liabilities	
Trade Payables	55,031
Tax Liabilities	21,108
	76,139
Total Liabilities	**276,139**
TOTAL EQUITY AND LIABILITIES	**726,074**

Calculate the following ratios to two decimal places (where appropriate):

Gross Profit Margin		%
Return on Capital Employed		%
Current Ratio		:1
Inventory Holding Period		Days
Trade Payables Payment Period		Days
Trade Receivables Collection Period		Days
Asset Turnover (net assets)		Times
Gearing		%
Interest Cover		Times

Task 7 (22 marks)

You work for Squirrel Ltd. The company has recently issued its financial statements for the year ended 31st March 20X8, and you have been asked by the Finance Director to analyse the company's performance in managing its resources, in comparison to Gopher Ltd, one of its major competitors. You have been provided with the following ratios which have already been calculated, along with a comparable set of ratios for Gopher Ltd which have already been prepared.

	20X7-X8 Squirrel Ltd	20X7-X8 Gopher Ltd
Inventory Holding Period (Days)	38	33
Trade Receivables Collection Period (Days)	39	35
Trade Payables Payment Period (Days)	64	49
Working capital Cycle (Days)	13	19

You are required to prepare notes which include:

- **An explanation of what each of the ratios shows.**
- **An explanation of whether Squirrel Ltd has performed better or worse than Gopher Ltd.**
- **Two practical measures which Squirrel Ltd could take to improve each of the first three ratios during the forthcoming year.**

Answer

APPENDIX ONE

List of Assessable Standards

The Financial Statements of Limited Companies is based on the following International Financial Reporting Standards (IFRS) and International Accounting Standards (IAS). These are the only standards of which you must be aware for your examination:

IFRS 3	Business Combinations
IFRS 10	Consolidated Financial Statements
IFRS 15	Revenue from Contracts with Customers
IFRS 16	Leases
IAS 1	Presentation of Financial Statements
IAS 2	Inventories
IAS 7	Statement of Cash Flows
IAS 10	Events After the Reporting Period
IAS 12	Income Taxes
IAS 16	Property, Plant and Equipment
IAS 36	Impairment of Assets
IAS 37	Provisions, Contingent Liabilities and Contingent Assets
IAS 38	Intangible Assets

This page is left intentionally blank.

Answers to Chapter 1 Activities

Answer to Activity 1.1

In preparing the financial statements for Anderson Ltd for the year ended 31 March 20X7, the managing director Julian Anderson has raised a number of concerns. These are:

1. The company bank account paid for an extension and swimming pool to be paid for at Julian's country house.
2. At 31 March 20X8 there is an unopened box of A4 paper in the stationery cupboard which have not been included in the figure for 'closing inventory', and Julian feels this is wrong.
3. Julian has said that he wants to include the proceeds of a large sale to a new customer in this year's accounts. Although the contract has not actually been signed yet, Julian is confident it should all go through in the next few weeks.
4. Anderson Ltd is experiencing significant cash flow problems and it is considered quite likely that the company will have to go into liquidation in the next few months.

Required

For each of the concerns, identify which one (or more) of the accounting concepts should be applied in determining the correct approach to dealing with them.

Concern	Accounting Concept
1.	*The **Business Entity** concept – there should be a clear distinction between business and private transactions.*
2.	***Materiality** – the value of the box of paper is not high enough that its omission from the financial statements to affect a user's decision making.*
3.	***Prudence** – profits should not be recognised until they have been made. Also **matching (accruals)** – transactions should be recorded in the period in which they occur.*
4.	***Going Concern** – the accounts are prepared on the assumption that the business will continue trading into the future – if this is not the case then the financial statements should reflect this.*

This page is left intentionally blank.

Answers to Chapter 2 Activities

Answer to Activity 2.1

Kelspa Ltd is preparing its year end accounts at 31st March 20X8. It has a number of adjustments which need to be. For each, identify the correct double entry to be made.

(a) Inventories at the close of business on 31st March 20X8 were valued at £182,000. Included within this figure is some inventory which had been valued at £6,000 but which is now only worth £3,500 due to damage.

Dr Closing Inventory (SFP)	**£179,500**
Cr Closing Inventory (SPLOCI)	**£179,500**

Note that inventories must be valued at the lower of cost and net realisable value (IAS 2).

(b) Depreciation has not yet been charged for the year ending 31st March 20X8.
The company had buildings which cost £4,000,000, and plant and equipment with a carried down value at 1st April 20X7 of £140,000.

Depreciation is to be provided for as follows:

i. Buildings 2% Straight Line Basis

ii. Plant and Equipment 20% Reducing Balance Basis

The Depreciation charge for the year is to be allocated 50% to cost of sales, 25% to distribution costs and 25% to administrative expenses.

Depreciation on buildings is £4,000,000 x 2% = £80,000.

Depreciation on plant and equipment is £140,000 x 20% = £28,000.
£80,000 + £28,000 = £108,000 depreciation for the year.

Dr Cost of Sales (50%)	**£54,000**
Dr Distribution Costs (25%)	**£27,000**
Dr Administrative Expenses (25%)	**£27,000**
Cr Accumulated Depreciation	**£108,000**

(c) Land (which is not to be depreciated) is included in the Trial Balance at a cost of £1,500,000. It is to be revalued to £1,670,000 and this revaluation is to be included in the financial statements as at 31st March 20X8.

Dr Land	**£170,000**
Cr Revaluation Reserve	**£170,000**

(d) Administrative expenses of £19,200 owing are to be provided for.

Dr Administrative Expenses	**£19,200**
Cr Accruals	**£19,200**

(e) An insurance contract for distribution lorries for the year 1st April 20X7-31st March 20X8 costing £5,800 is included in the Administrative Expense in the trial balance.

Dr Distribution Costs	**£5,800**
Cr Administrative Expenses	**£5,800**

(f) The Corporation Tax charge for the year of £23,000 is to be provided for.

Dr Corp. Tax (SPLOCI)	**£23,000**
Cr Corp. Tax Liability (SFP)	**£23,000**

(g) The provision for doubtful receivables is to be maintained at 2%. At 31st March 20X8, the balance of trade receivables was £138,000, and the provision for doubtful receivables was £2,520. Adjustments to the doubtful receivables account should be included in Administrative Expenses.

Dr Administrative Expenses	**£240**
Cr Provision for Doubtful Debts	**£240**
Notes - £138,000 x 2% = £2,760 - £2,520 = £240	

(h) Interest on a 6% loan of £200,000 for the period 1st October 20X7 to 31st March 20X8 has yet to be paid and must be provided for.

Dr Finance Costs	**£6,000**
Cr Accruals	**£6,000**
Notes: Annual interest = £200,000 x 6% = £12,000	
Adjustment = £12,000 x 6/12 = £6,000	

Answer to Activity 2.2

You are required to prepare the Statement of Profit or Loss for the year ended 31st December 20X4 and the Statement of Financial Position as at the same date.

ANSWERS - SPL – WORKINGS

Depreciation Charge	£000
Buildings *Workings* £3,250 - £850 = £2,400 x 5%	120
Plant and Equipment *Workings* £1,060 - £210 = £850 x 8%	68
Total	188
50% To Cost of Sales	94
25% To Distribution Costs	47
25% To Administration Expenses	47

Revenue	£000
Sales	841
Less Sales Returns	-18
Total	823

Cost of Sales	£000
Opening Inventories	198
Purchases	265
Less Purchase Returns	-7
Depreciation Charge	94
Less Closing Inventories	-204
Total	346

Distribution Costs	£000
Distribution Costs (from TB)	188
Depreciation	47
Accruals	16
Prepayments	-
Other Adjustments	-
Total	251

Administration Costs	£000
Administration Expenses (from TB)	107
Depreciation	47
Accruals	-
Prepayments	-3
Provision for Doubtful Receivables – Adjustment	2
Other Adjustments	-
Total	153

Finance Costs	£000
Interest Paid (from TB)	12
Accruals	12
Total	24

Taxation	£000
Tax charge for year (from notes)	27
Adjustments for under/over payment in previous year	-
Total	27

Statement of Profit & Loss and Other Comprehensive Income
For the year ended 31st December 20X4

	£000
Revenue	823
Cost of Sales	(346)
GROSS PROFIT	477
Distribution Costs	(251)
Administrative Expenses	(153)
PROFIT FROM OPERATIONS	73
Finance Costs	(24)
PROFIT BEFORE TAX	49
Tax	(27)
PROFIT FOR YEAR FROM CONTINUING OPERATIONS	22
Other Comprehensive Income	140
TOTAL COMPREHENSIVE INCOME FOR THE YEAR	162

STATEMENT OF FINANCIAL POSITION – WORKINGS

Property, Plant and Equipment	£000
Land and Buildings at cost	3,250
Land and Buildings – Accumulated Depreciation	-1,080
Revaluation	140
Plant and Equipment – at cost	1,060
Plant and Equipment – Accumulated Depreciation	-210
Depreciation Charge for the Year	-188
Total	2,972

Trade and Other Receivables	£000
Trade and Other Receivables	300
Prepayments	19
Provision for Doubtful Debts	-12
Total	307

Retained Earnings	£000
Retained Earnings at 1st January 20X4	1,480
Profit for Period	22
Dividends Paid	-465
Retained Earnings at 31st December 20X4	1,037

Trade and Other Payables	£000
Trade and Other Payables	104
Accruals	40
Accrued Interest	12
Total	156

Statement of Financial Position for Murray Mince Ltd as at 31st December 20X4

	£000	£000
ASSETS		
Non-Current Assets		
Property, Plant and Equipment		2,972
Current Assets		
Inventories	204	
Trade and Other Receivables	307	
Cash and Cash Equivalents	1,577	
		2,088
TOTAL ASSETS		5,060
EQUITY AND LIABILITIES		
Equity		
Share Capital	2,500	
Share Premium	200	
Retained Earnings	1,037	
Revaluation Reserve	740	
Total Equity		4,477
Non-current Liabilities		
Bank loans		400
Current Liabilities		
Trade and Other Payables	156	
Tax Payable	27	
		183
Total Liabilities		
TOTAL EQUITY AND LIABILITIES		5,060

Answer to Activity 2.3

You are required to prepare the Statement of Profit or Loss for the year ended 31st March 20X8 and the Statement of Financial Position as at the same date.

ANSWERS - SPL – WORKINGS

Depreciation Charge	£000
Buildings *Workings* £5900 - £1600 = £4300 x 4%	172
Plant and Equipment *Workings* £990 - £190 = £800 x 10%	80
Total	252
To Cost of Sales	126
To Distribution Costs	63
To Administration Expenses	63

Revenue	£000
Sales	1,085
Less Sales Returns	-10
Total	1,075

Cost of Sales	£000
Opening Inventories	208
Purchases	481
Less Purchase Returns	-14
Depreciation Charge	126
Less Closing Inventories	-270
Total	531

Distribution Costs	£000
Distribution Costs (from TB)	153
Depreciation	63
Accruals	19
Prepayments	-
Other Adjustments	-
Total	235

Administration Expenses	£000
Administration Expenses (from TB)	121
Depreciation	63
Accruals	-
Prepayments	-9
Provision for Doubtful Receivables – Adjustment	3
Other Adjustments	-
Total	178

Finance Costs	£000
Interest Paid (from TB)	20
Accruals	20
Total	40

Taxation	£000
Tax charge for year (from notes)	32
Adjustments for under/over payment in previous year	-
Total	32

Statement of Profit & Loss and Other Comprehensive Income
For the year ended 31st March 20X8

	£000
Revenue	1,075
Cost of Sales	-531
GROSS PROFIT	544
Distribution Costs	-235
Administrative Expenses	-178
PROFIT FROM OPERATIONS	131
Finance Costs	-40
PROFIT BEFORE TAX	91
Tax	-32
PROFIT FOR YEAR FROM CONTINUING OPERATIONS	59
Other Comprehensive Income	300
TOTAL COMPREHENSIVE INCOME FOR THE YEAR	359

STATEMENT OF FINANCIAL POSITION – WORKINGS

Property, Plant and Equipment	£000
Land and Buildings at cost	5,900
Land and Buildings – Accumulated Depreciation	-1,064
Revaluation	300
Plant and Equipment – at cost	990
Plant and Equipment – Accumulated Depreciation	-190
Depreciation Charge for the Year	-252
Total	5,684

Trade and Other Receivables	£000
Trade and Other Receivables	300
Prepayments	28
Provision for Doubtful Receivables	-9
Total	319

Retained Earnings	£000
Retained Earnings at 1st April 20X7	2,580
Profit for Period	59
Dividends Paid	-340
Retained Earnings at 31st March 20X8	2,299

Trade and Other Payables	£000
Trade and Other Payables	265
Accruals	49
Accrued Interest	20
Total	334

Statement of Financial Position for Chartwell Ltd as at 31st March 20X8

	£000	£000
ASSETS		
Non-Current Assets		
Property, Plant and Equipment		5,684
Current Assets		
Inventories	270	
Trade and Other Receivables	319	
Cash and Cash Equivalents	882	
		1,471
TOTAL ASSETS		7,155
EQUITY AND LIABILITIES		
Equity		
Share Capital	3,000	
Share Premium	280	
Retained Earnings	2,299	
Revaluation Reserve	710	
Total Equity		6,289
Non-current Liabilities		
Bank loans	500	
Current Liabilities		
Trade and Other Payables	334	
Tax Payable	32	
	366	
Total Liabilities		866
TOTAL EQUITY AND LIABILITIES		7,155

Answers to Chapter 3 Activities

Answer to Activity 3.1

a) Calculate the total number of issued shares after the rights issue.

Previously issued	=	**400,000 shares**	
Rights Issue	=	**<u>80,000 shares</u>**	*(400,000 x 1/5)*
Total	=	**480,000 shares**	

b) Show the double entry to record the rights issue.

Dr Bank	**£256,000**
Cr Ordinary Share Capital	**£ 80,000**
Cr Share Premium A/c	**£176,000**

c) Show the equity section of the Statement of Financial Position after the rights issue.

Equity Section (extract)

Ordinary Shares	**£480,000**
Share Premium A/c	**£272,000**
Retained Earnings	**<u>£120,000</u>**
Total Equity	**£872,000**

d) Calculate the total number of issued shares after the bonus issue.

Previously issued	=	**480,000 shares**	
Bonus Issue	=	**<u>48,000 shares</u>**	*(480,000 x 1/10)*
Total	=	**528,000 shares**	

e) Show the double entry to record the bonus issue.

Dr Share Premium A/c	**£48,000**
Cr Ordinary Share Capital	**£48,000**

f) Show the equity section of the Statement of Financial Position after the bonus issue.

Equity Section (extract)	
Ordinary Shares	**£528,000**
Share Premium A/c	**£224,000**
Retained Earnings	**£120,000**
Total Equity	**£872,000**

Answer to Activity 3.2

Prepare the Statement of Changes in Equity for the year ended 31st August 20X5.

	Share Capital £000	Share Premium £000	Revaluation Reserve £000	Retained Earnings £000	Total Equity £000
Balance at start of year	100	28	12	155	295
Changes in Equity:					
Comprehensive Income			92	63	155
Dividends				(31)	(31)
Issue of Share Capital	10	8			18
Balance at end of year	110	36	104	187	437

Answers to Chapter 4 Activities

Answer to Activity 4.1

1. Define 'depreciation'.

   "The systematic allocation of the depreciable amount of an asset over its estimated useful life."

2. Define 'fair value'.

   "The price that would be received to sell an asset or paid to transfer a liability in an orderly transaction between market participants at the measurement date."

3. What are the two models which an entity may choose by which to value its Property, Plant and Equipment?

   a. Impairment Model.
   b. **Cost Model.** ✓
   c. **Revaluation Model.** ✓
   d. Depreciating Model.
   e. Diminishing Model.
   f. Fair Value Model.

4. Which of the following costs could be included in the cost of a new industrial sanding machine?

   a. **Costs of site preparation.** ✓
   b. **Costs of testing the asset before being brought into use.** ✓
   c. **Cost of professional fees (e.g. architect or surveyor).** ✓
   d. Cost of ongoing maintenance contract for the machine.
   e. **Cost of initial delivery of the machine.** ✓
   f. Cost of replacement sanding discs for the machine.

5. If an asset is revalued upward, the double entry is to debit the bank and credit the revaluation reserve. True or False?

   False.

6. Which type of land may be depreciated?

   a. **A freehold quarry**. ✓
   b. Freehold land without planning permission.
   c. Freehold land with planning permission for industrial development.
   d. Freehold land with derelict property.
   e. **Leasehold land**. ✓

7. Which of these methods of depreciation would be most likely to result in equal depreciation expenses each year?

    a. Reducing Balance Method.
    b. Straight Line Method. ✓
    c. Units of Output Method.

8. Which of these is the depreciable amount of an asset?

    a. The total amount of depreciation charged to date.
    b. The amount at which the asset is shown in the financial statements.
    c. The original cost of the asset less any estimated residual amount. ✓
    d. The percentage rate at which depreciation is calculated in the diminishing balance method.

9. When, according to IAS 16, should an asset be recognised in the financial statements?

    a. When it is possible that it will result in future economic benefits flowing to the entity, and the value of the asset can be reliably measured.
    b. When it is probable that it will result in future economic benefits flowing to the entity, and an approximate estimate of the value of the asset can be made.
    c. When it is certain that it will result in future economic benefits flowing to the entity, and the value of the asset can be reliably measured.
    d. When it is probable that it will result in future economic benefits flowing to the entity, and the value of the asset can be reliably measured. ✓
    e. When it is possible that it will result in future economic benefits flowing to the entity, and an approximate estimate of the value of the asset can be made.

Answer to Activity 4.2

What is the definition of a lease in accordance with IFRS 16?

A lease - A contract, or part of a contract, that conveys the right to use an asset (the underlying asset) for a period of time in exchange for consideration. [IFRS 16 Appendix A].

What is the definition of a lessor and a lessee?

The <u>lessor</u> is usually a finance company that allows the right to use an asset for the stated period of time in exchange for consideration.

The <u>lessee</u> is the entity that gained the right to use the asset for the stated period of time in exchange for consideration.

Answer to Activity 4.3

PP Ltd is a sweet manufacturer. In PP Ltd's latest financial year, it undertook a number of lease agreements for assets as below. For each, you should identify whether it should be treated as a **lease, short term lease** or a **lease of a low value asset**.

Description of lease	Lease	Short term lease	Low value asset lease
Leased an machine on a six year contract. At the end of the six year period PP Ltd will own the asset.	✓		
Leased a Vauxhall car on a five year lease for use by a director. The list price of the car at the time of the lease is £25,000. The lease payments are agreed at £420 per month for the duration of the lease.	✓		
Leased a printer. The term of the lease is 3 years and the value of the printer is £2,000.			✓
Leased an industrial food mixer on a 10 month lease. The value of the mixer is £6,000.		✓	

Answer to Activity 4.4

Complete the following table to show the present value of the lease payments for each year. The discount factors have been entered

	20X1	20X2	20X3	20X4	Total
Lease payment	**£6,000**	**£6,000**	**£6,000**	**£6,000**	**£24,000**
Discount factor	1.000	0.890	0.840	0.792	-
Discounted amount	**£6,000**	**£5,340**	**£5,040**	**£4,752**	**£21,132**

Answer to Activity 4.5

a) Show the entries that will be recorded for the lease in the accounts at 1 January 20X2.

	Account	£
DR	**Plant, Property and Equipment**	**28,368**
CR	**Lease Liability**	**28,368**

b) Calculate the depreciation charge for the year using the straight-line method.

£28,368 / 4 years = £7,092

c) You have been asked to calculate the interest expense for each year of the lease, that is to be recorded in the Statement of Profit or Loss. Round your answers to the nearest whole pound.

	20X2	20X3	20X4	20X5
Lease liability (1 Jan)	**£28,368**	**£21,786**	**£14,875**	**£7,619**
Interest (5%)	**£1,418**	**£1,089**	**£744**	**£381**
Sub-total	**£29,786**	**£22,875**	**£15,619**	**£8,000**
Less Lease payment	**£8,000**	**£8,000**	**£8,000**	**£8,000**
Lease liability (31 Dec)	**£21,786**	**£14,875**	**£7,619**	**Nil**

d) Show the entries that will be recorded in the accounts at the end of the period for the interest charged.

	Account	£
DR	**Finance Costs**	**1,418**
CR	**Lease Liability**	**1,418**

e) Show the entries for the lease payment at the end of the period.

	Account	£
DR	**Lease Liability**	**8,000**
CR	**Bank**	**8,000**

f) Calculate the carrying amount of the asset that will be appear in the Statement of Financial Position, at the end of the year.

£28,368 - £7,092 = £21,276

Answer to Activity 4.6

What entries will be entered into the Statement of Profit or Loss at the end of the year. Round your answers to the nearest whole pound.

Entry	£	Workings
Depreciation charges	4,722	28,334 / 6 years
Finance costs	1,100	(28,334 – 10,000) x 6%

What entries will be entered into the Statement of Financial Position at the end of the year.

Entry	£	Workings
PPE	23,612	28,334 – 4,722*
Lease Liability	19,434	

*(*depreciate on useful life due to ownership at end of lease*)*

How will the lease liability be split between the non-current liabilities and the current liabilities in the Statement of Financial Position?

	£
Non-current Liability	9,434
Current Liability	10,000

Answer to Activity 4.7

Present your findings in an email to Vidrun Singh, the Managing Director of Battle-Hastings Ltd.

To: Vidrun Singh, MD
From: Accounting Technician
Subject: Impairment Review

Hi Vidrun

I have examined three assets with a view to identifying if there have been any impairment losses. My findings are:

- ***a) Machine 765/23 has not been impaired, because although its value in use is zero, its fair costs (less costs to sell) is £33,000, which is more than the carrying value.***
- ***b) The property has suffered an impairment loss as it's carrying value (£288,000) is higher than both its value in use (£80,000) and its fair value (less costs to sell) of £270,000. The impairment loss is £18,000. The accounting adjustment required is to credit the value of the asset by £18,000, and to debit the existing revaluation reserve by the same amount.***
- ***c) The motor van, again has been impaired; the carrying value (£4,500) is higher than both the value in use (£3,000) and the fair value less costs to sell (£3,600). The impairment loss is £900, which should be debited as an expense in the SPLOCI and credited to the carrying value of the asset.***

I hope this clarifies the situation; if you have any further questions please do not hesitate to contact me.

Kind regards

AAT Student

Answer to Activity 4.8

Scenario 1

How should the value of the staff be accounted for?

Staff are not included as an asset in the SFP; their wage costs etc should be shown as an expense in the SPLOCI.

Scenario 2

How should the value of Dexter be accounted for?

Because the image of Dexter was developed internally it is not possible to ascertain its cost accurately. Therefore, it should not be shown as an intangible asset in the SFP. IAS 38 prohibits the recognition of internally generated brands as intangible assets.

Scenario 3

How should this be accounted for?

As this is a purchased intangible asset with a finite life (four years), the £8 million cost should be shown in the SFP as an intangible asset. In 20X6, it would be recorded at cost of £8 million, and then this should be amortised over its four year useful life. This could be on the straight line basis (£2 million a year), or any other systematic basis the directors feel to be appropriate.

Scenario 4

How should this be accounted for?

This is development expenditure. The company (at this stage) cannot be certain that future economic benefits will flow to the entity, and so the expenditure (£28 million) should be shown as an expense in the SPLOCI. The costs of building the facility (£400 million) should be shown under Property, Plant and Equipment in the SFP.

If the project continues, and the company can demonstrate that it meets the criteria for capitalisation of development expenditure, future expenditure may be included as an intangible asset in the SFP.

Answer to Activity 4.9

What is the total valuation of closing inventory which should be included in Burghley Ltd.'s Statement of Financial Position at 31st March 20X8?

Zed =	**£18,540**
Wye =	**£21,110**
Exe =	**£22,450**
	£62,100

This page is left intentionally blank.

Answers to Chapter 5 Activities

Answer to Activity 5.1

Calculate the tax charge that Kickfish Ltd will show in the Statement of Profit or Loss and Other Comprehensive Income for the year ended 31st December 20X3, and the tax liability that will be shown in the Statement of Financial Position at that date.

The tax charge is £274,400 (*£268,000 + £231,400 - £225,000)*

The tax liability is £268,000

Answer to Activity 5.2

What are the steps of the 5 Step Model for IFRS 15 *Revenue from Contracts with Customers*?

Step 1:	**Identify the contract with the customer.**
Step 2:	**Identify the performance obligations in the contract.**
Step 3:	**Determine the transaction price.**
Step 4:	**Allocate the transaction price.**
Step 5:	**Recognise revenue when (or as) a performance obligation is satisfied.**

Answer to Activity 5.3

What is the amount of revenue to be recognised?

£63,750 *(£100 x 25% = £75   850 hoovers x £75 = £63,750)*

Answer to Activity 5.4

What is the amount of revenue that should be recognised in the financial statements in accordance with IFRS 15 *Revenue from Contracts with Customers?* Explain your answer.

£0

No revenue should be recognised. Magazine World Ltd has not performed any of its obligations yet and nothing has passed to the control of the customer. Another way to look at this scenario is that Magazine World Ltd has done nothing to earn it because the magazine is yet to be published and distributed.

Answers to Chapter 6 Activities

Answer to Activity 6.1

Produce the **Reconciliation of Profit Before Taxation to Net Cash from Operating Activities.**

Reconciliation of Profit Before Taxation to Net Cash from Operating Activities		
	£000	**Notes / Workings**
Profit before tax	**51,149**	*From Statement of Profit & Loss*
Adjustments For:		
Depreciation	**12,560**	*See notes*
Finance Costs	**104**	*From Statement of Profit & Loss*
Gain on disposal of PPE	**(56)**	*From Statement of Profit & Loss*
Dividends received	**(42)**	*From Statement of Profit & Loss*
Adjustment in respect of inventories	**(4,201)**	*15,483 – 19,684*
Adjustment in respect of trade receivables	**(5,768)**	*22,188 – 27,956*
Adjustment in respect of trade payables	**(601)**	*17,846 – 18,447*
Cash Generated by Operations	**53,145**	
Interest Paid	**(104)**	*From Statement of Profit & Loss*
Taxation Paid	**(2,156)**	*2,156 + 3,846 – 3,846*
Net Cash from Operating Activities	**50,885**	

Further Notes:

*Both inventories and receivables have **increased** during the year – these have both led to a reduction in cash in the business. At the same time payables have decreased – again leading to a reduction in cash in the business.*

*Depreciation is **always** added back.*

The non-current asset was sold for a profit – this must be deducted in the reconciliation. Had it been sold at a loss, this would have been added back.

Dividends received are not operating income, so must always be deducted at this stage.

In this situation, there is no information about any interest liabilities at the end of the year, and so it can be assumed that the interest charge for the year is the amount actually spent.

The cash spent on tax, on the other hand, must be calculated. The amount owing at the start of the year was £2,156, and the charge for the year was a further £3,846. However, £3,846 was still outstanding at the end of the year, and so the amount actually paid was £2,156.

Answer to Activity 6.2

Answer – Sadler Ltd

Proceeds on Disposal of PPE – WORKINGS W1	
	£000
Carrying amount of PPE sold	**360**
Loss on disposal of PPE	**-29**
	331

Purchases of PPE – WORKINGS W2	
	£000
PPE at start of year	**28,472**
Depreciation Charge	**-2,405**
Carrying amount of PP sold	**-360**
PPE at end of year	**-47,850**
Total PPE additions	**-22,143**

Reconciliation of Profit before Tax to Net Cash from Operating Activities	£000	Notes
Profit before tax	**21,235**	*From P&L*
Adjustments For:		
Depreciation	**2,405**	*Given in info*
Finance costs	**34**	*From P&L*
Loss on disposal of PPE	**29**	*From P&L*
Dividends received	**-77**	*From P&L*
Adjustment in respect of inventories	**-244**	*£5,810 - £6,054*
Adjustment in respect of trade receivables	**1,275**	*£5,964 - £4,689*
Adjustment in respect of trade payables	**-4,343**	*£6,932 - £11,275*
Cash Generated by Operations	**20,314**	
Interest Paid	**-34**	*From P&L*
Taxation Paid	**-1,060**	*£1,060 - £979 + £979*
Net Cash from Operating Activities	**19,220**	

Investing Activities		
Purchases of PPE	**-22,143**	*Working W2*
Proceeds on Disposal of PPE	**331**	*Workings W1*
Dividends Received	**77**	*From P&L*
Net Cash Used in Investing Activities	**-21,735**	
Financing Activities		
Increase in share capital & share premium	**3,000**	*(£18,500 - £16,300) + (£3,600 - £2,800)*
Decrease in loan	**-1,400**	*£3,700 - £5,100*
Dividends paid	**-965**	*From P&L*
Net Cash From Financing Activities	**635**	
Net inc / (dec) in cash and cash equivalents	**-1,880**	*£19,220 -£21,735 + £635*
Cash and cash equivalents at beginning of year	**2,476**	*From SFP 20X8*
Cash and cash equivalents at end of year	**596**	*From SFP 20X9*

Answer to Activity 6.3

Answer Template – Robson Ltd

Proceeds on Disposal of PPE – WORKINGS W1	
	£000
Carrying amount of PPE sold	**475**
Gain on disposal of PPE	**95**
	570

Purchases of PPE – WORKINGS W2	
	£000
PPE at start of year	**53,058**
Depreciation Charge	**-1,398**
Carrying amount of PPE sold	**-475**
PPE at end of year	**-62,124**
Total PPE additions	**-10,939**

Reconciliation of Profit Before Tax to Net Cash from Operating Activities	£000	Notes
Profit Before Tax	**10,229**	*From P&L*
Adjustments For:		
Depreciation	**1,398**	*Given*
Gain on disposal of PPE	**-95**	*From P&L*
Dividends received	**-195**	*From P&L*
Finance costs	**68**	
Adjustment in respect of inventories	**-1,358**	*£7,684 - £9,042*
Adjustment in respect of trade receivables	**-1,147**	*£6,957 - £5,810*
Adjustment in respect of trade payables	**-3,285**	*£8,053 - £11,338*
Cash Generated by Operations	**5,615**	
Interest Paid	**-68**	*From P&L*
Taxation Paid	**-965**	*£965 + £1,038 - £1,038*
Net Cash from Operating Activities	**4,582**	
Investing Activities		
Purchases of PPE	**-10,939**	*Working W2*
Proceeds on Disposal of PPE	**570**	*Workings W1*
Dividends Received	**195**	*From P&L*
Net Cash Used in Investing Activities	**-10,174**	
Financing Activities		
Increase in share capital & share premium	**6,419**	*(£28,470 - £22,300) + (£2,139 - £1,890)*
Decrease in loan	**-1,860**	*£6,140 - £8,000*
Dividends paid	**-820**	*From P&L*
Net Cash From Financing Activities	**3,739**	
Net inc / (dec) in cash and cash equivalents	**-1,853**	*£4,582 -£10,174 + £3,739*
Cash and cash equivalents at beginning of year	**486**	*From SFP 20X7*
Cash and cash equivalents at end of year	**-1,367**	*From SFP 20X8*

Answers to Chapter 7 Activities

Answer to Activity 7.1

You are required to produce the Consolidated Statement of Financial Position for the group as at 31st December 20X5.

CONSOLIDATED STATEMENT OF FINANCIAL POSITION as at 31st December 20X5	
Non-Current Assets	**£**
Investment in S Ltd	-
Property, Plant and Equipment	104,000
	104,000
Current Assets	
Inventories	22,700
Receivables	35,380
Cash & Cash Equivalents	16,220
	74,300
Total Assets	178,300
Equity	
Ordinary Share Capital	75,000
Retained Earnings	30,250
	105,250
Non-Current Liabilities	
Bank Loan	48,500
Current Liabilities	
Trade and Other Payables	24,550
Total Equity and Liabilities	178,300

Answer to Activity 7.2

You are required to produce the Consolidated Statement of Financial Position for the group as at 31st December 20X8.

Working – Goodwill Calculation

Consideration (amount paid)	**£88,000**
Value of Net Assets Acquired	**£65,600**
Goodwill	**£22,400**

CONSOLIDATED STATEMENT OF FINANCIAL POSITION as at 31st December 20X8	
Non-Current Assets	**£**
Goodwill	**22,400**
Investment in Kid Ltd	
Property, Plant and Equipment	**130,500**
	152,900
Current Assets	
Inventories	**25,030**
Receivables	**9,350**
Cash & Cash Equivalents	**6,900**
	41,280
Total Assets	**194,180**
Equity	
Ordinary Share Capital	**90,000**
Retained Earnings	**53,660**
	143,660
Non-Current Liabilities	
Bank Loan	**36,000**
Current Liabilities	
Trade and Other Payables	**14,520**
Total Equity and Liabilities	**194,180**

Answer to Activity 7.3

You are required to produce the Consolidated Statement of Financial Position for the group as at 31st December 20X3.

CONSOLIDATED STATEMENT OF FINANCIAL POSITION as at 31st December 20X3.	
Non-Current Assets	**£**
Goodwill	**10,000**
Investment in Child Ltd	
Property, Plant and Equipment	**538,600**
	548,600
Current Assets	
Inventories	**36,530**
Receivables	**39,530**
Cash & Cash Equivalents	**26,610**
	102,670
Total Assets	**651,270**
Equity	
Ordinary Share Capital	**400,000**
Retained Earnings	**174,900**
	574,900
Non-Current Liabilities	
Bank Loan	**48,500**
Current Liabilities	
Trade and Other Payables	**27,870**
Total Equity and Liabilities	**651,270**

Working – Goodwill Calculation

Consideration (amount paid)	**£140,000**
Value of Net Assets Acquired	**£130,000**
Goodwill	**£10,000**

Working – Retained Earnings Calculation

Parent – Retained Earnings	**£140,000**
Subsidiary – Post-Acquisition Retained Earnings	**£34,900**
Consolidated Retained Earnings	**£174,900**

Answer to Activity 7.4

You are required to produce the Consolidated Statement of Financial Position for the group as at 31st December 20X3.

CONSOLIDATED STATEMENT OF FINANCIAL POSITION as at 31st December 20X3	
Non-Current Assets	**£**
Goodwill	**80,000**
Investment in Kind Ltd	
Property, Plant and Equipment	**840,000**
	920,000
Current Assets	
Inventories	**68,000**
Receivables	**47,000**
Cash & Cash Equivalents	**25,000**
	140,000
Total Assets	**1,060,000**
Equity	
Ordinary Share Capital	**700,000**
Retained Earnings	**193,000**
Non-Controlling Interest	**49,000**
	942,000
Non-Current Liabilities	
Bank Loan	**72,000**
Current Liabilities	
Creditors	**46,000**
Total Equity and Liabilities	**1,060,000**

Working – Goodwill Calculation

Consideration (amount paid)	**£200,000**
NCI % at acquisition	**£40,000**
Less - Value of Net Assets Acquired	**-£160,000**
Goodwill	**£80,000**

Working – Retained Earnings Calculation

Parent – Retained Earnings	**£166,000**
Subsidiary – Post-Acquisition Retained Earnings *(£96,000 - £60,000 = £36,000 x 75%)*	**£27,000**
Consolidated Retained Earnings	**£193,000**

Working – Non-Controlling Interest

Share Capital attributable to NCI *(£100,000 x 25%)*	**£25,000**
Retained Earnings attributable to NCI *(£96,000 x 25%)*	**£24,000**
Value of Non-Controlling Interest	**£49,000**

Answer to Activity 7.5

You are required to produce the Consolidated Statement of Financial Position for the group as at 31st December 20X7.

CONSOLIDATED STATEMENT OF FINANCIAL POSITION as at 31st December 20X7	
Non-Current Assets	**£**
Goodwill	**264,000**
Investment in Monfils Ltd	
Property, Plant and Equipment	**3,850,000**
	4,114,000
Current Assets	
Inventories	**439,000**
Receivables	**456,000**
Cash & Cash Equivalents	**114,000**
	1,009,000
Total Assets	**5,123,000**
Equity	
Ordinary Share Capital	**3,000,000**
Retained Earnings	**1,275,000**
Non-Controlling Interest	**129,000**
	4,404,000
Non-Current Liabilities	
Bank Loan	**374,000**
Current Liabilities	
Creditors	**345,000**
Total Equity and Liabilities	**5,123,000**

Working – Goodwill Calculation

Consideration (amount paid)	**£1,200,000**
NCI % at acquisition *(£1,040,000*10%)*	**£104,000**
Less - Value of Net Assets Acquired *(£500,000 + £240,000 + £300,000)*	**-£1,040,000**
Goodwill	**£264,000**

Working – Retained Earnings Calculation

Parent – Retained Earnings	**£1,050,000**
Subsidiary – Post-Acquisition Retained Earnings	**£225,000**
Consolidated Retained Earnings	**£1,275,000**

Working – Non-Controlling Interest

Share Capital attributable to NCI *(£500,000 x 10%)*	**£50,000**
Retained Earnings attributable to NCI *(£490,000 x 10%)*	**£49,000**
Revaluation attributable to NCI *(£300,000 x 10%)*	**£30,000**
Value of Non-Controlling Interest	**£129,000**

Answer to Activity 7.6

Calculate the value of inventory for the group which should be included in the Consolidated SFP, and the adjustments that will be needed to the group's consolidated reserves and the non-controlling interest.

Answer

Adjustment to Inventory	**£10,500** *(£182,000 - £140,000) x 1/4*
Adjustment to Retained Earnings	**£7,875** *(£10,500 x 75%)*
Adjustment to NCI	**£2,625** *(£10,500 x 25%)*

** Workings for mark-up = £140,000 x 130% = £182,000. **

Answer to Activity 7.7

Prepare the consolidated statement of financial position as at 31 March 20X5.

CONSOLIDATED STATEMENT OF FINANCIAL POSITION as at 31st March 20X5	
Non-Current Assets	**£**
Goodwill	**68,000**
Investment in Tiny Ltd	
Property, Plant and Equipment	**1,625,000**
	1,693,000
Current Assets	
Inventories	**126,200**
Receivables	**69,000**
Cash & Cash Equivalents	**37,000**
	232,200
Total Assets	**1,925,200**
Equity	
Ordinary Share Capital	**500,000**
Retained Earnings	**787,400**
Non-Controlling Interest	**102,800**
	1,390,200
Non-Current Liabilities	
Bank Loan	**345,000**
Current Liabilities	
Creditors	**145,000**
Taxation	**45,000**
Total Equity and Liabilities	**1,925,200**

Working – Adjustment for Non-Realised Profit

(£27,000 - £18,000) = £9,000 x 20% = £1,800

Working – Goodwill Calculation

Consideration (amount paid)	£300,000
NCI % at acquisition	£58,000
Less - Value of Net Assets Acquired	-£290,000
Goodwill	£68,000

Working – Adjustment to Inventories

Inventories of Poppop Ltd	£70,000
Inventories of Tiny Ltd	£58,000
Less adjustment for unrealised profit	- £1,800
	£126,200

Working – Adjustment to Receivables

Receivables of Poppop Ltd	£50,000
Receivables of Tiny Ltd	£30,000
Less adjustment for intra-group trading	-£11,000
	£69,000

Working – Adjustment to Payables

Payables of Poppop Ltd	£82,000
Payables of Tiny Ltd	£74,000
Less adjustment for intra-group trading	-£11,000
	£145,000

Working – Retained Earnings Calculation

Parent – Retained Earnings	£610,000
Subsidiary – Post-Acquisition Retained Earnings	£179,200
Less adjustment for unrealised profit	-£1,800
Consolidated Retained Earnings	£787,400

Working – Non-Controlling Interest

Share Capital attributable to NCI *(£200,00 x 20%)*	£40,000
Retained Earnings attributable to NCI *(£314,000 x 20%)*	£62,800
Value of Non-Controlling Interest	£102,800

Answer to Activity 7.8

Complete the extract of the consolidated Statement of Profit or Loss shown below.

Consolidated Statement of Profit or Loss for the year ended 30th April 20X7	**£000**
Sales	2,528
Cost of Sales	1,056
Gross Profit	1,472
Distribution Costs	354
Administrative Expenses	399
Profit from Operations	719
Finance Costs	136
Profit Before Tax	583
Taxation	129
Profit for the Year from continuing operations	454
Attributable to:	
Equity Holders of the Parent *(balancing figure)*	433
Non-Controlling Interest *(£210,000 x 10%)*	21

Answer to Activity 7.9

Prepare the consolidated statement of profit or loss for the group for the year ended 31st October 20X9.

Consolidated Statement of Profit or Loss for the year ended 31st October 20X9	£000	Notes
Sales	**2,878**	*£2,148 + £1,580 - £850*
Cost of Sales	**779**	*£985 + £496 - £850 + £148*
Gross Profit	**2,099**	
Distribution Costs	**389**	
Administrative Expenses	**430**	
Profit from Operations	**1,280**	
Finance Costs	**138**	
Profit Before Tax	**1,142**	
Taxation	**287**	
Profit for the Year from cont. operations	**855**	
Attributable to:		
Equity Holders of the Parent	**765.4**	*Balancing figure*
Non-Controlling Interest	**89.6**	*£448 x 20%*

The unrealised profit on unsold inventory is calculated as (£850,000 - £480,000) = £370,000 x 40% = £148,000.

Answer to Activity 7.10

Prepare the consolidated statement of profit or loss for the group for the year ended 31st May 20X1.

Consolidated Statement of Profit or Loss for the year ended 31st May 20X1	£000	Notes
Sales	**8,340**	*£5,580 + £3,140 - £380*
Cost of Sales	**4,677**	*£2,962 + £1,960 - £380 + £135*
Gross Profit	**3,663**	
Distribution Costs	**1,153**	
Administrative Expenses	**912**	
Profit from Operations	**1,598**	
Finance Costs	**293**	
Profit Before Tax	**1,305**	
Taxation	**239**	
Profit for the Year from cont. operations	**1,066**	
Attributable to:		
Equity Holders of the Parent	**955.6**	
Non-Controlling Interest	**110.4**	*(£411 x 40% = £164.4) – (£135 x 40% = £54) = £110.4*

The unrealised profit on unsold inventory is calculated as (£380,000 - £200,000) = £180,000 x 75% = £135,000.

Answers to Chapter 8 Activities

Answer to Activity 8.1

(a) Calculate the following ratios to two decimal places.

	20X7	20X8	20X9
Gross Profit Percentage	66.32	64.02	63.58
Operating Profit Percentage	38.95	38.41	36.42
Return on Capital Employed	27.99	21.34	21.49

(b) Write a short note to your manager explaining the changes in the ratios over the three years.

Sales revenue and gross profit both fluctuated over the three years, suffering a drop in 20X8 before recovering in 20X9. However, gross profit percentage has fallen (from 66.32% to 63.58%) over the three years– this is because the cost of sales has risen at a faster rate than turnover.

Operating profit fell in 20X8 before stabilising in 20X9. However, the operating profit margin actually decreased by a small amount in 20X8 before falling more significantly in 20X9; this was by a significant decrease in expenses in 20X8. It may be that 20X7 contained an abnormal expense – for example, a particularly high-cost marketing campaign or redundancy costs. Marketing may have been repeated in 20X9 and explain the rise in expenses.

The return on capital employed has fallen from 20X7 to 20X8, and then stabilised in 20X9. The reason for this was partly the fall in operating profit, but also because of the increase in capital (caused by the increased equity) from 20X7 to 20X8.

Overall, the ratios would indicate that Flamingo Ltd encountered tough trading conditions in 20X7 which have continued, but improved slightly, in 20X9.

Answer to Activity 8.2

(a) Calculate the following ratios for 20X4 and 20X5 to two decimal places.

	20X4 £	20X5 £
Current Ratio	**1.44:1**	**1.28:1**
Quick (Acid Test) Ratio	**0.67:1**	**0.56:1**

(b) Write a short note explaining why both the quick ratio and the current ratio have fallen in 20X5.

There was a decrease in liquidity from 20X4 to 20X5 when measured using both ratios. This is primarily caused by the increase of over £10,000 in current liabilities rather than a decrease in current assets, which in total remained at roughly the same value.

There has been a change in the mix of the current assets, with less cash and more inventories in particular. This has also been a factor in the worsening acid-test ratio. There may be a legitimate reason for this, but the company should take care not to over purchase inventory, as this will lead to cash becoming 'tied up' and a worsening of the company's working capital.

Answer to Activity 8.3

(a) Calculate the following ratios (to the nearest day) for 20X7 and 20X8.

	20X7	20X8
Inventory Holding Period (days)	**81 days**	**92 days**
Receivables Collection Period (days)	**15 days**	**17 days**
Payables Payment Period (days)	**38 days**	**43 days**
Working Capital Cycle (days)	**58 days**	**66 days**

(b) Comment on whether the ratios have improved or worsened from 20X7 to 20X8, and what impact these changes will have on the company's working capital.

Inventory holding period and receivables collection period have both worsened from 20X7 to 20X8. The company is taking more time (11 days on average) to sell its products. It has also seen a small increase (two days) in the length of time its customers take on average to pay their bills. If the company's normal credit terms are fourteen days then its customers are failing to adhere to these terms. These changes will have a negative effect on the working capital and liquidity of the company.   ***The payables payment period has increased by 5 days. It is not clear whether the company's average credit terms from suppliers are 30 days, 45 days or 60 days – or perhaps a combination of all of these. Consideration should be given as to whether the company is simply taking better advantage of available credit terms, or the increase in payables days is due to liquidity issues.***   ***As a result of these changes, the working capital cycle has worsened from 58 days to 66 days. This usually indicates the company may be experiencing a worsening liquidity situation, as is demonstrated in the financial statements by the reduction in cash and cash equivalents over the year from £18,850 to £2,680. If the company continues to experience worsening working capital and liquidity in 20X9 it could result in a requirement for an overdraft, or even put the viability of the business at risk.***

Answer to Activity 8.4

Carry out an analysis of the ratios listed below for Tipping Ltd and comment on the results:

Ratio	20X8	20X9
Gross Profit %	**44.76%**	**41.75%**
Comments ***This has worsened over the period; this could be due to a fall in selling prices and/or an increase in the cost of sales.***		

Ratio	20X8	20X9
Operating Profit %	**11.93%**	**7.24%**
Comments ***Again, this has worsened. This is caused in part by the fall in the Gross Profit Margin, and also an increase in the expenses.***		

Ratio	20X8	20X9
ROCE	11.53%	6.92%

Comments

The ROCE has also fallen, reflecting the reduction in profitability for the company over the two years. The company increased its capital base but did not see a similar rise in profitability.

Ratio	20X8	20X9
Asset Turnover (net)	0.97 times	0.96 times

Comments

The asset turnover ratio has stayed about the same; this is because although the company increased its capital base its turnover increased at approximately the same rate.

Ratio	20X8	20X9
Current Ratio	3.91:1	11.76:1

Comments

The ratio is healthy in both years, suggesting few liquidity problems. The increase is primarily caused by the reduction in trade payables.

Ratio	20X8	20X9
Acid Test Ratio	3.08:1	9.13:1

Comments

The acid test ratio has also significantly increased, due mainly to the reduction in payables.

Ratio	20X8	20X9
Inventory Holding (days)	36.29 days	35.34 days

Comments

Has stayed broadly the same, with a fall of one day. This indicates that goods are being sold (slightly) quicker in 20X9 than the previous year, which is a positive indication.

Ratio	20X8	20X9
Receivables Collection Period (days)	35.92 days	32.34 days

Comments

The company has improved its receivables collection process by almost four days, which will have a positive impact on liquidity. However, if the credit terms offered by the company are 30 days then it is still not quite managing to get all customers to pay within these terms, and so further improvements could be sought.

Ratio	20X8	20X9
Payables Collection Period (days)	36.11 days	8.02 days
Comments ***There has been a rapid decrease in this ratio. Perhaps the company is deliberately paying early to take advantage of prompt payment discounts, or perhaps it is making more of its purchases on cash or 7-day credit terms. It is caused by the significant reduction in the value of trade payables over the year. This should be investigated as whilst there may be advantages of paying early, it can have a negative impact on the company's working capital management.***		

Ratio	20X8	20X9
Gearing Ratio	23.28%	25.21%
Comments ***There has been a slight increase in ratio, caused by the increase in long-term borrowing. However, the figure is still within a generally acceptable range and so is not likely to be a cause for concern.***		

Ratio	20X8	20X9
Interest Cover	21.68 times	11.90 times
Comments ***This has fallen quite significantly, due both to the fall in profitability and also the increase in borrowings. Nevertheless, interest cover of nearly 12 times is likely to be acceptable, although any further decreases may indicate an increase in risk exposure (e.g. to an interest rate rise) for the business.***		

This page is left intentionally blank.

Mock Exam - Answers

Task 1 (23 marks)

1a. Complete the following workings boxes to calculate the correct figures for Cost of Sales, Distribution Costs and Administration Expenses.

Cost of Sales	
	£000
Opening Inventories	31,958
Purchases	301,568
Closing Inventories	33,108
	300,418

Distribution Costs	
	£000
Distribution Costs	29,953
Doubtful Debts Adjustment	316
PPE	18
	30,287

Administrative Expenses	
	£000
Administrative Expenses	51,465
Prepayment	(162)
	51,303

1b. Draft the statement of profit or loss and other comprehensive income for Gerbil Ltd for the year ended 31st December 20X6.

Gerbil Ltd Statement of Profit or Loss and Other Comprehensive Income for the year ended 31/12/20X6	
	£000
Revenue	515,840
Cost of Sales	-300,418
Gross Profit	215,422
Distribution Costs	-30,287
Administration Expenses	-51,303
Profit from Operations	133,832
Finance Costs	-2,000
Profit Before Tax	131,832
Taxation	-8,245
Profit for the Year from Continuing Operations	123,587
Other Comprehensive Income for the Year	5,000
Total Comprehensive Income for the Year	128,587

1c. Draft the Statement of Changes in Equity for Gerbil Ltd for the year ended 31st December 20X6.

	Share Capital £000	Revaluation £000	Retained Earnings £000	Total Equity £000
Balance at 1st January 20X6	120,000	0	64,520	184,520
Changes in Equity				
Total Comprehensive Income	0	5,000	123,587	128,587
Dividends	0	0	(7,900)	(7,900)
Balance at 31st December 20X6	120,000	5,000	180,207	305,207

1d. Complete the following workings boxes to calculate the correct figures for Property, Plant & Equipment, Trade & Other Receivables, Trade & Other Payables and Retained Earnings.

Property, Plant and Equipment	
	£000
PPE at cost	324,980
Accumulated Depreciation	(41,185)
Revaluation	5,000
Distribution Costs	(18)
	288,777

Trade and Other Receivables	
	£000
Trade Receivables	31,160
Allowance for Doubtful Debts	(1,558)
Prepayments	162
	29,764

Trade and Other Payables	
	£000
Trade and other Payables	27,341
Accrual – Finance Costs	1,000
	28,341

Retained Earnings	
	£000
Retained Earnings @ 01/01/20X8	64,520
Dividends Paid	(7,900)
Profit for the Year	123,587
	180,207

1e. Draft the Statement of Financial Position for Gerbil Ltd as at 31st December 20X6.

ASSETS	£000
Non-Current Assets	
Property Plant and Equipment	288,777
	288,777
Current Assets	
Inventories	33,108
Trade and Other Receivables	29,764
Cash and Cash Equivalents	15,144
	78,016
Total Assets	366,793
EQUITY AND LIABILITIES	
Equity	
Share Capital	120,000
Retained Earnings	180,207
Revaluation Reserve	5,000
Total Equity	305,207
Non-Current Liabilities	
Bank Loans	25,000
	25,000
Current Liabilities	
Trade and Other Payables	28,341
Tax Liability	8,245
	36,586
Total Liabilities	61,586
Total Equity and Liabilities	366,793

Task 2 (17 marks)

2a. Complete the following workings boxes to calculate the correct figures for Proceeds on Disposal of PPE and Purchases of PPE.

Proceeds on Disposal of PPE	
	£000
Carrying amount of PPE sold	360
Gain / Loss on disposal of PPE	16
	376

Purchases of PPE	
	£000
PPE at start of year	33,108
Depreciation Charge	(2,275)
Carrying amount of PPE sold	(360)
PPE at end of year	(44,256)
Total PPE additions	13,783

2b. Prepare a reconciliation of <u>profit from operations</u> to net cash from operating activities for Hamster Ltd for the year ended 31st October 20X8.

	£000
Profit from Operations	18,407
Adjustments For:	
Depreciation	2,275
Gain / Loss on disposal of PPE	(16)
Dividends received	(101)
Adjustment in respect of inventories	(662)
Adjustment in respect of trade receivables	(3,615)
Adjustment in respect of trade payables	838
Cash Generated by Operations	17,126
Interest Paid	(66)
Taxation Paid	(3,105)
Net Cash from Operating Activities	13,955

Remember: starting from profit from operations we do not need to add the finance costs back to calculate the operating profit.

2c. Prepare the Statement of Cash Flows for Hamster Ltd for the year ended 31st October 20X8.

	£000
Net Cash From Operating Activities	**13,955**
Investing Activities	
Purchases of PPE	**-13,783**
Proceeds on Disposal of PPE	**376**
Dividends Received	**101**
Net Cash Used in Investing Activities	**(13,306)**
Financing Activities	
Increase in share capital & premium	**2,700**
Increase in loan	**3,100**
Dividends paid	**(1,200)**
Net Cash From Financing Activities	**4,600**
Net increase / (decrease) in cash and cash equivalents	**5,249**
Cash and cash equivalents at beginning of year	**(1,452)**
Cash and cash equivalents at end of year	**3,797**

Task 3 (8 marks)

a) What is the objective of Financial Statements, according to the IASB Conceptual Framework?

To provide information about the reporting entity that is useful to existing and potential investors, lenders and other creditors in making decisions about providing resources to the entity.

b) Define the three elements of financial statements which would appear in the Statement of Financial Position.

Asset – is ***"a present economic resource controlled by the entity as a result of past events. An economic resource is a right that has the potential to produce economic benefits".***

Liability – is ***"a present obligation of the entity to transfer an economic resource as a result of past events".***

Equity – is the residual interest in the assets of the entity after deducting all its liabilities.

Task 4 (12 marks)

a)

Event A – This is a non-adjusting event – The fire happened after the reporting date so no adjustments will be made.

Event B – This is a non-adjusting event under IAS 10 – it is litigation based on an event after the reporting date. There should be no adjustment to the accounts; the directors must take a view on the likelihood of loss and possibly disclose in a note to the accounts.

Event C – This is an adjusting event under IAS 10 as it relates to conditions in existence at the reporting date. Adjustment should be made in the accounts as an irrecoverable debt.

Event D – This is specifically identified as a non-adjusting event under IAS 10 – it should be shown as a disclosure in the notes to the financial statements.

b)

i. Which asset is impaired? **B**

ii. How much is the impairment loss? **£5,000**

c) Which of these is not a criterion for determining whether expenditure on development can be capitalised?

	✓
It is technically feasible to be able to complete the development so that the asset will be available for use or sale.	
The business has the intention to complete, and then use or sell, the asset.	
It is probable that the asset will generate future economic benefits	
The business has available resources to complete the development	
It is possible to measure all future income reliably	✓

d) According to IAS 2 *Inventories* what is the total valuation of Mole Ltd.'s inventory at the year end?

£67,935

e) An intangible asset is defined as:

"An ______1______, _________2________ asset without ________3___________"

Complete the missing words.

	✓
1. Identifiable, 2. monetary, 3. real form	
1. Invisible, 2. non-real, 3. identifiable value	
1. Identifiable, 2. non-monetary, 3. physical substance	✓
1. Identifiable, 2. non-physical, 3. ascertainable value	

f) How should Guinea Ltd show this in the accounts for the year ended 31st December 20X8?

	✓
Record an expense of £1.8 million in the SPLOCI, and show a payable of £1.8 million in the SFP.	
Record a provision in the SFP for £1.8 million, with an expense for the same amount in the SPLOCI.	
Disclose the possible liability in a note to the accounts, describing the situation.	✓
No disclosure at all.	

Task 5 (30 marks)

5a. Complete the following workings boxes to calculate the correct figures for Goodwill, Inventories, Retained Earnings and Non-Controlling Interest.

Goodwill	
	£000
Consideration	**2,000**
Non-controlling interest at acquisition	**180**
Net assets acquired (800+600+400)	**(1,800)**
Goodwill	**380**

Inventories	
	£000
Consolidated Inventories (before any inter-company adjustment)	**1,171**
Inter-company adjustment	**(8)**
	1,163

Retained Earnings	
	£000
Rabbit Ltd	2,950
Hare Ltd attributable to Rabbit Ltd (excluding any inter-company adjustment)	684
Inter-company adjustment	(8)
	3,626

Non-Controlling Interest (NCI)	
	£000
Share Capital Attributable to NCI	80
Retained Earnings Attributable to NCI	136
Revaluation Reserve Attributable to NCI	40
	256

5b. Draft the Consolidated Statement of Financial Position for Rabbit Ltd as at 31st August 20X8.

ASSETS	£000
Non-Current Assets	
Goodwill	380
Property, Plant and Equipment	7,008
	7,388
Current Assets	
Inventories	1,163
Trade Receivables	1,070
Cash and Cash Equivalents	506
	2,739
Total Assets	10,127
EQUITY AND LIABILITIES	
Equity	
Share Capital	3,800
Retained Earnings	3,626
Non-Controlling Interest	256
Total Equity	7,682
Non-Current Liabilities	
Bank Loans	920
	920
Current Liabilities	
Trade Payables	1,098
Taxation	427
	1,525
Total Liabilities	2,445
Total Equity and Liabilities	10,127

Task 6 (8 marks)

Calculate the following ratios to two decimal places (where appropriate):

Gross Profit Margin	**60.56**	%
Return on Capital Employed	**23.71**	%
Current Ratio	**1.20**	:1
Inventory Holding Period	**155**	Days
Trade Payables Payment Period	**152**	Days
Trade Receivables Collection Period	**23**	Days
Asset Turnover (net assets)	**0.51**	Times
Gearing	**30.77**	%
Interest Cover	**5.95**	Times

Task 7 (22 marks)

You are required to prepare notes which include:

- An explanation of what each of the ratios shows.
- An explanation of whether Squirrel Ltd has performed better or worse than Gopher Ltd.
- Two practical measures which Squirrel Ltd could take to improve each of the first three ratios during the forthcoming year.

Answer

The Inventory Holding Period shows the average number of days inventory is held in stock for. Squirrel Ltd.'s period (38 days) is five days longer than Gopher Ltd.'s, which suggests Gopher Ltd has performed better in this respect. Gopher Ltd sells its goods more quickly (on average) than Squirrel Ltd. This could be due to more aggressive marketing, or discounting, by Gopher Ltd. Squirrel Ltd could look to improve this over the coming year by reviewing the product lines held to identify and eliminate slow-moving product lines, increase or improve marketing activities to generate additional sales, or review purchasing and stock control to minimise stock-holdings.

The Trade Receivables Period shows how long it takes credit customer on average to pay their invoices. Squirrel Ltd has done poorly this year compared to Gopher Ltd, as its customers take an average of 39 days to pay against 35 days for Gopher Ltd. Squirrel Ltd could review their credit control procedures, identifying regular late payers and implementing stricter credit management for them, pro-actively managing very old debts (writing them off if necessary) and introducing more rigorous credit checks for new customers. They could also consider offering early settlement discounts to customers to encourage them to pay more promptly.

The Trade Payables Collection Period measures how long Squirrel Ltd take to pay outstanding creditors; the company took 64 days to pay bills on average in 20X7-X8, compared to 49 days for Gopher Ltd. Companies would usually look to ensure that the Payables Payment period is longer than the Receivables Turnover Period, and Squirrel

Ltd have achieved this. This will improve cash flow as the company is not having to pay suppliers before cash has been received from customers. However, there could be disadvantages such as damage to reputation, loss of available settlement discounts etc and possible withdrawal of credit facilities. Some suppliers may even turn away orders from Squirrel Ltd if the time they take to pay suppliers is considered inappropriately long – especially when compared to their competitors Gopher Ltd.

If Squirrel Ltd wish to shorten the Payables Payment Period it could introduce more regular or flexible payment runs, and monitor and take available settlement discounts.

The working capital cycle is the number of days it takes for a business to convert the purchase of raw materials or finished goods into a cash receipt from customers. Companies should aim for it to be as short as possible, and so Squirrel Ltd has actually achieved a shorter working capital cycle than Gopher Ltd. This is entirely due to the increased time the company takes to pay its suppliers, which actually outweighs the poorer performance in turning over inventory and collecting debts. If the extended payables period is caused (at least in part) by Squirrel Ltd encountering cash flow problems during the month, improved performance in turning over inventory and collecting debts would have a positive impact in this regard.